A Hurdler's Hurdler

# A Hurdler's Hurdler

*The Life of Rodney Milburn,
Olympic Champion*

STEVEN McGILL

McFarland & Company, Inc., Publishers
*Jefferson, North Carolina*

LIBRARY OF CONGRESS CATALOGUING-IN-PUBLICATION DATA

Names: McGill, Steve, 1966– author.
Title: A hurdler's hurdler : the life of Rodney Milburn, Olympic champion / Steven McGill.
Description: Jefferson, North Carolina : McFarland & Company, Inc., Publishers, 2018 | Includes bibliographical references and index.
Identifiers: LCCN 2018031326 | ISBN 9781476670973 (softcover : acid free paper) ∞
Subjects: LCSH: Milburn, Rodney, 1950–1997. | Track and field athletes—United States—Biography. | Hurdling (Track and field) | African American track and field athletes—United States—Biography.
Classification: LCC GV697.M3675 A3 2018 | DDC 796.42092 [B] —dc23
LC record available at https://lccn.loc.gov/2018031326

BRITISH LIBRARY CATALOGUING DATA ARE AVAILABLE

**ISBN (print) 978-1-4766-7097-3**
**ISBN (ebook) 978-1-4766-3242-1**

© 2018 Steven McGill. All rights reserved

*No part of this book may be reproduced or transmitted in any form or by any means, electronic or mechanical, including photocopying or recording, or by any information storage and retrieval system, without permission in writing from the publisher.*

Front cover: Rod Milburn (left) clears a hurdle during his sophomore year at J.S. Clark High School in Opelousas, Louisiana

Printed in the United States of America

*McFarland & Company, Inc., Publishers*
 *Box 611, Jefferson, North Carolina 28640*
 *www.mcfarlandpub.com*

To the memory of Rodney Milburn,
and to all who knew and loved him.

# Table of Contents

| | |
|---|---|
| *Acknowledgments* | viii |
| *Introduction* | 1 |
| One—Out of the Blocks: Up from Opelousas | 3 |
| Two—First Hurdle: Wooden Hurdles on a Grass Track | 10 |
| Three—Second Hurdle: Rod and Willie at Southern U. | 27 |
| Four—Third Hurdle: On a Winning Streak | 35 |
| Five—Fourth Hurdle: Reaching for the Gold | 47 |
| Six—Hurdle Five: Date with Destiny | 59 |
| Seven—Hurdle Six: From College to the Pros | 82 |
| Eight—Hurdle Seven: The ITA Blues | 96 |
| Nine—Hurdle Eight: Hero Without a Country | 110 |
| Ten—Hurdle Nine: The Quiet Champion | 126 |
| Eleven—Hurdle Ten: Into the Sunset | 138 |
| Twelve—Across the Finish Line: The Final Transition | 153 |
| *Chapter Notes* | 163 |
| *Bibliography* | 180 |
| *Index* | 189 |

# Acknowledgments

The author would like to thank the following people for the role they played in making this biography a reality:

Sue Deville, who has since passed, was the director of the Opelousas Cultural and Interpretive Museum in Rodney Milburn's hometown of Opelousas, Louisiana, at the time when I was doing my initial research. Sue put me in contact with several of Rod's family members and also organized both of my visits to Opelousas, where I was able to conduct multiple interview with friends, family members, teammates, classmates, and coaches. She also provided access to original copies of many newspaper articles and other sources that focused on Milburn's athletic achievements.

Jimmy Milburn, brother of Rodney Milburn, became a good friend of mine through the process of writing this book. He provided almost all of the information necessary for the first chapter that focuses on Rodney's childhood. In my second visit to Opelousas, he showed me around to many places, including the house where Rodney, Jimmy, and their sister Mary Ann grew up. He also drove me to visit Rodney's gravesite, which was a very powerful moment for me, enabling me to realize the magnitude of this project.

Ken Stone, the webmaster of the master's track and field site, masterstrack.com, proved to be immensely helpful throughout the entire writing and researching process. It would be fair to say that without Ken's help, this project would not have been completed. Ken helped to edit early drafts of early chapters; he went out of his way to dig up old copies of *Track & Field News*, scouring each issue for content that mentioned Milburn; and he also provided me with motivational peptalks when I felt discouraged that I might never find a publisher for the book.

Everyone whom I interviewed provided me with deeper insight not

*Acknowledgments*

only into Milburn's athletic career and accomplishments, but also into his character. Interview after interview revealed to me that Rodney was indeed a truly special human being, not just an outstanding athlete. Time and time again, the themes that kept coming up were that Rodney was extremely humble, extremely caring, and extremely giving. He went out of his way to make people feel better about themselves, he took a special interest in the youth, and he carried himself in a manner that was dignified and understated. The list of people I would like to thank for taking the time to talk with me include family members such as the aforementioned Jimmy Milburn, Rodney's sisters Lillie and Alice, Rodney's wife Betty, and Rodney's cousin Joseph Stanislars Milburn; Sue Deville's husband Gil Deville; former high school teammates and coaches Vont Dabney, Oliver Jackson, Harry Meuillion, and Coach Morrison; former professors at Southern University Dr. George Whitfield and Dr. Raymond Lockett; Bob Hersh of *Track & Field News*; former hurdling rivals/friends including Tom Hill, Larry Shipp, Leon Coleman, Marcus Walker, Charles Foster, Renaldo Nehemiah, and Tonie Campbell; other athletes and executives who knew of Rodney and who were prevalent during his prime in the 1970s including Dwight Stones, Cliff Wiley, the deceased Brian Oldfield, and Ollan Cassell; and *Opelousas Daily World* newspaper reporter Herman Fuselier.

Michael J. Daniels, who graduated from the same (now defunct) J. S. Clark High School that Milburn graduated from, provided the photos that appear in the book. Milburn graduated in 1969. Daniels graduated in 1967. Daniels is the project leader of the J. S. Clark Memorial Walkway.

This book is infused with the spirit of two people whom I never got to meet but who are an integral part of this story: Rodney's mother Mary and Rodney's rival/friend/mentor/teammate in the hurdles, Willie Davenport.

# Introduction

I am not old enough to remember the hurdling career of Rodney Milburn. Nor did I ever meet him personally. I had just turned six years old when he won Olympic gold in the 110 meter high hurdles in Munich, Germany in 1972, and I have no recollection of that race. Yet when I heard the news of his tragic death in November of 1997, I was deeply saddened. Why? Because Milburn was the hero of my heroes. I grew up watching hurdling greats like Renaldo Nehemiah, Greg Foster, and Tonie Campbell. Even though all of them ran against an older Milburn in the late 70s and early 80s, they considered him a role model and a mentor—not just in the hurdles, but in living the life of a world-class athlete, and in being a person of dignity and honor.

As someone who ran the hurdles myself in high school and college, and as someone who has coached hurdlers throughout my adult life, I was quite familiar with the history of the event at the time of Milburn's passing. All hurdling experts agreed that Milburn was one of the best ever, if not the best. Many, including Nehemiah, considered Milburn to be the first modern hurdler—the first hurdler to truly sprint between the hurdles, as opposed to taking three steps and a jump.

So, living in my own personal bubble where everything revolves around the hurdles, I assumed that a book and/or a movie would soon come out about Milburn's outstanding achievements on the track. But it never happened. Finally, in 2005, the thought hit me: Why don't I do it myself?

In that moment, I decided I was going to try to write a book on Rodney Milburn. I started by calling Sue Deville, now deceased, who was the curator of the Cultural and Interpretive Museum in Milburn's hometown of Opelousas, Louisiana. Sue loved my idea, and she promised to put me in contact with family members. Soon thereafter, Rodney's brother Jimmy

# Introduction

contacted me and expressed enthusiasm for such a project. From there, I visited Opelousas twice to gather research and to conduct interviews. By 2008, I had completed a full draft of the biography and was ready to seek an agent.

After sending out dozens of query letters and receiving a few responses, I noticed a consistent theme in the responses: we love your research, we love your writing style, etc., but who is Rodney Milburn? Silly me, I thought everybody knew who Rodney Milburn was.

Disheartened, and busy with my life as a full-time high school English teacher and track coach, I put the book to the side. Three years later, because people were still asking me about it, I uploaded the chapters of the book to my website, which is dedicated to all things hurdle-related.

Someone saw it there and asked me if I had ever heard of McFarland Publishers. No, I hadn't, I responded. After receiving their contact information, I emailed them with an explanation of the book I had written and asked if they had any interest in publishing it.

And now, here we are.

This book is a tribute to a great man, a great human being, not merely a great hurdler. From all the interviews I conducted and all the research I gathered, one major theme stood out: Rodney Milburn was a humble champion who never flaunted his success. He mentored younger teammates, younger rivals, and young children. When he lost races, he congratulated the victor. When he won, which was often, he shook hands with every opponent in the spirit of true sportsmanship. As he grew older and was moving toward the downside of his career, he gracefully accepted the decline of his skills even as he continued to compete fiercely. After his athletic career ended, he coached at his alma mater, Southern University in Baton Rouge, where he molded young minds and developed the program. In his last years of life, even as he faced financial struggles, he remained a man of integrity to the end.

People loved Rodney Milburn. Even the white people in his segregated hometown loved him and claimed him as one of their own. And for those who knew him well, the loss of him still stings terribly. It is my hope that this book can serve to provide a measure of healing for those who think of Rodney every day and miss his presence. I also hope that it can let those who didn't know him appreciate this very special human being.

# ONE

# Out of the Blocks
## *Up from Opelousas*

"It's not the size of the place that matters. It's the size of the individual that matters. I've never been ashamed of being from Opelousas."[1]

—Rodney Milburn

Rodney Milburn was born in the small, segregated town of Opelousas, Louisiana, whose name derived from the Native American tribe that inhabited the land when French traders arrived in the late 1600s.[2] His father made a living building houses from scratch. His mother worked six days a week in white folks' homes. She washed dishes, cleaned shelves and cabinets, and took care of the laundry. She earned two dollars a day. As a child wandering the streets of the housing-project neighborhoods in the black section of Opelousas, or running with his cousins through the open fields of nearby Bayou Teche, Rodney Milburn did not know he would grow up to be a world record holder and Olympic gold medalist in the 110 meter high hurdles. He did not yet even know what a hurdle was.[3]

In 1951, before Rodney had reached the age of two, his parents' divorce split apart the family. His father, Rodney Sr., moved to Galveston, Texas, and started a carpentry business, taking four of Rodney Jr.'s older siblings with him. Wilfred, Clary, Alice, and Lillie moved to Galveston, while Rodney Jr., his sister Mary Ann, and his brother Jimmy stayed with their mother in Opelousas. Throughout his life, Rodney Jr., the youngest of the seven siblings, would remain close to all his family members and to all the impoverished people in the dusty town of his childhood. Even after becoming an internationally famous track athlete who brought home victory medals from foreign countries, he would never stop referring to Opelousas as home.

## A Hurdler's Hurdler

Located an hour's drive west of Baton Rouge and a three hour's drive northeast of Houston—the two cities where Milburn lived throughout most of his adult life—Opelousas in the 1950s and 1960s was a diverse town ethnically, but most of the blacks lived in an isolated part of town. They rarely came into contact with the white population and struggled to survive on an income that kept them below the poverty line. Very few blacks in Opelousas had college degrees; the women did what was called "day's work" as maids for the wealthier white families in town, while the men scrounged for whatever manual labor jobs they could find. For the most part, that meant either picking cotton, cutting sugar-cane, or working in the local oil-refining factory.

"Guys that didn't have a factory job," Jimmy Milburn said, "had to either go out and catch these cotton-picking trucks or cane-cutting trucks. They'd go out and pick cotton or cut cane to earn a living. It was a tough life, but they had to do it." The trucks would roll through town in the morning looking for workers, and the men would hop on for a day of labor in the fields. "When they were old enough to get on the back of a truck," Jimmy said, "they had to catch one; they had to work." Some began such work as early as age ten. Rodney Jr.'s older sister Lillie noted that "a person would have had to have been around in that era of time to know the prejudices of a Southern town that kept a lot of people from being anything and doing anything."[4]

By the time Jimmy and Rodney Jr., who was called Russell by family members, were old enough to attend school at the all-black J. S. Clark Elementary School, they spent the school year in Opelousas with their mother. During the summers, they stayed with their father in Galveston, helping with his self-made carpentry business. Traveling from job to job with Rodney Sr. and sweating under the hot Galveston sun, Jimmy and Russell quickly learned to appreciate the value of hard work. "We'd go out there in the summer," Jimmy said, "and we'd do a little painting. We were little handy-man boys, you know. We'd help the people who were working for my daddy. Sometimes we'd handle pieces of lumber, sometimes we'd do a little nailing ourselves." With the money they made assisting their father, Jimmy and Rodney Jr. made enough money to pay for their schooling and to buy new clothes for the upcoming school year.

Rodney Sr., a light-skinned man who stood 6-feet-1 and weighed 180 pounds, had grown up in a family of sharecroppers in Bayou Teche, a farming community about a mile or two outside the city limits of Opelousas.

## One—Out of the Blocks

So, unlike his son, Rodney Sr. never had time to find out if he had any athletic ability. His parents were sharecroppers, as were his brothers and sisters, so the only thing they had time for was work.

Rodney Sr. would grow up to become a masterful carpenter. "In carpentry," Jimmy said, "my daddy was a genius." Rodney Sr. built many homes in Galveston; he built them from scratch, "not like they do it today," Jimmy said, "where they put everything together just like a puzzle. He built them from the ground up. Solid, you know." In a town like Galveston, which was often ravaged by storms during hurricane season, Rodney Sr.'s services were in high demand by both whites and blacks.

"When hurricanes ran through," Jimmy said, "they wiped houses out. I'll never forget one time Daddy rode us around Galveston. There were a lot of homes that had been damaged. He drove us around, pointing to certain houses, and he'd say, 'Ya see, these are the houses I built. The hurricane didn't damage them.' He built a lot of homes out there that were pretty solid, that the hurricanes didn't destroy."

In addition to building homes, Rodney Sr. also did remodeling work, add-ons, and all kinds of assorted carpentry jobs, particularly for people whose homes had been damaged by hurricanes. Over time, his business expanded simply because of the quality of his product. Jimmy recalled, "When people would drive by and see him painting a house or building a house, they would stop and say, 'Could you do mine? Could you come paint my house?' He had so much work that he couldn't get to everybody."

Upon returning to Opelousas during the school year, Jimmy and Rodney Jr., who was only thirteen months younger, entered a more hostile social climate, and a harsher economic situation. Although it's true that, in the 1950s, the South was the South, the two boys found that racial tensions in Opelousas were much more pronounced than they were in Galveston. While segregation existed in both places, the prowess of Rodney Sr. shielded the two youngsters from any overt racism that they may have otherwise faced. In Opelousas, "they still had signs out there saying this was for whites only, this was for coloreds," Jimmy said. "It was up until we were about in the seventh or eighth grade that we experienced these things."

Once they reached high school in the early 1960s, racial tensions in Opelousas began to ease up. The civil rights movement had finally begun to creep into the town's consciousness. Still, integration in schools did

## A Hurdler's Hurdler

not take place until 1969, after both Jimmy and Rodney had graduated from all-black J. S. Clark High School.

Jimmy remembers one particular incident that took place when he and his younger brother were in their early teens, and they entered a local restaurant called The Kettle. The policy was for black patrons to order their food in the front, then go around in the back to pick it up. On one particular winter day, Jimmy recalled, "we were ordering our food, and it was cold that night, so we said we didn't want to stand outside and wait for our food. We wanted to wait inside, like everybody else." With them was their cousin Curtis, who lived in Bayou Teche and who was neither as friendly and pleasant as Jimmy nor as quiet and mild-mannered as Rodney Jr. "Curtis had about enough of it," Jimmy said, "so he told the lady behind the counter that he wasn't leaving." She called him a racial slur, and he took a glass and threw it against the back wall. The three boys had to leave before the police came. "All we wanted to do was wait inside instead of waiting outside in the cold."

Rodney's unwillingness to make a stand was not surprising. It was in his make-up to avoid conflict. He was a quiet boy. Not necessarily shy nor lacking in self-confidence. Not necessarily taciturn or anti-social. He just didn't like trouble; he didn't like ugliness in people's behavior, and, when confronted with it, he preferred to turn away from it. Rodney's attitude toward racism was this: "If you don't want me here, then I don't want to be here," not "I am going to force you to tolerate my presence." This basically peaceful nature remained with him throughout his life, at times to his own detriment. But it also endeared him to many of the locals in Opelousas, and to the many athletes, officials, and reporters who would later come to know him as "hot Rod" in the track world. The nickname was more a reference to his speed than his personality.

In the neighborhood and in the schoolyard, it was up to Jimmy, Curtis, and a few other schoolmates to keep the bullies away from Rodney. When it came to choosing between fight versus flight, the young Rodney definitely preferred to run away, and he was not ashamed of that. "Rodney was the type," Jimmy said, "who didn't like to get in fights. It was the kind of thing he stayed away from. So me and my cousin kind of kept the bullies away from him. He didn't like confrontations."

To escape the racism, bullies, concrete streets, and narrow confines of his mother's one-floor house on 749 Myrtle Street in the Opelousas projects, Rodney took off for the wide-open spaces of Bayou Teche. There,

## One—Out of the Blocks

he played and ran around with his cousins. On Friday afternoons after school, instead of walking the six blocks home with Jimmy and Mary Ann, Rodney caught the bus to the country. Out there, on the grassy fields where the autumn winds whistled through the pecan trees, Rodney first began to develop his athletic ability. "That was a big thing for Rodney," Jimmy said, "every Friday before the weekends. He could just run around, play around, and have fun." Rodney and his cousins would run mock races—to the pecan tree and back, to the fence, to a spot on the ground, or they'd chase after the horses that roamed the rolling plains. Here there were no bullies, racists, nor one-way streets. Just endless space.

"That's where he liked to have fun," Jimmy said. "All them kids out there, all his cousins. Curtis was one of them, and he ended up being faster in the sprints than Rodney when they got older, although nobody could beat Rodney in the hurdles. But yeah, they'd make up all kinds of games to see who could run the fastest. Those kids would just run, run, run. All day long." Until he was ten years old, an asthma condition prevented Rodney from showing the type of speed that he would later display to his cousins, to Opelousas, and to the world. "I had asthma real bad," Rodney once told a newspaper reporter. "I couldn't participate in anything because of a shortness of breath. It was very frustrating."

When Rodney first started to go on his Friday afternoon excursions throughout his elementary school years, Rodney's mother Mary worried, wondering aloud as the sky grew dim and the bats began to flutter through the humid, smoky air, "Now where's that little Russell?" Because Mary did not own a telephone, the only way for her to find news of Rodney's whereabouts was for one of her cousins from the bayou to come to her house in Opelousas saying, "Oh, Russ is at his auntie's house in the country. You don't have to worry. He caught the bus." Mary would heave a weary sigh, relieved to know that Rodney Jr. was not involving himself in any dangerous activities.

Mary's motherly instincts for her youngest child would endure into his adulthood, even into his glory years as a track athlete. Bobby Ardoin, a reporter for the Baton Rouge *Advocate* who covered much of Rodney's hurdling career, once marveled at the fact that when he talked to Mary on the day Rodney won his Olympic gold medal, she did not express much elation over his remarkable accomplishment, but "all she could talk about was what a good son he had been and how he had never gotten in trouble."

## A Hurdler's Hurdler

Harry Meuillion, a pole-vaulter on the J. S. Clark High School track teams in the mid–1960s who graduated two years ahead of Rodney, tells another childhood story that reveals the raw physical ability of the young Rodney in his formative years. One day, Dice—as Rodney was called by his peers and neighbors because of his ability to shoot dice so well—had a craving for watermelons, and he told Harry of a place where they could find some without getting caught. "So he says to me, 'Let's go over here and get some watermelons,'" Harry recalled. "Well, it started raining real hard, and the guy who owned the place wasn't too cool about us going into his yard, so he yells at us to get out of there. Next thing I know, Dice is *gone*. He left me there by myself. Thing is, because of the rain, there had been some flooding, so we were in water knee-high tryin' to get them watermelons. But when Dice heard that man yell at us, he just *took off*. That's when I realized how fast he was. The fact that he could move like that in water up to his knees, my goodness! After that, I said to him, 'I ain't never doing nothing you say ever again.'"[5]

Such harmless adventures marked the limits of Rodney's deviant behavior. Rodney, along with Jimmy and Mary Ann, was living with their mother in what Jimmy described as a shop-shoot house. "When you can see through the front door," he explained, "you can see through the back." From the time Rodney was four months old until his sophomore year of high school, the one-floor shack on Myrtle Street was his home. The living conditions that he, his mother, and his two siblings had to endure were quite severe, almost unfathomable in the post-industrial age. "We didn't have no electricity, no gas, no toilet in the house," Jimmy said. "We had an outdoor toilet, in what they call an out-house. We had wood heaters; we had to go out and cut our own wood in order to have heat. For light, we used kerosene lamps. That's how we'd do our studying—by the kerosene lamps."

While the money Jimmy and Rodney made over the summer working with their father in Galveston helped them to pay for some of their school clothes, it didn't pay for everything, and it didn't last all year long. Their mother Mary did her best to make ends meet by taking on employment in the homes of white Opelousas residents. She took care of their daily house-cleaning tasks and helped to raise their children. Mary worked, at different times, "for about four different families," Jimmy said. "She would earn about two or three dollars a day. Maybe five sometimes, you know. Back then, if they made like two dollars a day, it was a lot of money." Still, it didn't go far. Mary had to make tremendous sacrifices to ensure that her daughter and two sons looked presentable at school. They also needed money for food.

"Back then, our lunch money was like fifteen cents," Jimmy said, laughing grimly at the memory. "Our mother would give us our little change for the day. Fifteen cents for Rodney, fifteen cents for me, fifteen cents for Mary Ann, and that was all the lunch money we went to school with." Still, the three Milburn children never looked like ragamuffins when they walked to J. S. Clark. Their mother made certain of that. "She would starch our clothes," Jimmy said. "She made sure our socks matched with our shirt. We were living in this little shop-shoot house, but people never knew it. By what we wore to school, they couldn't tell, you know. Because our mother, with the little money she was making, sacrificed for us, and bought us good stuff."

Rodney Milburn, Jr., would never lose the ability to look refined when times were hard, to mask his personal difficulties with a warm smile, easy laughter, and a stylish wardrobe. He was usually successful in convincing family and friends that everything was okay, even when it was not. "He always had that comforting smile that he wore," said long-time friend Woodrow Thompson. "It was a comfortable feeling to be around him." Milburn never liked others to feel sorry for him. He preferred to believe in people's good nature, and he didn't want anything given to him that he didn't earn. On the track, personal difficulties would never be an issue; that was the one place where he always remained in control, where he still stood as an electrifying and awe-inspiring figure even late into his career, even when he was no longer the consistent winner he had been in his glory years. As long-time Opelousas resident Gilbert Deville said, looking up to the sky, trying to recapture a distant memory that he hoped he might find drifting through the air, "My word, that boy could run like a deer."[6]

Oh yes he could. And once he joined the J. S. Clark track team in the ninth grade, everyone in Opelousas knew.

# Two

# First Hurdle
## *Wooden Hurdles on a Grass Track*

> If you go out there and you got it in your heart, you can do something with it. If you don't got it in your heart, then it can't get done."[1]
>
> —Rodney Milburn

The hurdles were made of wood. They were built by kids in the industrial arts class. The track was a grass field. Coach Claude Paxton regularly mowed it and lined it himself. If you knew what was good for you, you had better not get caught walking on Coach Paxton's field.

Over hand-made hurdles, on a grass track, Rodney Milburn, Jr., became one of history's greatest high school hurdlers. But if the best hurdler at J. S. Clark High School hadn't gotten sick the day of a race early in the spring of 1966, Rodney might never have become a hurdler at all.

Coach Paxton gathered all the team members around him prior to the start of the meet and informed them that Fulton Lewis, the team's star hurdler and one of the fastest hurdlers in the state of Louisiana, was feeling sick and wouldn't be able to run. He then asked if anyone would be willing to step in for Fulton.

At first, nobody spoke up. As Jimmy Milburn later explained, nobody wanted to risk injury. Unlike other track events, the hurdles didn't just involve fatigue; the hurdles involved pain. Sure, the wooden hurdles made by assistant coach Oliver "Chief" Jackson's shop class were sturdy, well-designed, and built according to specifications,[2] but the thought of a knee or an ankle smacking into one of those heavy crossbars intimidated the boys even more than Coach Paxton's rumbling voice.

## Two—First Hurdle

The freshman, Rodney Milburn, raised his hand. "I said 'Boy, get away. You can't hurdle,'" Paxton later recalled in a 1993 interview with Bill Campbell of *The New Orleans Times-Picayune*.[3] But the young kid didn't relent. Rodney explained that he had been training over the hurdles after practice every day after the team's practice had ended. Those words, Paxton recalled, "hit me like a paddle."[4] Despite his misgivings, he decided to give the young kid a chance.

So he let Rodney run. It was the 180-yard low hurdles. Those hurdles were only 30 inches in height, compared to the 39-inch height of the 120-yard high hurdles. In his first race, Rodney hit every hurdle. "He ran through them all," Rod's brother Jimmy recalled. "He hit every last one."[5] But he won the race. That's when Paxton and assistant coach Eddie Guilbeaux realized they may have something special on their hands. They just needed to let him work on his technique, teach him how to really run the hurdles. And that's what they did.

Track was only one of Rodney's three sports: he also played wide receiver and defensive back on the football team, plus guard on the basketball

Milburn (*on the far left*) clears a hurdle during his sophomore year of high school while racing against J. S. Clark teammates on the school's grass track, over wooden hurdles made by the school's shop class.

## A Hurdler's Hurdler

team. His speed was his greatest asset, and it was quite obvious early on that track would become his best sport. Robert Morrison, head coach of the varsity basketball team said, "He couldn't dribble. He was too fast; he'd outrun the ball. So I'd tell the guys, if you want to give Rodney the ball, throw it way down there and let him go get it."[6] In football, Milburn never had much of a problem getting open, but he wasn't reliable when it came to making catches. Huey Hawkins, an alderman in Opelousas who used to referee J. S. Clark football games, remembers that "Rodney was fast, very fast. If he caught a pass you could forget keeping up with him."[7] Milburn's gift was his speed and his ability to step over those high hurdles with an uncommon grace and ease that belied the remarkable power of his densely-muscled frame.

Maybe Paxton saw himself in Rodney. In the 1930s, Paxton, too, had been a hurdler while running for Long Branch High School in New Jersey. Paxton perhaps was looking for athletes who had the physical tools and mental toughness required to excel in his own specialty. At 5-feet-11, 170 pounds, and having enough motivation to practice hurdling on his own, Rodney fit the bill.

Paxton, who graduated in 1938, is one of the best prep hurdlers ever to come out of New Jersey. He went on to Xavier University in New Orleans, where he starred in both football and track. His collegiate career was interrupted when he served in the U. S. Army during World War II. His Olympic hopes also ended; he would have been a heavy favorite to make the USA's 1940 Olympic team in the high hurdles had the Games been held.[8]

In the late '40s, after the war, Paxton starred as a two-sport athlete at Xavier. He and teammate Isaac Tatum graduated together in 1948, then Tatum came to J. S. Clark the following fall and started the first football, basketball, and track teams for blacks in Opelousas. Paxton followed Tatum to J. S. Clark in 1951. They worked together in coaching the football team, and Paxton took over as head track coach, quickly developing Clark into one of the most consistent and well-respected high school track programs in the South. He also organized and directed the J. S. Clark Relays—an annual relay carnival that he created in 1951. More than thirty black schools in pre-segregation Louisiana, Texas, and Mississippi participated each year.[9]

Coach Jackson assisted Paxton with the track program on a volunteer basis, but he is most proud of the fact that his students built the hurdles that Rodney skimmed over on his way to becoming a high school legend. The work was done after school hours. The kids, hand-picked by Jackson himself, did the work in addition to their usual class work. They built enough hurdles for six lanes, ten flights, for a total of sixty hurdles.[10]

Jackson's students made the hurdles light enough to do minimal damage to a hurdler's legs. "We checked them out," Jackson said, "to make sure that if a guy hit one of them, it didn't stand up to hurt him. It'd tip over."[11] Still, after knocking into every single one in his first race, Milburn wasn't feeling sure he wouldn't be better off returning to the sprints. "At first I started to quit. My legs took an awful beating," Milburn told the Opelousas *Daily World* in May of his senior year.[12] But when Milburn informed his coach that he didn't want to hurdle anymore, Paxton "gave it to me good," Milburn said in a *Boys' Life* interview with Frank Litsky in August of 1972. "He said I had the speed and height, but I wasn't dipping my body over the hurdles and that's why I was getting hurt. He said I could be one of the best hurdlers who ever lived. I liked that. He said I'd have to have the desire, that it wouldn't just come to me. He talked real loud, and all of us were afraid of him. We thought he was mean. He wasn't. He was really a nice guy."[13]

Stories of Paxton's quick temper and in-your-face style of coaching have reached mythic proportions among those in Opelousas old enough to remember him in his robust, boisterous prime. "If you knew Claude T. Paxton," Jackson said, "you knew that everybody around him has got to do something. And don't come half-stepping." Jimmy Milburn, who also ran on the track team, concurred: "Paxton was the type who would come at you," he said. "He was a screaming coach, and everybody felt threatened by him. When he hollered, he didn't need a microphone. You heard him from one end of the field to the other."

Being such a quiet, sensitive kid, Rodney didn't seem like the type who would respond well to Paxton's coaching methods, but Rodney was quickly able to see through his coach's gruff exterior and to recognize that Paxton genuinely cared about him. In his first race, Rodney had "banged my legs, my ankle, my knee, and my heel,"[14] yet Paxton still believed in his potential.

Paxton also understood the technical complexities of the hurdling events, as well as the fragile confidence and emotional ups and downs that hurdlers often experience. He understood that it would take time for Milburn to overcome his fear of hitting the barriers, to coordinate his lead leg (the leg that clears the hurdle first) with his trail leg, to coordinate the

## A Hurdler's Hurdler

arms with the legs, to adapt his raw speed to the limited space between the hurdles, and to then cohesively put all these factors together in a race. Paxton allowed Milburn the practice time he needed to learn the subtleties of hurdling mechanics. Instead of requiring that Milburn hurdle a certain way, he gave him the freedom to experiment with multiple technical ideas. Although Rodney was fast enough that he probably could have been a champion in the 100-yard dash, he was pleased to have found an event that required more than speed. His enjoyment of the intellectual challenge that hurdling presented explains why he stuck with it—that and the fact that Paxton wouldn't let him quit.

\* \* \*

"Hold on a second, Dice." Coach Paxton fished in his pockets and pulled out three dimes. He placed one atop each of the first three hurdles.

**Milburn (*third from left*) with coaches Claude Paxton (*far left*), Robert Morrison and Eddie Guilbeaux.**

## Two—First Hurdle

Rodney had finished third in his first race over the 120-yard distance,[15] and Paxton felt that his young protégé needed to learn to step over the hurdles. The coach's logic was typically straightforward: you can't run fast if your feet aren't on the ground. So he created a workout that would help Milburn learn to clear the hurdles on more of a horizontal plane. In this workout, the "dime method," Paxton instructed Milburn to drive the foot of his lead leg directly at the dime, trying to get as close to it as possible without knocking it off the crossbar.

Through use of this method, demonstrating the steady perseverance that he learned from his mother and father, Rodney gradually learned to hurdle more efficiently, but he was not an overnight success. He spent many hours with Paxton and by himself refining his technique. Coach Morrison noted that Milburn "was self-motivated. During the summers, Rodney would get out there on that grass track and mow the straightaway himself when the grass grew too high, so he could practice." Over time, the hard work would pay off, but as a sophomore, he still had a long way to go to catch Lewis. Milburn was also entering the beginning stages of what would later become an intense rivalry with Spencer Thomas of George Washington Carver High School in New Orleans. Thomas, more of an all-around athlete than Milburn, excelled in the long jump, triple jump, and both hurdling events.

In May of 1967, in the Zone 1 AAA Track & Field Championships, Milburn finished fifth in the 120-yard hurdles; he was beaten by Thomas, who finished fourth. Milburn's time of 14.7 was respectable for a sophomore, but he would have to continue to work very hard if he ever hoped to defeat the very talented Thomas, who was also a sophomore.[16]

In 1968, Milburn's junior year, he improved his personal best in the high hurdles to 13.9, which he ran twice, making him the third-fastest high school hurdler in the country.[17] In the lows, he dropped down from 19.5 to 19.0.[18]

On Saturdays, he could be found working out over three flights of hurdles. He figured that if he could get those first three hurdles down without too much trouble, then chances are he would win. Which he did, almost all of the time. Rodney also developed his own unique pre-race warm-up routine. In addition to running wind-sprints, stretching, and doing calisthenics, he would "go down all ten hurdles, clearing them with just his trail leg," Jimmy said, "then he'd turn around and come back, clearing them with just his lead leg, all in one motion. All the other hurdlers, when they'd warm up, they would go over like, three or four hurdles, or

## A Hurdler's Hurdler

they would just do some stretching over the first one. But Rodney, he would line up and go over ten hurdles. Boom! Trail-leg, trail-leg, trail-leg over ten hurdles, turn around, and boom! Lead-leg, lead-leg, lead-leg over ten hurdles. Continuous, like in a race. All full speed." Milburn's intensity in his race preparation added a new level of excitement on the track at J. S. Clark. The sight of this muscular figure striding over those hurdles with his wide, circular afro blowing in the wind put the fans into a fever pitch before the race even began. "The technique with which he could do it was amazing to see," Jimmy said.

Astoundingly, Milburn's warm-up didn't leave him too exhausted to race. He knew how much work his body could handle, and he knew what he needed to do to get himself primed to compete. Also, because most local meets did not include any preliminary rounds, the need for a full, highly powered warm-up was more important than in the bigger meets, which usually included one or two rounds prior to the finals. Since hurdlers usually run faster with each succeeding round, meets that included no rounds made them prepare so that the actual race *felt* like it was their second or third race of the day. Typically, right before the race, Milburn would go off by himself somewhere—under the shade of a Catawba tree, behind the bleachers, or on the other side of the track—to be alone with his thoughts, to quietly concentrate before heading to the starting line. Then, "when that gun would go off," Coach Jackson said, "he became a jet-plane."

Milburn clears a hurdle during his junior year on the grass track at J. S. Clark High School.

## Two—First Hurdle

Still, Milburn had trouble beating Spencer Thomas in the early part of his junior year. At the J. S. Clark Relays in March, Clark won the shuttle-hurdle relay, anchored by Milburn, but he finished second to Thomas in the high hurdles. Milburn did not run the low hurdles.[19] Later in the season, Milburn defeated Thomas at the LIALO (Louisiana Interscholastic Athletic and Literary Organization) State Championships in both hurdle races. (The LIALO consisted solely of black schools in Louisiana; the white schools belonged to the LHSAA, or Louisiana High School Athletic Association; the black schools and white schools had separate state championship meets).[20] Then, at the NORD (New Orleans Recreational Department) Meet of Champions in New Orleans, Milburn won both races again. His time of in 13.9 in the high hurdles made him the second Louisiana prepster to ever break the 14.0 barrier.[21] To close out the season, he ran the exact same times at the Preptacular meet in Alexandria,, setting himself up for what promised to be a dominant senior year.[22]

* * *

Rodney still played football in his final year but dropped basketball to concentrate on track. It was looking as if he'd be that rare black male Opelousan to attend a four-year college instead of catching cotton trucks or cane trucks or being drafted into the army and marching off to Vietnam as a draftee. Quitting basketball was more Coach Morrison's idea; Rodney was willing to play, despite his limited skills, if only to contribute to the team. Morrison saw Milburn's obvious potential in track and encouraged him to pursue it. "I told Rodney we weren't going to win no basketball championships," Morrison said. "The best thing for him to do was get ready for track, because that was his love."

In high school, Milburn was shielded from the draft. And with major track programs nationwide recruiting him, he'd be safe from Uncle Sam as a collegian. Schools seeking his services included some of the best in the country—the University of Southern California, the University of Tennessee, Grambling State University, Cornell University, the University of Florida, Michigan State University, and the University of Texas at El Paso. Some had been recruiting Milburn since his sophomore year at J. S. Clark. "Letters arrived daily from coaches offering full scholarships—tuition, books, room, board, and the legal limit of $15 a month in spending money," Frank Litsky wrote.[23] Most young black males in Opelousas in the late 1960s weren't so fortunate. While the Vietnam War didn't destroy

## A Hurdler's Hurdler

**Milburn (*third from left*) receives his 1st place award after defeating Spencer Thomas (*second from left*) in the NORD Meet of Champions in his junior year.**

Opelousas in the form of heavy loss of life, the psychological damage done penetrated into the daily lives of many families that were already struggling at or below the poverty line. "Probably about eighty percent of the guys who came back were mentally disabled," Jimmy said. "Maybe about twenty percent were functional."

## Two—First Hurdle

Rodney made the most of his senior year at J. S. Clark by having an outstanding spring season. He assaulted the record books on local, state, and national levels, making it increasingly clear that Paxton's initial prediction might well turn out to be accurate. The difference between Rodney's senior year and his previous years, besides the natural progression that he made, lie in a subtle shift in attitude. Before, Rodney would work hard in order to please Coach Paxton and because of the intellectual challenges that hurdling presented; by his final year, he had developed a true passion for the event, as the accomplishments of his junior year made him realize that he did have the talent to become a good hurdler. "I started to get used to it," he told the *Daily World* in May of 1969. "The legs didn't hurt half as bad. Then I began to enjoy it. Now I love it."[24]

Even the solo workouts were increasing in frequency. In his sophomore and junior years he would train on his own on Saturdays and a couple days during the week. Now he was doing it every day. Sometimes, instead of training all by himself, Milburn would grab his best friend on the team—fellow hurdler Vincent Hall—and practice with him over the first three hurdles. If he couldn't find Hall, then he'd get some younger sprinters to run alongside the hurdles. They wouldn't have to jump over them; he would just try to beat them to each one, which helped him to develop his lead leg quickness.[25]

The younger kids were glad to be practicing with Rodney, and he was glad to have them there. Their presence compelled him to focus more on his speed between the hurdles. It also inspired him to come up with the technical innovation of the double-armed lead. Rodney was having problems employing Paxton's dime method. In the attempt to forcefully drive his lead leg at the crossbar, he would flail his arms wildly, delaying the upward motion of his trail leg. The loss of balance was messing up his rhythm between the barriers, causing him to hit a lot of hurdles. To compensate, Milburn began to exaggerate the forward lean of his torso and drive both arms forward, not just the lead arm.

The exaggerated lean helped him to keep his momentum moving horizontally, and the double-armed action helped him to balance his weight. He was generating so much force in his dive into the hurdle that, once his lead foot touched the track, he was able to take a propulsive first stride toward the next hurdle. "The intensity of Rodney as he would go over those hurdles," Coach Morrison said, "was like nothing else I'd ever seen. Every time he hit the ground with that lead leg, it looked like he was just exploding off the track. Even the competition was looking at him like they didn't know what was going on."

Coach Paxton was also glad to see Rodney's progress. Although he had guided plenty successful athletes in his tenure as head track coach at J. S. Clark, none had reached Milburn's level of prominence. Paxton's affection for his star pupil did not come in the form of pats on the back or laudatory comments; it came in his devotion to keeping the grass track mowed and lined to perfection. "He did it all himself," Jimmy said, shaking his head at the memory, "he did everything. He mowed the field himself, he put the lines down himself. He wanted to be sure Rodney had a good surface to practice on."

Vont Dabney, who was a freshman sprinter in Rodney's senior year, vividly recalls Paxton's zeal in keeping the track in pristine condition for Rodney. "That field was just for Dice," he said. "When anybody else would walk on it, Paxton would be like, 'Get off that field!' He had one of them riding mowers, and he'd cut the grass all the way around, backward and forward, two times. And the whole time he's mowing it, he's turning around making sure nobody's walking on it. Then he'd line that track himself, and you better believe those lines were straight."[26]

They certainly were straight for the 51st running of the J. S. Clark Relays. Thousands of spectators filled the bleachers and lined the edges of the track. The local buzz that Friday afternoon centered around the impending showdown between Milburn and Thomas. It would be their first meeting of the season. "Dice got his hands full today," the Opelousas residents said to each other, the tense expressions on their faces revealing their concern. After his semi-final race, Thomas pumped his fist in the air, having run a faster time in his heat than Rodney had run in his. Rodney, after his race, followed his usual routine of quietly rejoining his teammates in the bleachers, where he started mentally preparing for the next day's competition.[27]

Many observers gave Thomas more than a fighting chance to beat Rodney. He had run a faster semi-final time, he was from the big city of New Orleans, and he had been hurdling longer than Rodney. In spite of Milburn's previous success and his status as one of the top hurdlers in the nation, there was still a widely-held belief throughout Louisiana that nothing good came out of Opelousas. The idea of a track star from Opelousas being better than one from New Orleans just didn't make sense, and many people couldn't make room in their minds for the possibility that Thomas would let Milburn beat him again. Like Milburn, Thomas was receiving scholarship offers from many universities and getting all kinds of national recognition, so very few people bought the idea that he might lose to a country boy from Opelousas.

An even larger crowd arrived for the finals. Everybody had come to see the race between Rodney and Spencer. The shuttle-hurdle relay earlier in the day had served to add tension to the race. Carver High School, anchored by Thomas, easily defeated Clark, anchored by Milburn. Clark's slowest man ran two seconds slower than anybody else, so when Rodney got tagged to take off, he was already five hurdles behind Spencer. He closed the gap, but Clark still lost by more than a full hurdle.[28] Rodney didn't take the loss well, and was intent on gaining revenge in the open hurdle final. "He was incensed," Morrison said. "Rodney was a calm guy, but if you beat him, he was coming after you. So when it came time for the individual race, Rodney was ready to blaze."

The 120-yard high hurdle final was run in the middle of the football field. When the time came for the big race, everybody in the bleachers was standing up. When Rodney's name was announced over the loudspeaker, he gave a short, quick wave and continued shaking out his legs. "Runners take your marks," the starter said. The athletes settled into their starting blocks and awaited the next command. "Set."

The gun went off, and Milburn and Thomas began to pull away from the rest of the pack. It was a two-man race from the start. Rodney and Spencer were sprinting stride-for-stride, hurdle-for-hurdle, for the first seven hurdles. The people of Opelousas were screaming for the local hero to come through. At the eighth hurdle, Rodney gained an edge, and pulled away further at the ninth hurdle. He carried the lead over the tenth hurdle and to the finish line, where he pushed his torso through the tape.

The crowd erupted into a frenzy. "Told you Dice would get him! Told you Dice would get him!" Thomas's 13.7 broke the all-time Louisiana record of 13.8 set by Jimmy Upton of Minden High School in 1967. Milburn, who finished two tenths of a second faster in 13.5, tied the national high school record set by Richmond Flowers of Alabama in 1965.[29] And they did it on a grass track, on the softest part of the field.

Milburn did not lose a race the entire season. At the prestigious Pelican Relays, held at Southern University in Baton Rouge, he and Thomas engaged in another electrifying battle, this time over the collegiate 42-inch hurdles. Milburn won in 14.1, with Thomas right behind him in 14.2.

## A Hurdler's Hurdler

The winning time in the college division was only a 14.4.[30] Because of all of his success on the track, Milburn was becoming a heroic figure throughout all of Opelousas, but particularly among the young black males. Milburn's victory over Thomas at the J. S. Clark relays, and his dominant season throughout the spring of 1969, was proving to these youths that something good *could* come out of Opelousas, that someone from this poverty-stricken town could take on the big dogs of New Orleans. Most importantly, Milburn was doing it with a quiet dignity and grace that made the young kids aspire to be just like him. In spite of his reserved mien and introverted approach to life, Milburn cared greatly about his status as a role model.

"Rodney was a few years older than me," said Stanislars Joseph Milburn, a second cousin. "I was still in the elementary school when Rodney was in High School. I used to go to a lot of football games and track meets, and I was watching Rodney all the time. Now you talk about exciting. I wanted to be just like him, and compete in Track & Field, but I kinda picked up some bad habits running the streets here with the guys in my neighborhood. Rodney would come by my house sometimes, he'd talk to me, to my mom, try to help get me straight. He was great with kids, man."[31]

Vont Dabney, who was old enough to share the same track space with Milburn for a year, remembered a time during his freshman year:

> Everybody wanted to be like Dice. One time a group of us younger guys were sitting around after practice. And you know, Dice was quiet, and he was a great runner, so we didn't think he paid us any mind. So we [were] sitting around after practice when all of a sudden Dice walks up to us. He must've heard what we was talking about 'cause we was all talking junk about who was better than who, then Dice walks up to us and says, "If you go out there and you got it in your heart, you can do something with it. If you don't got it in your heart, then it can't get done." And I'll never forget that, man. For as long as I live, I'll never forget that. And the thing was, he *never* talked to *nobody*. But he took the time to talk to us.

Such moments were typical. "He led by example," Coach Morrison said. "You would never find him arguing. And he was always influencing you to improve yourself. And I've never known him to have any vices at the time of when he was in high school. Not smoking, drinking. Nothing."

Another time, Dabney and one of his friends decided one day after practice that they wanted to give the hurdles a try. So, just like Milburn used to do, they grabbed a set of blocks, set up a hurdle, and prepared to go at it with no coaches around. "Next thing you know," Dabney said, "there's Dice standing behind us. Just looking, not saying anything. I don't

## Two—First Hurdle

know how long he'd been standing there. 'Cause you know what they used to say about Dice—if you didn't see him, you didn't hear him. So then he says to us, pointing to the hurdle, he says, 'Y'all wanna try that?' We was like, 'Yeah, we wanna try.' He was like, 'Okay, let's see what you can do.' And that was all he said. Didn't give us no instructions. He wanted to see if we *really* wanted to do it."

On a national level, many black athletic stars were coming into prominence. Jim Brown in football, Muhammad Ali in boxing, Tommie Smith in track, and Lew Alcindor in basketball were just a handful of the African-American athletes who were rapidly changing the complexion of sports in the United States. But in Opelousas, where schools were *still* segregated, the hero of choice was not any of the professional superstars who could only be seen on television; the only hero who mattered was the one who could be seen on the track at J. S. Clark High School striding over wooden hurdles with the grace of an equestrian horse.

"One time Coach Guilbeaux had us younger guys out there on the grass for a time trial in the 100," Dabney recalled. "So Paxton comes out and sees us out there in our regular shoes, and he says to Guilbeaux, 'Why the hell you got these guys out here doing time trials with no track cleats on?' Then he gets all the varsity guys to lend their shoes to one of us junior varsity guys. So everybody's looking at Dice 'cause we all want Dice's shoes. But Dice didn't have his shoes with him. So Sugar Bear—he was another sprinter—he didn't have his shoes with him either. So Dice goes into the locker room and comes back out with a pair of shoes and gives them to me. I went out there and won that time trial, boy, because I was *Dice*. I wasn't no Vont Dabney. I was *Dice*. Then I found out later they wasn't Dice's shoes, they was Sugar Bear's shoes!"

Rodney finished his senior year with two brilliant performances. On May 30, he ran another race over the 42-inch hurdles, this time at the Meet of Champions in the Houston Astrodome. This meet featured many collegiate stars. Although a senior in high school, Rodney was nineteen years old at the time (having repeated a grade during his elementary school days). Except for his lack of experience over the 42-inch barriers, there was no reason to believe that he couldn't compete with the nation's premier collegians. Rodney won the race in a blistering 13.7, four tenths of a second faster than his first race over the collegiate height a month earlier. In the process, he tied the meet record and broke the national high school record of 13.8 set by Richmond Flowers in 1965.[32]

## A Hurdler's Hurdler

Rodney was already the most accomplished high school hurdler in history, but his performance at Houston convinced him he could run with anybody. At 5-feet-11, he couldn't be sure that he'd be able to make a smooth transition to the higher hurdles. Although the 14.1 he had run at the Pelican Relays was quite impressive, such a time wouldn't hold up among the world's best. But the 13.7 would. It was only five tenths of a second off the world record. On May 30, 1969, Rodney Milburn, Jr., emerged as a force to be reckoned with in the 120-yard high hurdles. "That race was a turning point for me," Milburn told Frank Litsky a month before the 1972 Olympic Games. "That was the first time I thought I was good."[33]

Milburn's final meet was the Golden West Invitational in Sacramento, CA. In its tenth year of existence, the Golden West was the season's premier schoolboy meet—the unofficial high school national championships. Just being invited was a tremendous honor, since only the eight best seniors in each event receive an invitation to take part. Milburn was only the second J. S. Clark track athlete to ever have the opportunity to compete against the nation's elite; he was preceded by sprinter Aaron Thompson two years earlier.

Ironically, Milburn had been invited to the nation's premier high school track meet even though his national high school record of 13.5, run at the J. S. Clark Relays, was not officially acknowledged because the LIALO was not recognized by the National High School Federation as a legitimate state association; in Louisiana, only the LHSAA was recognized by the National Federation.[34]

Milburn wanted to go to the Golden West Invitational, Paxton wanted him to go, and so did the colleges that were bidding to land him as a prize recruit. The problem, of course, was money. Thompson's trip had cost $500, and Milburn would need at least that much for airfare and other expenses. If Milburn was going to make his first trip to the West Coast, he was going to need a lot of help from a lot of people.

Paxton first turned to the City of Opelousas for financial backing, but the bulk of the money was donated by the school community at J. S. Clark. "Everybody asked how much we needed," Jimmy said. "For the flight, the hotel room, the entry fee, and meals, it was something like six hundred dollars, but that was like five thousand back then. The teachers [at J. S. Clark] donated the money. No city council, none of that, because they didn't know anything about track; they didn't realize how significant it was to get invited to a meet like that. Turns out we were still forty dollars short right before it was time for Rodney to leave. A teacher came up and said 'I got it,' and they sent him over there." According to Jimmy, a total of $560 was raised among the people of Opelousas. Without a doubt, Milburn's trip to this prestigious race in California would never have been possible without a lot of help from many people in the J. S. Clark community.

In Sacramento, Milburn did not let down the people who pitched in to send him there. Milburn won the 120-yard high hurdles in 13.4, bettering the time that he ran at the J. S. Clark relays by a tenth of a second. His time would have broken the national record, but the tailwind was too strong to allow for a legally-established mark.[35]

Milburn also ran the 330-yard intermediate hurdles, since the 180-yard hurdles was being phased out of the sport in most states. In this race, over 36-inch hurdles, Milburn finished fourth in 39.1.[36] Not bad for someone who had never competed in the event before. But he didn't like the longer race, and vowed to never run it again. With his high school career complete, Milburn was ready to leave behind the 39-inch high hurdles and take on the best hurdlers in the nation over the 42-inch height. The only question was, what college would he be running for?

There was no reason to assume that Milburn would be going to college at all. His biggest obstacle was neither the war nor the track record of local black males, but his inability to read at twelfth-grade level. He had to go to all-white Opelousas High School for summer classes. Coach Guilbeaux paid for the classes out of his own pocket. Rodney had never been around white people before, and integration of schools had just started, so Guilbeaux would walk him over there. Lawrence Emerson, principal of J. S. Clark at the time, also helped to make sure Milburn got through the special remedial reading classes.[37] The day after Milburn won the Olympic gold medal in Munich, Emerson explained to the *Daily World* that "it is up to us in school administration to see that the athlete make it in school."[38]

Surely, if Milburn hadn't had such a reliable support system, he wouldn't have been prepared to handle the academic rigors of college; he may not have been able to meet college admissions standards to begin with. While Milburn was certainly a model student of hurdling, and a very serious student of life, he wasn't much of a student in the classroom. "He did his athletics, and he did his academics," Coach Morrison said. "He was not the type of athlete to look for an easy ride. In college, he wasn't an A student, but he was a good, solid C student."

## A Hurdler's Hurdler

The college that he ended up choosing was the one he had gone to for several of his greatest moments on the track—Southern University, a school of 7,000 students. Several factors led Rodney to attend Southern, not the least of which was that his coach would go with him.

On August 9, 1969, Paxton was officially named interim head Track & Field coach at Southern. One week earlier, Rodney had signed an athletic scholarship to attend the university. Paxton would be filling in for Dick Hill, who was taking a one-year sabbatical from his coaching duties in order to complete his doctoral studies.[39] Southern being nearby was another factor. Rodney was very close to his mother and sister, and didn't want to move too far away. Besides, he had no reason to trust the hundreds of coaches pursuing him. Did they have his best interests in mind? Or were they just under severe pressure to win? Success at the major collegiate level often had more to do with recruiting well than coaching well. A program that stockpiled the best athletes could be assured of contending for conference and national titles. In such programs, athletes were often treated as commodities.

Rodney was not a great student or an enthusiastic one. But he did want an education. As he told Litsky, "I decided I wanted three things: a good education and a degree because I knew there was a life after sports, a good track program, and a school where I would be accepted as a person and not just an athlete. Southern University gave me all of these, and it was close to home."[40]

Rodney's decision came down to two schools—Southern and Texas Southern, both of which were smaller schools with low athletic budgets. He was strongly considering Texas Southern since it was in Houston, home to his sisters Lillie and Alice. So, why did he choose Southern over Texas Southern? Paxton.

It was now time for coach and athlete to make the 45-minute drive down Route 190 to Baton Rouge.

# Three

# Second Hurdle
*Rod and Willie at Southern U.*

> We're all given a talent, and mine happened to be the hurdles.... That's what I did better than everybody else.
> —Willie Davenport[1]

In his first year at Southern University, Rodney became friends with the best high hurdler in the world. Willie Davenport, 1968 Olympic champion, had graduated from Southern shortly after his Olympic victory. When Rodney arrived, Willie still trained there and coached as a volunteer. From the beginning, Rodney and Willie developed a close relationship. The twenty-six-year-old Willie mentored Rodney as the young freshman adapted to college life and the higher hurdles.

Willie's journey to stardom had begun at Howland High School in Warren, Ohio.[2] His hurdling career took flight like Rodney's: filling in for a sick teammate. In 1961, Willie's junior year, his coach asked him to step in at the 120-yard highs. Willie, who preferred baseball over track anyway, figured he had nothing to lose. He covered the distance in 15.8. Very fast for a first try.[3]

He made it to the semi-finals of the State Championships that May, then won the state championship as a senior. His time of 14.2 was fast enough to earn an invitation to the U.S. Army track team in 1963.[4] At first, Willie was just glad to get out of some of the usual work duties. But then "I saw a film of Hayes Jones," he said years later, "and decided I could beat him."[5] Jones, bronze medalist in Rome in 1960, was the world's best hurdler and a favorite to win gold in Tokyo in 1964.[6]

The army had selected a small group of athletes to prepare for the 1964 Olympic Trials. Willie began to take track more seriously. "I was young and could run like a damn deer," he said. "I was training with Bullet

## A Hurdler's Hurdler

Bob Hayes.... Bob Hayes was the fastest son of a bitch that I ever saw."[7] Hayes, who went on to win the 100 meter gold in Tokyo, was coached by Dick Hill at Florida A&M before Hill moved on to Southern.

At the Trials in Los Angeles, Willie finished first in 13.6. Jones finished second in the exact same time, and Blaine Lindgren finished third in 13.8.[8] Willie's victory was a shocker. Experts had been predicting a showdown between Hayes and Lindgren. Willie had made himself a favorite for the gold. But he strained a muscle in an early round of the Games and could only muster a seventh-place finish in his semi-final heat. Jones won the gold in 13.6.[9]

Determined to gain redemption, Willie enrolled at Southern in 1965 after being discharged from the army.[10] Dick Hill had recruited Willie to Southern. Known for his meticulous approach and scientific knowledge of the sprints and hurdles, Hill began to correct Willie's technical flaws and mold him into an Olympic champion.

By 1968, the hurdling landscape had changed dramatically. Jones and Lindgren had ridden off into the sunset, replaced by Leon Coleman of Winston Salem State, Erv Hall of Villanova, and Richmond Flowers of Tennessee. Earl McCullough of the University of Southern California had tied the world record of 13.2 in 1967, but quit track before the Trials to play for the Detroit Lions of the National Football League.[11] So one of Willie's chief rivals was out of the picture.

Early in the 1968 season, Flowers looked like the biggest threat to Willie's hopes. At the Pelican Relays on April 19, on Willie's home track in Baton Rouge, he lost to Flowers, 13.3 to 13.7. The following day, running into a strong headwind, Flowers defeated Willie again, 13.8 to 14.0, at the Dogwood Relays on Flowers' home track in Knoxville.[12] Willie soon quit the Southern track team.[13] Doing the team thing was hurting his Mexico City chances.

He had Hill's blessing. Having coached the mercurial Bob Hayes, Hill knew that great athletes need to be given a fair chance to display their greatness. Freed of the shackles of the team schedule, Willie could now gear his training and racing schedule toward the Trials, which would be held in September. Since 1964, he had clearly established himself as the best hurdler in the world. He had won two Amateur Athletic Union titles and had cut his personal best to 13.3. But after Flowers had humbled him two days in a row in April, Willie knew he could take nothing for granted.

## Three—Second Hurdle

In June, Flowers tore his hamstring in a training session. In September, he showed up at the Trials in Echo Summit, California, ready to compete, but the muscle had yet to fully heal. Had the stakes been lower, he probably wouldn't have been running at all.[14] With Flowers hobbled, Willie's stiffest competition would come from Coleman and Hall.

After winning his quarter-final and semi-final heats in 13.3 and 13.5, Willie took the top spot in the finals in 13.4. Coleman and Hall finished right behind, both in 13.5. Willie had gotten out slow, but caught Coleman and Hall by the fourth hurdle and held his slight lead the rest of the race. Flowers fought gamely but managed only fifth in 13.7, ending his Olympic dreams and his track career. Like McCullough, he joined the pro football ranks. Willie headed off to Mexico City for his second chance at Olympic glory.[15]

At the Games, the 110 meter hurdle competition took place over two days. The first round was held on October 16. The semis and finals were held one day later. Willie won his first round heat in 13.6. The next day, he won his semi-final heat in 13.5. Coleman and Hall looked strong in their heats, too.[16] It was shaping up to be an American sweep.

Willie ran a flawless race, winning in an Olympic record of 13.3. Crossing the finish line, he raised his arms in jubilation. The smile on his face revealed his relief. He had gained redemption. He had won the gold.[17] "From the first step, the gun," he said years later, "I knew I had won the race. It was perhaps the only race I ever ran that way, but that first step was so perfect, right on the money."[18]

Hall claimed the silver medal in 13.4. Eddy Ottoz of Italy broke up the American sweep by narrowly defeating Coleman for the bronze.[19]

Willie Davenport, reigning Olympic champion, greatest sprint hurdler in the world, is the man Rodney Milburn met when he stepped foot on the campus of Southern University in the fall of 1969. Rod, the best prep hurdler in history, admired Willie, wanted to break his records, and longed to earn a gold medal.

Willie was the perfect mentor for Rodney. He embodied the personality traits that Rodney lacked. Willie was affable, outspoken, witty, and comfortable in social situations. Dr. George Whitfield, a retired professor who taught Willie in public speaking in 1966, pointed out that even before arriving at Southern, "Willie's military experience made him more outgoing, because he had been forced to deal with all kinds of people. Plus he had done track exhibitions all over Europe, so he was more mature than your average college student."[20]

## A Hurdler's Hurdler

Willie also had a huge ego. "When you ran against him," Leon Coleman said, "he'd tell you you got second place before the gun went off."[21] But he wasn't possessive of his territory. It would've been easy for him to shun Rodney as a potential threat to his status, but for all his brash egotism, Willie liked to help people. In the beginning, he was more mentor than peer for the introspective Rodney. Along with Paxton, he showed Rodney ways to adjust to the 42-inch hurdles and gave him plenty of positive reinforcement. Off the track, "Willie was kind of hip," Dr. Whitfield said. "A sharp dresser. So was Rod. They were alike in a lot of ways. They were both confident guys. They knew what they could do and they did it."

While Rodney's confidence was limited to the track, Willie's extended to all aspects of life. Unlike Rodney, who kept to himself and avoided conflict, Willie was acutely aware of social issues and never hesitated to make his opinions known. Like many black track athletes in the 1960s, Willie felt that there were major disparities between white and black athletes. They were treated worse by the press, meet directors, and the sport's governing bodies. In March 1966, Willie beat Richmond Flowers in a national indoor championship meet. Flowers' father, the attorney general of Alabama, was a despised figure among racist locals for advocating integration. Despite Willie's victory, Flowers ended up on the cover of *Sports Illustrated*. "Here I am," Willie recalled, "I win the national championship, and the whole story was about him and his father."[22]

Among the black athletes, such slights, whether intentional or not, were considered commonplace. The athletes began to see their status as second-class citizens reflected in the plight of blacks throughout the country. That's why, in 1967, the Olympic Project for Human Rights was born, led by sociology professor Harry Edwards at San Jose City College in California. Edwards found three track athletes at San Jose who agreed with his contention that sports gave the black race in America one of its only platforms to create change. World-class sprinters Lee Evans, Tommie Smith, and John Carlos all experienced racism at school. In trying to find on-campus housing or get into required courses, they kept running into roadblocks.[23]

Under the leadership of the fiery Edwards, the project began to threaten boycotts of major track meets, including the 1968 Olympic Games. A Games boycott never took place, but the infamous black-fist protest of Smith and Carlos did. On the victory stand after the 200 meter dash, Smith and Carlos bowed their heads and raised black-gloved fists toward the cloudy sky. It was a symbolic protest against social and economic inequities in the United States. It was interpreted as a threat of violence and an insolent display of disrespect for the American flag. The United States Olympic Committee, under orders from the International Olympic Committee to severely punish the two athletes, expelled them from the Olympic village and banned them for life from any further Olympic competition.[24]

After his victory in the hurdles, Willie made no similar protest. And the thought of taking part in a boycott had never entered his mind. He was a sergeant in the Army. He had loyalties to his country that other athletes didn't have. Plus he was an individual. Willie wouldn't do anything just because someone felt he should. Though the media considered him one of the more militant blacks on the Olympic team, Willie quickly grew annoyed with the fact that, at his post-race press conference after his medal ceremony, all of the questions were about politics and protest. "I noticed that no one was asking me about the race," he said years later. All they were interested in asking were racial questions. So I said, 'Hey, I came here to do a job, and I did it. If you don't have a question about my [hurdle] race, I don't have anything more to say.'"[25] He wasn't criticizing Carlos and Smith; he didn't like how the media was pitting the black athletes against each other. He also felt bitter about the black athletes' limited chances to cash in on their Olympic success. Years later, when asked what he got for winning the gold, he responded with a surly, "I got ran out of town. I got a ticket back home."[26]

Clearly, he was not satisfied with his Olympic experience. But he did believe in the Olympic spirit. He preferred to show his activism at Southern, where he led many demonstrations protesting segregation. He also accepted a position as director of the Mayor's Council for Youth Opportunity in Baton Rouge. In that role, he and his staff set up child-care centers, made sure underprivileged kids received healthy meals, and provided job training for single mothers.[27]

Willie's sincere concern for the poor children of Baton Rouge was a contrast to the other aspects of his character. Brian Oldfield, a shot-putter who traveled throughout Europe on the same circuit as Willie for many years, said in 2006 that Willie "was a smoker and a drinker. He was a womanizer. He could find a new girl in every port. I was like, whoa, I wanna be like him."[28] Vince Matthews, the 1972 400-meter gold medalist, detailed in his biography that athletes spent much down time on planes and in hotel rooms gambling. Willie was one of the major players.[29]

Willie also passed time on the road by playing pranks on the younger athletes. Charles Foster, the 1974 NCAA champion, recalled an incident from his first year on the European tour. He and Willie were walking outside the stadium in Munich, looking for a quick bite to eat:

> We walk out, they got concession stands to buy bratwurst, and Willie offers to buy me lunch. I get a frankfurter on a little plastic plate, with a Kaiser roll beside it. The guy offers me a choice of mustard, ketchup, some other condiments. I didn't know anything about German mustard. Willie was in the military, he could speak a little German, so he picked it out for me. He got the hottest mustard they had, but I didn't know. Then he asked me, "Do you know how to eat a frankfurter?" I said, "Yeah, it's just like a hotdog." He said, "No, it ain't like a hotdog. You gotta put the mustard in real good, then bite the bread. That's how they do it over here." Well I did like he said, and when I bit into that thing, I damn near burned my nose. I was on the ground trying to catch my breath. And Willie was on the ground laughing.[30]

For someone as low-key as Rodney Milburn, following in the footsteps of a dynamic, charismatic character like Willie Davenport was no easy task. Anybody who knew anything about track knew who Willie Davenport was. Anybody who followed the hurdles knew that Willie was the best in the world. Who was Rodney Milburn? A freshman.

Said Leon Coleman: "I give Rod a whole lot of respect, man. Coming up, running the hurdles behind somebody like Willie was tough. I used to run behind Willie, so I knew what it was like. People didn't even know my name. They would call *me* Willie. And Rod, when he was first coming up, they sometimes wouldn't notice him. If you're a novice runner, no matter how good you were in high school, you gotta show them what you can do."

But by 1970, Willie was no longer the only man to beat. He could still run with anyone, but two new Americans stood beside him as the nation's best hurdlers: Marcus Walker of Colorado and Thomas Hill of Arkansas State. Hill had graduated from Walter Cohen High School in New Orleans two years ahead of Rodney, but they had never raced each other as preps. Back then, Hill had focused on the high jump and long jump. He switched to the hurdles because his college coach offered him a scholarship. "It didn't make any difference to me," Hill said at the time. "I wanted a college education and if I had to hurdle to get it, I'd hurdle."[31] Another contender was Guy Drut of France. Drut rarely ran against the Americans, but he was making a name for himself in Europe.

And then there was Rodney. Exceptionally talented, but raw and unproven. At this level, one-on-one duels with Spencer Thomas were a thing of the past. Up here, everybody could run like Spencer Thomas. In his first major indoor meet, the CYO National Invitational in Maryland, Rodney finished fifth in the 60-yard hurdles. He wouldn't have been invited to compete at all if Willie hadn't asked the meet promoters to let him in. Willie set an indoor world record in the race,[32] but afterward he spoke of Rodney. When asked if he felt he was on pace for another Olympic victory, Willie said, "I'll probably still be hurdling in 1972, but I doubt if I'll be able to win another gold medal. You see, there's this young fellow I brought with me here from Louisiana. He finished fifth tonight, but by 1972, nobody is going to be able to beat him. He's going to be the best high hurdler in the world."[33]

Willie's words would prove prophetic. More important, they revealed that his initial impressions of Rodney's talent were no different from Paxton's four years earlier. Once the outdoor season hit, Rodney began to show that Willie's wild prediction might come true. In his first competition, a dual meet against Southwest Louisiana in Lafayette, Rodney won easily in 13.6. His time placed him among the top ten in the world, announcing that this schoolboy standout planned to wreak havoc on the college ranks as well.[34]

At the Martin Luther King Games in Philadelphia, Milburn lowered his best to 13.5. He came very close to beating Willie, who ran the same time but was given the nod.[35] Rodney and Willie rarely ran against each other that first year. Willie competed in open meets and invitationals, while Rodney raced in meets on Southern's schedule. The King Games marked only the second time all season they faced each other. The first time, at the Pelican Relays in April, Willie had defeated Rodney soundly. Rod's improvement the second time hinted that he was learning to look at Willie not as a mentor but as a rival.

In early June Rodney won his first collegiate national title with a 13.7 at the NAIA championships.[36] It was a good tune-up for the two national championship meets later in the month to close out the year. First came the United States Track and Field Federation championships in Wichita. There he finished second to Tom Hill, who tied the world record of 13.2. Rodney's 13.5 equaled his best. Even more encouraging was his consistency. He posted wind-aided times of 13.4 and 13.3 in the prelims and semi-finals.[37] He was getting the hang of these higher hurdles, and he was performing well under pressure.

## A Hurdler's Hurdler

Rodney's last competition was the AAU championships the last weekend in June. Since the AAU was the official governing body of track and field, this meet was considered the peak of the domestic season. Usually, the top three finishers in each event would be chosen to represent the United States in international competition the rest of the summer. All the heavyweights showed up in Bakersfield, California. For the first time, Rodney would compete against Hill, Walker, and Willie—all in the same race.

There were three semi-finals heats. In the first, Rodney ran a methodical 14.0, four tenths of a second behind Paul Gibson of UTEP. Walker edged Hill in the second heat. Willie outran Leon Coleman in the third. In the final, Rodney finished fourth in a relatively poor 13.7, behind all three of his main rivals. Hill won in 13.3, followed by Walker in second and Willie in third.[38]

With the national title under his belt, Hill was now the top dog. In just his third year of hurdling, he had become the best in the country. Walker had dropped his personal best by three tenths of a second, and could now claim to be the equal of Hill and Willie. Willie, who had been leading for most of the race before Hill and Walker overtook him at the fifth hurdle, had to concede that he was no longer king of the mountain.

For Rodney, the disappointment was profound. In his biggest meet of the year, he performed below his own personal standards. Instead of peaking, he ran the same time he had run in the Houston Meet of Champions as a high school kid. Perhaps being stuck way over in Lane 1 had something to do with his weak showing. Maybe he had succumbed to the pressure of facing so many top-notch opponents. Or maybe he still needed to fine-tune his technique. Whatever the case, his season was over.

Willie, along with Walker and Hill, traveled throughout Europe all summer. Rodney went home to Opelousas.

With the recent arrival of integration, old J. S. Clark had been renamed and remade as East Junior High. On his first day back, Rodney walked to the grass field and hopped aboard Paxton's riding mower. He cut the tall grass, and then he changed into his running clothes.

# Four

# Third Hurdle
## *On a Winning Streak*

> "Rodney didn't care whose ass he was whuppin,' he just loved whuppin' ass."
>
> —Charles Foster[1]

A funny thing happened in Southern University's first home meet in 1971. Rodney ran a pedestrian time of 14.1. He didn't understand why. There was no headwind, no rain. The tartan track felt soft and firm beneath his spiked shoes. The race felt quick. More like a 13.6 or 13.7. Something had to be wrong. Walking back to gather his warm-up clothes, he noticed where the timers were standing. The finish line was too far back. Rodney had run 127 yards.[2]

Another spring had arrived. The pain of last year's AAU meltdown had faded, but the desire to redeem himself had increased. He had spent the winter months training. With no races. If it had been up to Rodney, he would've been running indoor meets all winter long. But Dick Hill, back from graduate school, decided that Rodney needed to address his technical flaws before battling the likes of Willie Davenport, Tom Hill, and Marcus Walker again. He also declared that Rodney needed to build up his late-race strength, so he had him running over-distance. Rodney hated over-distance. He was a sprint hurdler, not a distance hurdler. He wanted to be an indoor champion, and Hill was preventing that from happening.

Rodney had no idea why Hill was keeping him out of races. At the time, Bert Nelson of *Track and Field News* wrote: "Rodney saw Davenport taking off every weekend and returning with prizes and stories to tell, and he wanted some of the action."[3] Why was Hill making Rodney run quarter-miles in practice? Would these workouts help him to hurdle faster? "The

## A Hurdler's Hurdler

one thing I most dislike about track is running the quarter," Rodney said in the *T&FN* article.[4] But Hill had him running quarters almost every day.

Accustomed to Paxton's improvisational approach to coaching, Rodney neither liked nor grasped Hill's more detail-oriented style. Hill told Nelson, "My philosophy is that in the technical area of the hurdles, a guy has to have a scientific background, so when they approach the level Rodney is at now, you can talk about things that are highly critical with the terminology you need to use. There are a lot of terms I use that he wasn't able to grasp during the turbulent time we ran into."[5] Rodney wasn't stupid. But technical jargon didn't appeal to him. Hearing it made him suspicious. He had grown so comfortable with Paxton as a mentor that he wasn't sure he could trust Hill the same way. Did Hill have his best interests in mind? Or was he one of these coaches who was just looking to pad his resume?

But Hill's credentials were beyond question. He had coached two gold medalists. Both Paxton and Willie advised Rodney to have faith in Hill, so Rodney tried, despite his own misgivings. Since Rodney wasn't running races, he had no way to be sure Hill's method's were working. Did his coach not have confidence in him? "Rod more or less felt he was being put down," Hill said. "He realized his great potential, and I realized it too, but I didn't want him to just go out there and start trying to prove greatness when he still had all these flaws."[6]

Rodney also had to accept that he was a member of a team. Willie wasn't. Willie could set his own schedule. As good as Rodney was, he had to put the team first. "He and I talked about some of the advantages and disadvantages of the team being just average while he was great," Hill said. "He had to subordinate a lot of his own personal desires for the benefit of the team."[7]

Hill recognized Rodney's work ethic, and knew their mutual efforts would pay off shortly. "Rodney is very coachable," Hill told Frank Litsky, "because he is willing to pay the price. What he has done is a reflection of that." Hill also compared Rodney favorably to his first Olympic champion, Bob Hayes. "Both realized they had awesome power, but neither sat back. Both thrived on competition. As the competition got better, they got better."[8]

May 16, 1971, was the first day Rodney beat Willie in a hurdles race. On a cold, damp, drizzly afternoon at the Martin Luther King Games in Philadelphia, Rodney ran a wind-aided 13.2 for the victory. Willie finished third in 13.5. Tommy White of Southern California snuck in for second in 13.4.[9] For Rodney, the triumph over Willie marked a turning point similar to the Meet of Champions victory after his senior year of high school.

"After that race," Rodney told *T&FN*, "I knew I could run a 13.2 anytime, with or without a wind. It was just a question of how much faster I could go."[10] In another *T&FN* interview he stated, "My goal when I got out of high school was to at least tie the world record. It wasn't until after Philadelphia that I started thinking I could go all the way."[11]

Hill agreed, noting that Rodney's 13.4 in the prelims came so easily, it didn't even look fast. Then, after he beat Willie, "he realized that he was strong," Hill said. "His whole attitude seemed to change because he started noticing the benefits that he was achieving. He became inquisitive and very interested in what we were trying to do." Hill admitted, though, that "if Rodney had fallen flat on his face in that meet he might have questioned a lot of things I was doing."[12]

All the quarters Hill made Rodney run gave him the endurance to maintain form over all ten hurdles. Before, when he would work only on his speed, start, and lead leg, his technique would get very sloppy toward the end of a race. Now, the tenth hurdle was looking as good as the first.

To Willie, the inevitable had finally happened. "It felt bad to lose," he said. "I had to tell Rodney he was the greatest. But I was happy to congratulate him after the race."[13]

Larry Shipp, who would enter LSU two years later and ran against Rodney and Willie, was a high school junior at the time, watching the race from the stands. The duel between the two rivals, and their mutual sportsmanship, left an impression on him. "One of the most heart-warming things I saw," he said, "was when Rodney beat Willie, and Willie gives him the biggest hug you've ever seen. Here I was a young guy; I had always been taught to have that boxer's mentality. But here was Willie showing me that you could be a warrior without hating your opponent. It teaches you a lesson. You go out, you work hard, you compete."[14]

The magnitude of Rodney's victory was enormous. "No one ever really heard of him before then," Shipp said. "The dominant hurdler was Davenport. To see Rodney win that race and beat Willie just changed everything. At first you think it's a fluke. Next thing you know, no, he's just dominating."

Rodney's break-out win was overshadowed by a duel between Marty Liquori of Villanova and Jim Ryun of Kansas in the "dream mile." Newspaper headlines the next day focused on the two middle-distance runners.

Both finished in an astounding 3:54.6, but Liquori was credited with the victory. In the wire service article that appeared across the country, the epic battle between Liquori and Ryun was described in detail, including mile splits and quotes from both athletes. Rodney's defeat of Willie was mentioned in a short paragraph at the bottom.[15] It wouldn't be the last time that a brilliant performance of Rodney's would go virtually unnoticed.

But Rodney was moving up in the hurdling ranks. Prior to the King Games, he had won at the prestigious Drake Relays in Iowa, setting a new meet record of 13.5.[16] Meanwhile, Marcus Walker and Tom Hill were falling off the map. Both had incurred injuries that threatened their careers. Walker, sadly, was never able to return to his old form. "I pulled a muscle in my hamstring," he said years later, "and I didn't wait long enough for it to heal. I just came back too soon, and it just caused more of a problem than anything. I developed a hematoma in the bone of the muscle, and that was it for me."[17]

Walker had managed to get in a couple races before his disaster struck, but Hill missed the entire season after tearing the anterior cruciate ligament in his right knee before the outdoor season even started. "I get a little depressed about it," Hill said of the injury at the time. "I really don't know what will happen and I just hope I'll be able to run well again."[18]

The injuries of the world's two top-ranked hurdlers from 1970 opened the door even wider for Rodney. At the California Relays in Modesto during the last weekend in May, Rodney beat Willie and Tommy White again.[19] The win itself wasn't a big deal, but how he won it was. Rodney got out slow and was having trouble settling into a rhythm. Then he clobbered the third hurdle and almost fell. The rest of the field flew past him. "The first thing that hit me," he told *T&FN*, "was that I had lost it. Then I figured I'd better get going, and I went on at it."[20] His time of 13.5 was nothing spectacular, but, as Coach Hill said, "I felt I'd just seen him run his worst race ever and still win. That was a pretty good indication that bigger things were on the way."[21]

At the NAIA championships the following week in Billings, Montana, Rodney turned out a stunning but wind-aided 13.0 to win by four tenths of a second over Ron Draper of North Carolina Central.[22] Wind-aided or not, it was the fastest sprint hurdle race ever run. There could be no doubt that Rodney was ready to challenge the world record of 13.2 set by Germany's Martin Lauer in 1959. "I felt then," Coach Hill said, "it was just a matter of time when the legal 13-flat would take place."[23]

## Four—Third Hurdle

The meteoric rise that Willie had predicted was coming true. Rodney was growing more consistent with his hurdling technique. As the victories piled up, his confidence soared. He stayed humble and mild-mannered, but the change in attitude showed in his appearance. Throughout high school and his first year at Southern, he had kept his afro haircut neatly trimmed and shaped. Now he let it grow out. Sometimes he added a part in the middle so that half of the afro swung to one side, and the other half swung to the other. In races, he often added a headband to the look. He also let his sideburns grow, abandoning the clean-shaven look of his "Dice" days. "He had all the self-confidence after the Modesto meet," Coach Hill said. "*He* even talked like it then."[24]

"That's when we started calling him Hot Rod," Leon Coleman said, "because we never knew when he was gonna put the rod on you." Rodney didn't talk trash to his opponents, but he did play subtle mind games with them. Always one to go off by himself in the moments leading up to a race, this habit started to get into his opponents' heads.

"You wouldn't see him until the starter said strip down," Charles Foster said. "Then he'd show up. He'd just appear from behind the bleachers. You'd think he's not coming, and then there he is."

Maybe Rodney chose to materialize out of the blue because he was growing annoyed with Willie's habit of running off at the mouth. Rodney was starting to beat him regularly, but that didn't lessen Willie's swagger in the least. Nothing, really, could affect Willie's confidence. "Willie was the kind of guy," Tom Hill said, "who felt he could beat your butt any day of the week."[25]

More than anyone, Willie could see that Rodney was becoming a superior hurdler. He trained with him. He saw how hard Rodney worked, and he knew that Rodney practiced harder than he himself did. Dr. Raymond Lockett, a history professor at Southern who assisted with the track team in the early '70s, claimed that "Willie never trained. He'd come out and go over two hurdles and that's it."[26] Willie already had a gold medal around his neck, so he wasn't nearly as hungry for Olympic success. "He worked," Dick Hill said, "but not on the same level as Rodney."[27] But because Willie was so highly skilled and such a tremendous competitor, he remained a constant threat. Before races, he liked to chatter at Rodney to break his concentration. "They'd jaw-jack back and forth all the time," Foster said.

But Rodney wouldn't let trash-talk get to him. He was a master at

## A Hurdler's Hurdler

shutting out distractions and focusing on the task at hand. "I've usually got butterflies prior to a meet," he told *The Advocate* of Baton Rouge. "I'm pretty tense, but that's good. It makes me run better. It helps me get up for a race. When getting ready for a meet I try to put everything else out of my mind. I think about each opponent individually. And I always like to think positively. That's the *only* way I think. Once the gun sounds, I'm all right."[28] With his sideburns, afro, headband, well-defined muscles, and explosive double-armed hurdling style, he was an intimidating figure. People didn't want to run against him. And there was nobody he was afraid to run against. "He was just taking names," Foster said. "He didn't care whose ass he was whuppin,' he just loved whuppin' ass."

Rodney and Coach Hill were pleased with the improvements, and credited them to their training sessions. Of course, because Rodney was heading toward a number-one world ranking, everyone wanted to know the secret to his success. "I believe the key is my start," Rodney said. "I have a good, quick start. Then I build up momentum between the hurdles.... As a freshman, I ran mostly off of strategy. My technique wasn't down. Now I can control my arm better, my trail leg is much quicker, and I stay down on the hurdles closer. I don't hit them as often."[29]

Hill was more analytical in his assessment: "He's developed a tremendous amount of technique in terms of lead leg, trail leg coordination, lift coming off the hurdles, use of the arms, and the sprint between the hurdles." Predictably, Hill saw more room for progress. "Rod still has a few rough spots," he said. "We definitely have to get rid of his lateral movement, and his left arm coordination is not exactly perfected. But he has overcome these deficiencies by having an overwhelming amount of strength and speed."[30]

Rodney was getting to know his body better. As part of his studies for a physical education degree, he took a physiology class. It helped him understand how the systems within the body function and interrelate. Based on his discoveries, he developed a new warm-up routine that involved more stretching and jogging than the one he used during his J. S. Clark days. Back then, he would just blast over the hurdles at full speed instead of building up gradually. Now he was warming up for 45 minutes before he even took off his sweat pants. "Every muscle needs to be loose," he said. "Hurdlers usually do more warm-up exercises than other participants in order to get the blood circulating good."[31]

Leading up to the AAU championships at the end of June, he took

## Four—Third Hurdle

on more of the college ranks, moving beyond the tiny schools of the NAIA. First came the NCAA College Division national meet in Sacramento. He ran a 13.5 into a fierce headwind, winning handily over Draper, yet again providing hope that, under the right conditions, the world record would fall.[32] Next came the NCAA University Division in Seattle. Here he faced athletes from all the major conferences around the country. He and Draper finished 1–2 again. Unfazed by the Notre Dames and UCLAs of the world, Rodney ran 13.5 in the prelims and semis, then finished things off with a smooth and easy 13.6 in the finals, slowing down at the tape.[33]

With Walker and Tom Hill on the shelf, Rodney was the clear-cut favorite at the AAU championships in Eugene, Oregon. Other contenders were Tommy White, Lance Babb, and Jerry Wilson, all of USC. Then there was Draper, and of course, Willie, who presented the stiffest challenge because of his proven ability to exceed expectations in big races. Draper had finished second to Rodney in just about every race they had run, so there was always the possibility he could come up with an upset. White, too, had lost a couple close ones to Rodney. In American hurdling, old faces might die out, new ones might replace them, but the level of competition always stayed the same. Even with Walker and Tom Hill gone, Rodney would have to run a near-flawless race if he expected to win.

\* \* \*

Prior to the semi-final race, Willie was doing his usual "jaw-jacking," but Rodney ignored him and focused on preparing. Their semi-final heat was stacked. Making the finals wasn't a lock. Wilson, Babb, Dick Taylor of Northwestern, and 1968 silver medalist Erv Hall joined Willie and Rodney at the starting line.

Rodney blasted out of the blocks and took command of the race. He never looked back until he broke the tape in a world record time of 13.0. Willie also qualified for the final, coming in three tenths behind Rodney in 13.3. Wilson, Babb, and Taylor all crossed the line in 13.4, with Hall's 13.6 good only for sixth and a seat in the bleachers. The Eugene fans, famous for their knowledge and enthusiasm, roared their approval when the world record announcement came over the loudspeaker. Rodney smiled and waved. He felt elated to have broken the record, but he still had more work to do.[34]

In the final, he sped to another easy victory in a wind-aided 13.1. Draper nipped Willie for second, 13.3 to 13.4. Babb finished fourth, also

## A Hurdler's Hurdler

in 13.4. Tommy White, who had finished second to Draper in their semi-final heat, hit a hurdle early and didn't complete the race.[35]

It was a glorious day for Rodney. The Eugene crowd gave him a standing ovation as he jogged a victory lap. Only their local hero, distance runner Steve Prefontaine, received a larger ovation. In the three-mile run, Prefontaine, spurred on by his fanatical hometown fans, willed himself to a dashing, daring triumph over big-named rivals Frank Shorter and Gerry Lindgren.[36]

Now there was no question that Rodney was king of the high hurdles. He wasn't just winning, he was dominating. He had swept the three collegiate championships, and then topped it off with an emphatic performance in Eugene. He had smashed a twelve-year-old record by a full two tenths, leaving many to wonder if he could go even faster.

Said Willie immediately after the finals: "I wasn't surprised by the 13-flat. I predicted he'd run 12.8." Willie also hinted that the student had become the master: "I still help him and he still has some flaws, but I learn things from him now too."[37] He also predicted even better things to come for his protégé: "Milburn can run 12.7 and that 13.0 won't last as long as a snow cone."[38]

Surprisingly, with the wind at his back, Rodney didn't run sub-13 in the finals. "My best times come in the trials," he told Frank Litsky. "I'm more relaxed. I don't like the pressure of a final. In my 13.0, everything went nice all the way. I even eased up over the last hurdle."[39] Describing the race to the *Daily World* years later, he said he felt "just like a ballet dancer out there going through the routines. I had so much finesse I could almost stand on top of the hurdle."[40]

Rodney had risen to the level of superstar. He was the greatest high hurdler in the world, maybe even in history. And he was arguably the best track athlete in the world. He had yet to lose a race all season. He could no longer go anywhere without someone recognizing him, asking for an autograph, encouraging him to break 13-flat, wishing him well in his quest for Olympic gold.

Although he tried to remain calm and approachable through it all, he had trouble adapting to his sudden fame. He viewed himself as the same ordinary guy he had always been. He'd been winning races all his life. Why should winning them now change anything? As Litsky pointed out, "He was a bright new star, a modest hero whom fans could respect and admire and cheer."[41]

## Four—Third Hurdle

Milburn relaxes in the infield during the UTEP Invitational in 1971.

Being a Southern gentleman played a big role in Rodney's increasing national popularity. He didn't go out of his way to make anyone like him, and many mainstream audiences saw him as a refreshing change from the militant black sports heroes of the 1960s: you didn't have to worry about Rodney Milburn raising a black-gloved fist to the sky. Still, he had the respect of blacks because of the adversity he had overcome in making it this far. Plus he was good friends with many of the "rebels" from the '68 Olympics, like Willie and Leon Coleman. And he had the respect of whites because he carried himself with dignity.

As he told Litsky, "I'm a fairly easy person to get along with. I guess I'm happy. But I don't enjoy being a celebrity. Everybody pressures me. I

## A Hurdler's Hurdler

want to get away from people. Since I set my world record, I won't even go to basketball games at school."[42]

Clearly, Rodney didn't have the charismatic personality of a Muhammad Ali, a Wilt Chamberlain, or even a Willie Davenport. If anything, fame made him even more reclusive. He suspected the motives of people who praised him without knowing him. He felt most comfortable when visiting family and friends in Opelousas during holidays and breaks, or when hanging out with Willie and his track teammates.

The only outside admirers he trusted were kids. At Southern's home meets, he spent hours after races signing autographs and talking with them. He liked going to local high school meets in Baton Rouge and watching the young athletes compete. Occasionally he attended their practices and offered instruction on the basics of sprinting and hurdling.

Rodney wasn't a typical college student. Besides being a star athlete, he was married. He and his wife Carolyn had known each other since childhood. They tied the knot early in Rodney's freshman year at Southern. They lived in separate dorms at first, but then moved together into on-campus housing reserved for married students. Rodney spent most of his time away from the track with Carolyn.[43] No partying, no drinking. Those kinds of pastimes didn't appeal to him. He didn't join a fraternity. The Greek tradition may have been a staple of social life at black colleges, but Rodney wasn't a fraternity kind of guy. As Litsky wrote, "When people aren't bugging him, Milburn is relaxed. He is soft-spoken, shy, and not excitable. He smiles easily. He talks easily with friends, not quite so easily with strangers."[44]

The strangers he trusted least were reporters. Perhaps he opened up to Litsky because that interview was for *Boys' Life*, a kids' magazine. But it was not in Rodney's nature to speak openly with sportswriters. "He was one of the more taciturn athletes that I ever met," said Bob Hersh of *T&FN*. "I once had to interview him and it was not the easiest interview in the world."[45]

In his own quiet way, Rodney was an idealist. He was a dreamer. If any cultural movement from the '60s stayed with him into the '70s, it was not the spirit of revolution, but the spirit of peace and love. At the top of his list of favorite musical groups was the Fifth Dimension. Their hit, "Aquarius," was an astrological anthem celebrating the vision of a shift into a new age of spirit consciousness. An age of "harmony and understanding, sympathy and trust abounding." Rodney believed in that vision, and he studied astrology intently. He did so on his own, outside the classroom.

"Astrology is very interesting," he told *The Advocate*. "It makes everything seem so real. I've got a whole set of books on astrology. I feel like many of the readings concern me in some way and I believe it reveals something about your future."[46] When asked by Litsky's eleven-year-old son to identify the thing he would ask for if granted one wish, Rodney answered simply, "Everybody should live forever."[47]

Not your typical college student. Not your typical world-class athlete.

\* \* \*

Unlike 1970, Rodney's season continued after the AAU meet. He didn't travel to Europe, but he faced international competition on domestic soil. He ran two races in July, the first against Russia, then against Africa two weeks later. He won both races handily. Draper finished second in each race.[48] Rodney closed out the season with another victory at the Pan-American Games in California the first weekend of August. He won by a wide-enough margin that he looked back at his opponents as he crossed the finish line. "Just wanted to see where they were," he said.[49]

Rodney's 1971 was one of the greatest campaigns ever for a track athlete. He didn't lose a race. Including the 127-yard mistake, he won 29 straight races in total, including 16 finals. "To win even three races in a row is incredible," Shipp said, "because those other hurdlers don't go into a race thinking, 'I'm going for second place today.' When you have that type of attitude coming after you and you can win more than twenty in a row, that's something you're not supposed to be able to do."

The accolades Rodney received at season's end included some of the most prestigious available. *Track & Field News*, in its annual year-end issue, named Rodney its Athlete of the Year. He was the first hurdler to ever receive this honor. Of course, the magazine also rated him as the #1 ranked hurdler in the world.

Locally, Rodney won the Jim Corbett award, given to the best amateur athlete in Louisiana. The award had been in existence since 1965; Rodney was its first black recipient. In Opelousas, August 28th was designated Rodney Milburn Day. It was the first time the town had ever organized a special day to honor a black citizen.[50]

On the morning of the 28th at City Hall, dressed in a button-down shirt, sports coat, and pin-striped slacks, Rodney autographed pictures

## A Hurdler's Hurdler

**Willie Davenport, Milburn, and another Southern University teammate pose for a photograph during an awards ceremony in 1971.**

for kids and shook hands with many politicians. After breakfast came a parade and Rodney's acceptance speech. The breakfast, parade, and ceremony were attended by blacks and whites.

"The white people here," his sister Lillie said, "they really loved Rodney. They loved to put on a show that they loved him and cared about him. I think they really respected him because he was a good person."[51]

Rodney's appeal, certainly, was his quiet nature. "He was good people," Gil Deville, a local white resident, said. "They're all good people, that whole family. This was a man who was brought up with good manners, had a good reputation in the community. Very polite, very well-reared."[52]

Rodney had bridged the racial divide. The only thing left now was to win a gold medal.

# Five

# Fourth Hurdle
## *Reaching for the Gold*

"A track man is like a flower. You have to bloom again every spring. I've got to go to work and do it all over again."
—Rodney Milburn[1]

In track, the three years between Olympics matter only because they lead up to the Games. In Milburn's day, this was even more true. There were no world championships every other year, and there was no professionalism. The sole motivation for the best athletes was Olympic glory. That was the only way to validate the training, traveling, and financial sacrifices. Only a gold medal made it all worthwhile.

Heading into the outdoor season of 1972, Rodney was feeling the pressure. His dominance the previous year wouldn't mean a thing if he didn't follow it with Olympic success. His undefeated season made him the favorite, but it provided no guarantees. He would have to train, race, and hope for the best, just like everybody else. No longer raw and unproven, he wasn't chasing Willie Davenport anymore. He was chasing a dream.

Though Rodney was protective of his privacy, the "Hot Rod" persona was taking over his life. Reporters and fans were making increasing demands on his time, and Rodney didn't like all the attention. When Frank Litsky's son asked him where he'd like to live if he could live somewhere else, Rodney answered, "Billings, Montana," the rural town where the 1971 NAIA national championships were held, because "it's a lot quieter there."[2]

On the track, Rodney was coming off an indoor season in which he had lost a couple races over the 60-yard distance. Willie beat him once, and in another he finished third to Tom Hill and Tommy White. Hill, now back from knee surgery, was picking up where he left off in 1970, when he was the world's best. Like Rodney, Hill also dreamed of Olympic gold, and he wasn't convinced that Rodney was better. "Rod's win streak didn't affect me," Hill said in 2006. "I felt that if I had been running in '71, he wouldn't have been undefeated. My thinking was, he lucked out that I had been injured. So going into '72, coming off the injury, I wanted to compete everywhere he competed. I wanted to get him because, having an undefeated competitor in your event, that's not cool."[3]

Rodney wasn't about to concede anything either. His first race over the 120-yard distance took place indoors, at the Houston Astrodome on February 12th. He set a new indoor record of 13.4, taking advantage of a quick start and finishing one tenth ahead of Willie, who tied the old record.[4] With Hill back at top form and Willie still running fast, it was looking more and more like Rodney, Willie, and Hill would be the three favorites to make the Olympic team. The trials were set for the first weekend in July.

At the Southwest Louisiana Relays in Lafayette on April 15th, Rodney ran another wind-aided 13.0.[5] That he did it in an early-season college meet against no big-named opponents proved that he was on his way to another dominant season.

After victories in the Drake Relays and the SWAC conference championships, Rodney had another astounding performance at the second annual El Paso Invitational in Texas. There, on May 20th, he beat Willie again, 13.3 to 13.5, into a blustery headwind of more than three meters per second.[6] Under normal conditions, he would've easily run 13.1, maybe 13.0.

The following weekend was the California Relays in Modesto. All the American hurdlers who held hopes of making the Olympic team were at the meet. Willie, Tom Hill, Tommy White, Ron Draper, Paul Gibson of UTEP, and young Charles Foster—a freshman sensation at North Carolina Central under the direction of coaching legend Dr. Leroy Walker. It was the first outdoor meeting between Rodney and Hill since the AAU championships two years earlier. Both entered the meet undefeated.

Rodney easily won his semi-final heat in a wind-aided 13.3.[7] In the final, he lined up in the middle of the track in lane four. Willie was beside him in lane five, with Hill one lane over in six. Wearing his aqua-blue Southern uniform, Rodney had all his accessories in place: wedding ring on his left hand, wristwatch, knee-high socks, and headband surrounding his untamed afro.

## Five—Fourth Hurdle

In the biggest race of the year up to that point, and facing the stiffest competition in the nation, Rodney dominated the field. He blasted out the blocks and gained a slight advantage by the first hurdle. He continued to increase his lead until he crossed the finish line in a blazing but wind-aided 13.0, the third such race of his career. Willie and Hill came in a half-second behind in 13.5. White and Draper both fell after colliding into each other off the seventh hurdle. Foster finished a distant fifth.[8]

Hill's presence didn't make a difference. He was just another member of the trailing pack. Rodney's superiority was clear. Not just to spectators, but to the other competitors. Recalling the race in a 2005 interview, Foster noted, "Rod was off the last hurdle running toward the finish line, and I was still between hurdles nine and ten."[9] Rodney seemed almost a sure bet to win the Olympic Trials and Games. The only contender outside of the U.S. was Guy Drut, dubbed "The Frenchman" by the American hurdlers. He had run a wind-aided 13.3 in a European meet and had finished 1971 ranked fourth in the world.[10]

Rodney faced Foster again at the NAIA championships the next weekend in Billings, Montana. Despite his performance in the Modesto race, Foster went into the meet feeling confident that he could hold his own. Except for Rodney, Foster was the best hurdler in the NAIA. The top freshman hurdler in the country, he had run 13.7 to win the Penn Relays in Philadelphia in late April.[11] The past successes of his coach, Dr. Walker, gave him instant credibility. Walker had coached Lee Calhoun to two Olympic gold medals in the high hurdles, in 1956 and 1960.[12]

"But Rod didn't give a damn," Foster recalled. "Mine was just another ass to kick, from his perspective."

Both hurdlers easily won their preliminary rounds. In the finals, they lined up side by side, Rodney in lane four, Foster in five. Said Foster years later: "I figured I'd put it to the test and see what I could do."

He got out evenly with Rodney and they touched down together off the first hurdle. From there it was all over. "I've never seen anybody in my entire life run like that from the first hurdle to the second hurdle," Foster said in 2005. "That changed my entire perspective on hurdling. It was like, how does he *do* that?" Rodney ran away from Foster and won in 13.5, glancing back to see where Foster was as he crossed the line.[13]

Rodney's secret, which he later shared with Foster, was that he didn't look at the first hurdle. He looked past it, to the second one. "His thinking was," Foster explained, "you know it's there, and you've practiced your

## A Hurdler's Hurdler

start enough times, so why don't you run at the next one? The moment I started doing that, my times dropped drastically. So that's how I coach my athletes now. You never have to look at the first hurdle."

The NAIA race was also memorable for the comical accident that befell Rodney. Said Foster:

> Back then, all you really wore beneath your shorts was a jockstrap, so your cheeks were completely exposed, and you just had a little cup to hold your package. Rod must have hit one of those hurdles, because he caught the crotch of his shorts. By the time he hit the finish line it looked like he had a skirt on. He was holding his package like Michael Jackson. His whole ass was exposed. Somebody threw him some warm-ups and he put them on. He and I got a good chuckle after that one. He thought it was funny too.

On June 9th, Rodney traveled to Los Angeles for the VONS Invitational, where he won in 13.4, defeating Willie, Hill, and Guy Drut.[14] The following day, at the Kennedy Games in Berkeley, he took Willie's best shot, holding on for a 13.3–13.4 victory. Rodney got out to a big lead in the early part of the race. Willie came back with a huge late-race surge, but it wasn't enough to catch Rodney.[15]

Rodney was maturing as an athlete. In earlier years, being tracked down by Willie would've caused him to lose his nerve. "I felt Willie coming up on me," Rodney said after the race, "but I didn't fold. If I really went to pieces, I could have lost. But I was able to concentrate and I just pumped that much harder."[16]

The AAU championships were next, in Seattle, Washington. Usually the biggest domestic meet of the season, this year it served as just another tune-up for the Olympic Trials that would arrive in two weeks. Adding interest to the meet was the presence of Drut. It was very rare for a foreign athlete to be invited to compete in the American national championships. That the AAU was allowing him to compete in an Olympic year, when dreams and medals were at stake, did not go unnoticed by the American athletes. According to a Chicago Tribune report at the time, some "wondered out loud" why Drut was being given such an opportunity.[17]

Whether Rodney was among the hurdlers who protested the Frenchman's presence is unclear, but, considering his success in the past year and a half, there is little reason to believe he felt concerned that Drut might be able to beat him.

Rodney breezed to a first-round win in 13.5, but it turned out to be a pointless race. The other two heats had several scratches, so only fourteen athletes entered in the event. Which meant that all would qualify for the semis. Once the officials realized how low their numbers were, they decided to automatically qualify all athletes. But Willie, protesting in behalf of Rodney, argued that if the guys in the first heat had to run a qualifying round, then they all should. So two more meaningless heats were run, with no one running faster than 13.9.[18]

The shocker came in the semi-finals. Rodney lost to Tom Hill, 13.5 to 13.8.[19] It was Rodney's first outdoor loss since the 1970 AAU final, when he finished fourth. Still, because it occurred in a preliminary round, it didn't count as an end to his winning streak. He easily qualified for the finals, but the loss was significant because it came at the hands of Hill. It was clear now that Hill had fully come back from his injury, and that he had the mental toughness necessary to compete against Rodney.

Still, while the press was making a big deal out of Hill's defeat of Rodney, neither of the two athletes seemed impressed. To Hill, it only proved that anybody can be beaten. One victory, especially in a semi-final, did not mean he could reclaim the title of world's fastest hurdler. What it did mean was that he was still a formidable opponent and gold medal contender. He seemed annoyed that his win surprised people.

"He's human," he said a week later, referring to Rodney. "Willie could have got him. Anybody could have got him. If I didn't think I'd win, I wouldn't have come."[20]

Rodney, for his part, blamed his semi-final performance on having discovered the day before that $257 had been stolen from his wallet while taking a shower. His mind wasn't on his race, he said, but on his lost money.[21]

He regained focus an hour after the semis and stepped into the starting blocks for the final. There, he gained a bit of redemption by claiming first place in 13.4, into a strong headwind. Once again, he showed his ability to concentrate under stressful conditions. Besides losing his cash, his blocks slipped in the final, forcing him to catch himself by putting both hands on the track. He quickly held up his hand to the starter, who shot the gun a second time. No false start was charged, and Rodney saved himself from a certain defeat. On the next attempt, he got out behind Hill and Tommy White, but ate up ground between the hurdles and won comfortably. Willie and Hill both finished in 13.6, with Willie getting the nod for second. Drut did not even finish the race. After suffering a mild thigh injury during warm-ups, he hit the first hurdle, crashed into the second, and knocked down Ron Draper in the lane next to him before falling out of the race.[22]

Rodney's winning streak was still intact, and so was his confidence. Heading into the Trials, he had defeated the best the world had to offer. Some observers in the media noted that he may have grown complacent at this point and eased up his training schedule. His brother Jimmy claims that that is not the case. Certainly, though, Rodney was growing tired of track, despite his dominance. He was growing tired of the politics, the travel, and the fickleness of the press and fans.

Even before the AAU meet, Rodney felt frustrated that his superstardom wasn't making him any wealthier, while athletes of comparable abilities in other sports were making tens and even hundreds of thousands of dollars a year. He was also feeling uncomfortable with the pressure the world record had brought. Now, instead of being a contender for Olympic gold, he was the favorite. Such weighty expectations, along with being stuck in a sport where he could not make a living, was wearing him down.

"I wish I had lost somewhere along the line," he said in the days leading up to the AAU meet, "because I am feeling the pressure of this streak."[23]

After the meet, he was already talking about retiring from track and trying his hand at pro football. "Six more races and then it's over," he told *Track and Field News*. Three rounds at the Trials, then three more at the Games. "I'm not getting anything out of track. For three years now it's all I've done. I'm always thinking track. I'm traveling here for this and that meet, and everybody's hassling me."[24]

"Everybody" included the media, whose demands on his time were cutting into his training regimen. "The media people have kept me on the run and have interrupted my schedule," he said. "But that's okay," he added with unconvincing diplomacy, "these are things you have to live with."[25]

It also included the fans. Suddenly thrust into the spotlight, he was getting a crash course on the American public's penchant for building up and then tearing down its stars. "People don't realize an athlete goes through changes," he told Frank Litsky. "And they demand just too much. First, everyone wanted me to beat Davenport and all the others. Then when I broke the world record, they wanted everyone to beat me. They said they were my friends, but friends don't do that. And when I lost a race," he added, referring to the AAU semi-final, "all of a sudden they weren't my friends."[26]

## Five—Fourth Hurdle

Heading into the Trials, his mind was distracted and fatigued. He was thinking about football as much as track, even though he hadn't played a down since his senior year at J. S. Clark. He was already planning to play cornerback and wide receiver for Southern upon returning to Louisiana after the Olympics.

"You do a lot of work," he told Frank Litsky, expressing his frustration with track, "but get nothing in the pocket. At least I could make a living in pro football. Another thing I don't like about track is the training. If I could do without training I would skip it."[27]

Strange words for someone admired for his work ethic. He was obviously feeling the strain of being a world record holder. But he realized he was on the verge of something special, and remained determined to earn a gold medal. He didn't want to let down the people in Opelousas and Baton Rouge who were counting on him. "I know you gain from everything," he told Litsky. "You've got to pay the price. And now, with my world record, I have a responsibility. I'm the Olympic favorite. I just hope I can get there. I've got to avoid injury. And I've got to make the United States team, which probably will be tougher than the Olympic competition. I've got to prove to myself that this is all real and not just a dream."[28]

The Trials were held at Hayward Stadium in Eugene, Oregon, the same venue where Rodney had run his world record 13.0 the year before. He eagerly looked forward to competing on the soft tartan surface again, in front of knowledgeable, enthusiastic fans. "On that track," he told *Track & Field News* in the days leading up to the meet, "there is no reason I can't run 12.7, or even 12.6 for that matter. That's the best track I've ever been on."[29]

The rounds of the 110 hurdles were spread out over four days, July 6th through 9th. The heats and quarter-finals took place on the 6th, the semis were on the 7th, then after a day of rest, the finals were set for the 9th.

All the heavyweights in the high hurdles arrived in Eugene healthy and ready to race. Rodney, Willie, and Tom Hill were the favorites to make the Olympic team, but there was also Foster, Draper, White, Babb, and Coleman. Youngsters to look out for included Charles Rich of California, Jeff Howser of Duke, and Jerry Wilson of USC. Veterans Erv Hall and Paul Gibson, both victims of minor injuries at the AAU meet the previous week, did not show up. All prognosticators were predicting that Rodney would come out on top.

The first round consisted of five heats. Rodney ran in the second heat,

## A Hurdler's Hurdler

and won easily in 13.6. Hill and White also won their heats in the same time. Willie also ran well, finishing behind White in 13.7.[30]

Willie asserted himself in the quarter-finals, winning the first heat in 13.6. Rodney followed suit by winning the next heat in 13.5. But there was cause for concern, despite his fast time. He hit seven of the ten hurdles en route to winning the race.[31] No big deal for an early round, but he would have to run a much cleaner race once it came time to line up against Hill and Willie in the finals. Rodney's "dime method" of skimming over hurdles made him quicker than all of his competitors, but it also made him more susceptible to making contact with the barriers.

Tommy White won the third quarter-final heat in 13.7, and Hill matched Rodney's 13.5 in the last heat.[32] It was looking like Hill had the best chance of anyone to upset Rodney. Not nearly the technician that Rodney was, Hill relied on his height and athleticism. "I've still got a lot to learn," Hill said after the quarter-finals. "My form isn't good. I'm not that fine a hurdler yet. Guys talk about knocking a dime off a hurdle. If I tried to do that, I'd flatten the hurdle."[33] In a 2006 interview, Hill explained that "my challenge was to not overstride. Tailwinds wreaked havoc on me. I'm 6–2 with a 36-inch inseam. Getting over hurdles was never a problem for me. My technique was not very good, but I knew it was sufficient to negotiate the barriers."[34]

It was sufficient, in fact, to tie the world record of 13.2 in his semi-final race. Rodney's record of 13.0 was run over the 120-yard distance, which is a few centimeters shorter than 110 meters. Back then, races in the United States were all measured in yards, except during Olympic years. Hill's time was not counted as a record because the wind at his back was slightly over the allowable legal limit.[35] Still, he was running better than Rodney so far at Eugene, and he was now looking like the man to beat.

Rodney also handled business in his semi-final heat, posting another 13.5, but he did more of his timber-toppling. This time he smashed the third and ninth hurdles.[36] Definitely, the aura of invincibility he had built over the past year and a half was diminishing.

With a day off between the semis and finals, Rodney had plenty of time to think about the stress he was under. The Olympic Trials was unlike any other meet he had ever attended. The pressure was enormous. His winning streak didn't matter. His world record didn't matter. That he could beat Willie, Hill, and all the others nine times out of ten didn't matter. If he didn't finish in the top three the next day, he was done. His Olympic dreams would be dead, his hard work wasted. Still, he knew without question that he was the best hurdler in the field. No one could beat him at his best. "The only way they were going to beat me," he recalled years later, in 1993, "was on technicalities. I'd have to have a bad race. If I had my race, I'd beat them."[37]

Hill, though confident, was feeling the pressure too. "In this country," he said in 2006, "making the team is a very difficult process. You can't save anything. You have to be sharp for the Trials or else you will never make it to the Games. So you try to run your best race at the Trials and hope you can equal it or top it at the Games. You don't even worry about the Games because if you're saving something you might be saving it for the next four years. You could be the best in the world and not make it through the U.S. Olympic Trials."[38]

One athlete who certainly had no doubts about making the team was Willie Davenport, who stood on the verge of going to his third Olympics. As Hill says, "Willie was always confident. I don't care about time of day, year, how old he was. If you ever stepped on the track with Willie Davenport, he thought he could beat your butt."[39]

The other finalists were Draper, White, Rich, and Howser. None could be written off. Another sloppy race could easily leave Rodney out of the running.

Though he had won his semi-final heat, Rodney was assigned lane eight. In track today, heat winners are given the preferred lanes in the middle of the track—lanes 3 through 6. But back then, lanes were assigned randomly. In races run on the straight-away, such as the 100 meter dash and the 110 meter hurdles, lane assignments didn't really matter much because all athletes would be running the same distance, with no curve involved and no staggered start. But mentally, lane assignments were very important. The way it works now, with the fastest athletes in the middle lanes, the favorites run beside each other, where it's easy for them to keep close tabs on each other. Plus, being in the middle lanes gives them the psychological advantage of knowing they're one of the favorites.

Lane eight must have made Rodney feel awkward. Hurdlers and sprinters get used to having an opponent on either side of them. In lane eight, Rodney had no one to his right, just a wall with billboards on it. Fortunately, Willie was to his immediate left, in lane seven. Hill, though, on the other side of the track in lane two, would be hard for Rodney to see.

## A Hurdler's Hurdler

"Runners take your marks."

Rodney eased his feet into the starting blocks, placed his hand behind the starting line, took a long, slow breath, and waited for the next command.

"Set."

He raised his butt and rolled his shoulders forward.

Boom!

Willie got out the fastest and held a slight lead over the first hurdle. Rodney touched down a fraction of a second behind him. Hill was in the thick of the hunt as well. By the fourth hurdle, the three favorites had created separation from the rest of the pack. The long-legged Hill was just beginning to crank it into another gear. "Getting started presented a challenge for me," Hill said in 2006. "But this time I got a good start. I used to judge the first half of my race by the distance I was behind the leaders. If I could minimize that distance, the second half of the race was mine. If I'm with you at the fifth hurdle, you're gonna have a problem with me, because I'm coming."[40]

Sprinting into the seventh hurdle, the three favorites continued to battle for first. That's when Rodney ran into some trouble. "He hit the hurdle with his lead leg," recalled his brother Jimmy, who watched the race on television. "He hit it hard. And then, like, it knocked him back a little."[41]

Hill and Willie surged ahead. The young Charles Rich in lane five also capitalized on Rodney's mistake. Rodney was in fourth place. As he would later reflect, this was his "bad race."[42]

Rodney had no speed going into the eighth and ninth hurdles. He was just trying to recover his balance. White and Wilson were gaining ground on him. Hill and Willie were pulling further away. Rodney finally regained balance and attacked the tenth hurdle aggressively, but he struck it with the foot of his lead leg, throwing him off-course yet again. By the time he landed he was in sixth place. There was not enough space to catch Hill and Willie, but he still had a chance to grab the third spot. Making a frantic dash toward the finish line, he thrust forward his torso in a desperate lunge at the tape.

The final results listed Hill as the winner in 13.5, Willie in second in 13.5, and Rodney in third in 13.6. He had made the team. He was going to Munich. The fourth, fifth, and sixth place finishers—Rich, Wilson, and White, all ran the exact same time as Rodney. His lunge at the finish proved to be the difference.[43]

## Five—Fourth Hurdle

Back in those days there was no such thing as digital photography, and electronic timing was still in its experimental stages, used only at the Olympic Games. Ties were decided by the finish line officials, who took a manual photo. It could be argued that the judges gave Rodney the third-place nod simply because he was Rodney Milburn and they knew he had the best chance of capturing gold at the Games, but Rodney's lean was perfect. That final lean is all about timing. If you lean too soon, you'll slow down before crossing the line. If you lean too late, you'll already be past the line. Rodney leaned at exactly the precise moment he needed to.

Also, he thrust his torso forward, not his head. The torso that crosses the line first gets the nod, regardless of where the head is. Despite running a technically flawed race, Rodney had survived the Olympic Trials. Still, his performance raised some serious questions. Firstly, what had gone wrong? He had been running on his favorite track, against the type of competition that had usually brought out the best in him, but he couldn't stop bulldozing hurdles. Why?

"I don't think it had anything to do with losing focus," his brother Jimmy said. "I think it was just one of those things that happens in a hurdle race. He just made a mistake and hit that seventh hurdle."

Rodney himself admitted in a 1993 interview to being caught up in the moment. As he put it, "I felt a lot more pressure in the Trials than I did in the Olympics. The sheer psychological intensity was like nothing I'd ever experienced."[44]

Now, with the Trials behind him, was Rodney still the favorite to win the Games? Did he still consider himself the best hurdler in the world?

"His confidence didn't waver any after that race," Jimmy said. "Going into the Games, his confidence didn't waver at all."

Rodney himself said in 1993 that, after making the team, the Olympics two months later "were easy. I never considered for a moment that I might not win."[45]

He had reason to be confident. The winning time of 13.5 was slower than he had run in most of his races all year, even in the preliminary rounds of many meets. He knew that when he ran his best, no one could beat him. There was no other hurdler who could make such a claim. Still, when there are hurdles in the way, anything can happen. And his poor showing at the Trials validated Hill's belief that Rodney's winning streak was largely the result of his absence, not Rodney's superiority.

Hill now held the title of national champion. One year after tearing

## A Hurdler's Hurdler

ligaments in his knee so badly that there had been talk of amputating the leg, Hill had not only returned to competition, but he had made it all the way back to the top. Overcome with emotion, he let out a whoop when the official results of his finals victory were announced. "I had no idea I won it," he said afterward. "I thought I was tied for third. I gave it everything I had. This is the greatest thing that's ever happened to me. By far."[46]

Reflecting on the race years later, Hill said that he "felt good from start to finish. At that level, you're on a mission. You stay focused on what you came to do. And that's what I did. And I believe I wasn't expected to win it anyway. Which was okay, because after coming off the season Rod had, he was clearly the guy to beat. After being out a solid year, there were some question marks as to whether I could recapture the old form. That's why you run the race, though. I'm really clear about that."[47]

Looking forward to the Olympics, Hill's faith in his ability was at an all-time high. "I went into the Games expecting to win," he says. "I was at a point in my career [that] whenever I stepped on the track I expected to win."[48]

Then there was Willie. At 29, he was the grand old man of the hurdles. In that era, very few track athletes competed past their collegiate years. Even fewer competed past the age of 26 or 27. But Willie had a combination of will and skill that can only be found among the top tier of elite athletes. As defending Olympic champion, the brash, ebullient veteran was going to be a formidable foe in Munich.

As for Rodney, his football plans would have to be put on hold a little while longer. His destiny awaited him on the track.

# Six

# Hurdle Five
## *Date with Destiny*

"Unless you're on that [victory] stand, you can't know the pride that comes from winning something for America."
—Rodney Milburn[1]

Following the near-disaster of the Trials, it was time to regroup. Rodney was no longer the clear-cut favorite he had been before his upset defeat. Hill was the Olympic Trials victor. And Willie was the defending Olympic champion. Rodney's Athlete-of-the-Year campaign of 1971 was already a distant memory, as was his 28-race win streak. All of a sudden, he had something to prove.

But at the same time, the worst was over. He had survived the enormous pressure of his first Trials. He had made the Olympic team. Despite the third-place finish, most experts still believed he was far and away the best hurdler in the world. Jim Bush, head coach of UCLA at the time, said of Rodney in the weeks leading up to the Games, "If he's healthy, and I think he will be, nobody will touch him."[2]

Stan Wright, an assistant coach of the 1968 Olympic Team, dismissed the significance of Rodney's sub-par Trials performance. In his autobiography, Wright wrote that those who believed Milburn had lost his edge were wrong. Rodney, he said, had simply had a bad day in Eugene.[3]

That Wright was not the head coach of the 1972 Olympic team was a point of contention among many of the black athletes. They felt he should've been chosen over Oregon's popular distance coach, Bill Bowerman. Racial tensions weren't nearly as high as they had been four years earlier, but it would be fair to say that the 1972 squad was a divided bunch, largely along color lines.

Quarter-miler Vince Matthews explained in his autobiography that,

## A Hurdler's Hurdler

of the five initial nominees for the head coaching spot, the United States Olympic Committee narrowed down its list to two—Wright and Bowerman.[4] No black man had ever served as head coach of the United States Olympic Track and Field team, although several black coaches—most notably Wright and Leroy Walker—had achieved plenty of success coaching Olympians. After the racial discord surrounding the Mexico City Games, now seemed like a good time for the USOC to alter the course of history by awarding the prestigious position to a well-deserving black coach. The steady, agreeable, and highly experienced Wright was certainly someone who could handle the various personalities on the team and also deal with all the political hassles that came with the job.

Wright had been a long-time coach at Texas Southern—a SWAC rival of Southern—although Wright had left TSU by the time Rodney had arrived in Baton Rouge. During Wright's tenure, TSU had conquered much larger schools at prestigious meets such as the Texas Relays and Drake Relays. Wright's biggest claim to fame was that he had coached the 1968 Olympic 100 meter gold medal winner Jim Hines, who won his gold in a world-record time of 9.95.[5] Because of his past success as a sprint coach, and because many members of the 1972 team were familiar with Wright from their time together on the 1968 team, they—Matthews and Davenport in particular—wanted him as head coach..

But it wasn't to be.

Matthews wrote that the USOC was deadlocked in its vote, but ultimately decided upon Bowerman. Their logic was that the older Bowerman had earned the right due to his three-plus decades of coaching excellence. Wright was young enough that he could wait another four years. So he would be an assistant once again.[6]

In preparation for the Games, Bowerman took the team to Bowdoin College in New Brunswick, Maine.[7] Plenty of hills and trails for the distance runners, but not a very popular place with the black athletes. There was nowhere to go and nothing to do. Rodney, though, didn't complain about Bowerman being head coach, and he didn't complain about being stuck up in Maine. He was on the Olympic team, one step away from making his dream come true. He preferred quiet places anyway, so Maine was fine. Plus the cool Northeastern summer air was a welcome change from the pestilent heat of Baton Rouge. The campus of Southern University got awfully "boring and hot" in the months when no students stayed on campus.[8]

## Six—Hurdle Five

From Maine, the group traveled to Europe for more training and a few tune-up meets.[9] Again, all the planning and preparation seemed geared toward the distance runners, increasing the frustration among the sprinters. Matthews pointed out Oslo, Norway as a particular dead zone for the black athletes, stating that they could not feel comfortable in such a foreign environment, and that there was nothing there for them to do when not training on the track.[10]

How much the tension affected Rodney is unclear, but it seems apparent that none of his black teammates felt he needed to be more vocal, and none of the whites felt he was too militant. Rodney got along with everybody. As 1968 Olympian Leon Coleman said in 2005, "Rod was just a cool dude, man."[11] Probably Rodney was more focused on getting his form back together than he was on getting caught up in any drama. Just like he avoided conflict as a youngster, he also steered clear of it as an adult.

But the political commotion leading up to the Games only increased as the opening ceremonies drew nearer. Four days before the competition was set to begin, the African country of Rhodesia was expelled from participating in the Games. Now known as Zimbabwe, Rhodesia had been a British colony until declaring its independence in 1965. At the time of the Munich Games, it was ruled by a white minority in a system of apartheid. Several African nations were threatening to boycott the Games if Rhodesia were allowed to compete. Even after the Games had begun, countries such as Ethiopia were threatening to withdraw if their athletes were made to compete against Rhodesians.[12]

The United States track and field team also issued a statement supporting the African nations and threatening withdrawal. While Matthews and the other 400 meter runners were prepared to boycott if Rhodesia competed, Rodney for his part didn't support such a measure, feeling that the Olympics was not the place to play world politics. Yielding to the pressure, however, the International Olympic Committee finally voted to ban Rhodesia.[13]

The IOC's decision severely disheartened its leader, Avery Brundage. President of the IOC since 1952, Brundage had what many considered an obsessive desire to keep the Olympic movement free of anything that smelled of professionalism or politicism. To him, barring Rhodesia from the Games was much more unethical than the governmental policies that led to the ban. Throughout his career as IOC president, and AAU president before that, he zealously fought to protect the sanctity of the Games.

## A Hurdler's Hurdler

His stubbornness, which often came in the form of racist decisions and policies against blacks, Jews, and Indians, made him one of the most reviled figures in all of sports.[14]

The list of athletes whose lives were damaged by Brundage's unyielding nature included some of the best who ever lived, most notably Jim Thorpe and Jesse Owens. Thorpe, a Native American, won Olympic gold in the pentathlon and decathlon at the 1912 Olympics in Stockholm. One of the athletes he defeated in the decathlon was a young Avery Brundage. Shortly after, the IOC stripped Thorpe of his medals for having played semi-professional baseball prior to his Olympic triumphs, which made him a "professional" athlete at the time of the Games. Thorpe, though innocent of any intentional wrongdoing, was forced to return his medals, and his name was erased from the amateur record books. Forty years later, as president of the IOC, Brundage had the opportunity to overturn that decision and to give back to Thorpe the two medals he had fairly earned. But Brundage refused. To give Thorpe his medals would be to condone professionalism in amateur sports, and Brundage was unwilling to do that.[15]

As for Owens, no African-American athlete, with the possible exception of Joe Louis, had done more to bring blacks into international prominence than he did when he won an unprecedented four gold medals at the 1936 Olympic Games in Berlin, Germany. Now commonly known as the "Nazi Olympics," the Berlin Games are remembered as much for the proliferation of Nazi propaganda as for the achievements of the athletes. Adolf Hitler, the leader of this new, frighteningly powerful regime, watched much of the track competition from a press box in the upper regions of the stadium. During each day's events, he would come down for medal ceremonies to congratulate the medalists. But when Owens won the 100 meter dash, Hitler stayed in his box.

Owens went on to win three more golds, and Hitler didn't shake his hand once. Through his graceful running and jumping, as well as his graceful dignity in dealing with the turmoil surrounding his success and Hitler's snub, Owens proved to the world that Aryan superiority was a myth, and so was Negro inferiority.

To celebrate Owens' victories, or to cash in on them, the AAU, led by president Avery Brundage, mandated that he travel throughout Europe and continue to compete. Owens, exhausted from the Olympics, refused to go. As punishment, the AAU banned him from any competitions that it sponsored. Which basically meant he couldn't run anywhere.[16]

## Six—Hurdle Five

In *Heroes without a Country: America's Betrayal of Joe Louis and Jesse Owens*, author Donald McRae portrays Owens as expressing extreme frustration with the fact that the AAU benefited financially from the achievements of athletes, basically exploiting the athletes without any consideration for the athletes' careers or livelihoods.[17] In a desperate attempt to make some money, Owens accepted an offer to run a series of exhibition races against horses. The AAU then labeled him a professional, and his amateur track career was over.[18]

Thorpe and Owens notwithstanding, Brundage is perhaps most well-known for the rigid stance he took against all things political in the 1968 Mexico City Olympics. The Olympic Project for Human Rights was threatening to boycott the '68 Games. In February of that year, the OPHR did stage a boycott of a major indoor meet at Madison Square Garden in New York City. The meet was sponsored by the New York Athletic Club, which was celebrating its 100-year anniversary. The NYAC didn't admit blacks as members. So the OPHR saw this meet as a key opportunity to flex its muscles. While a few notable black athletes did end up competing, enough prominent names didn't show up to prove to the powers-that-be in amateur track that the OPHR was a force to be reckoned with. The success of the boycott also led credence to the possibility that the OPHR might be able to pull off a boycott of the Games.[19]

The OPHR hoped that boycotting the Games would force America to recognize blacks as equal citizens. The athletes sought to be regarded as more than just entertainers. The thinking among the athletes was: Why should we go win medals for a country that doesn't even acknowledge our humanity? Because there were so few blacks in positions of power in the United States, the athletic arena was virtually the only one where blacks had a platform. An Olympic boycott would draw world-wide attention to the plight of the black American, and potentially force America to do something to address the racial strife that was polarizing the nation.

Ultimately, there was no boycott, because most athletes weren't willing to let go of their Olympic dreams. But the OPHR members agreed that they could each, as individuals, decide upon some symbolic form of protest if they made it to the medal stand.[20]

Meanwhile, in Mexico City, all hell was breaking loose in the months leading up to the Games. Student protesters were clashing with riot police on a regular basis. The confrontations were escalating in intensity, to the point where they might destroy Brundage's vision of a peaceful Games.

## A Hurdler's Hurdler

On October 2nd, less than two weeks before the Games were to begin, a firestorm erupted as army troops opened fire on a group of 3,000 demonstrators at a rally in the city's downtown area. At least 100 demonstrators were killed, and many more were wounded.[21]

Obviously, Mexico City, caught in the throes of chaos and bloodshed, was looking like a town unfit to hold a major international sporting event. But Brundage remained unfazed. Claiming that the student uprising had nothing to with the upcoming Olympic Games, he announced that the Games would not be canceled or even postponed, but would take place as scheduled.[22]

The Games did take place as scheduled, but not without more controversy. Much more.

In the finals of the men's 200 meter dash, USA's John Carlos was ahead as he raced into the final straightaway. Compatriot Tommie Smith and Australia's Peter Norman followed closely behind. Then the long-legged Smith switched into another gear and swallowed Carlos whole as Carlos looked around nervously, hoping he could hold off the charging Smith long enough to hang on for the gold. But Smith, known as a strong finisher, used his 6–3 frame to speed by Carlos with ridiculous ease. Norman, too, snuck past Carlos at the finish line to claim the silver medal.

Before the meet had even started, Smith and teammate Lee Evans had bought black gloves. Unable to bear the thought of their flesh touching that of the unashamedly bigoted IOC leader, they planned to wear the gloves in case they might have to shake hands with Brundage, who shook the hands of all medalists. Before the medal ceremony for the 200 meter dash, Smith grabbed his pair of gloves, gave the left one to Carlos and instructed him, "Do what I do."[23]

What transpired next—the infamous black-gloved fist protest—would go down as one of the most memorable moments in Olympic history. To some, it was one of the darkest moments; to others, it was one of the most triumphant.

The immediate reaction of the crowd was to boo and jeer vociferously. And Brundage was enraged. These two black athletes had brought their political agenda into the arena of his sacred Games. The retribution needed to be swift and severe. The USOC initially decided not to punish the athletes, but, in a prepared statement, gave a clear warning that if any other athlete engaged in a similar activity, the consequences would be harsh. But after being pressured by Brundage and the IOC, the USOC quickly hardened its stance and kicked Smith and Carlos out of the Olympic village, suspending them from the team and giving them forty-eight hours to leave Mexico City.[24] Brundage wouldn't have it any other way.

Heading into the Munich Games, which would probably be his last as president of the IOC before heading into retirement, Brundage was determined that politics would not upstage athletics this time around. He had lost the battle to allow Rhodesia back into the Games, but he wasn't about to let any upstart Negro athletes ruin his utopia again. On the U.S. track team, those who had been members of the '68 team still held bitter feelings toward the USOC and IOC. They particularly despised Brundage in particular, whom they had uncerenomiously dubbed "Slavery Avery."[25]

Some were still plotting protests, but one person Brundage wouldn't have to worry about was Rodney Milburn. Rodney was in Munich for one reason: to capture Olympic gold. Like many Southerners, even those who'd been on the '68 team, Rodney had no desire to take part in any social protests. Like Jesse Owens in his time, Rodney felt that there were many financial injustices in track. And like his friend Willie Davenport, Rodney was quite aware that there were many racial inequities in the United States and in the sport of track. But Rodney was a simple man. Not an activist, not an intellectual. He was a hurdler, and he would do his talking on the track.

\* \* \*

On August 26, 1972, female discus thrower Olga Connolly carried the American flag as she led the U.S. team into Munich's Olympic Stadium for the opening ceremonies of the Games of the XX Olympiad. Formerly of Czechoslovakia, Connolly won the gold medal in 1956, when her name was still Olga Fikotova. At those Games, she met American hammer thrower Hal Connolly, later married him, and would compete for the U.S. thereafter.[26]

The new Olympic Stadium, with a seating capacity of 80,000, was a state-of-the-art venue for its time. The centerpiece of Olympic Park, the stadium featured large, sweeping canopies of acrylic glass stabilized by steel cables. The open, inviting design of the stadium was intentionally created to erase memories of the 1936 "Nazi Olympics," and to inspire an image of a new, democratic, welcoming Germany.[27]

For Rodney, the opening ceremonies represented the fulfillment of a dream. Though he'd competed in Europe before, he'd never taken part in

## A Hurdler's Hurdler

an event so spectacular. As he walked into the Olympic Stadium with his teammates, seeing how it was filled to capacity, hearing the roar of the crowd, and feeling himself surrounded by athletes of every shade and color from all over the world, Rodney felt an overwhelming pride. He was at the *Olympic Games*, representing the United States.

A whirlwind of thoughts must have run through Rodney's mind as he waved to the crowd and walked around the track he would be racing on in a few days. The family he left behind to come here, his wife Carolyn getting ready to start up another semester at Southern University, his mother Mary and sister Mary Ann back home in Opelousas, his brother Jimmy in Houston, his father in Galveston, all his other brothers and sisters, the teammates and friends he grew up with during his days at J. S. Clark. He was here for all of them. He was representing all of them.

Amidst these thoughts, Rodney knew he was taking part in something that was of enormous significance. Growing up in segregated Opelousas, and then attending all-black Southern U., Rodney had never been in an environment where there wasn't division between black and white. Even on the U.S. Olympic track team, the predominantly-black sprinters, hurdlers, and jumpers didn't associate much with the predominantly-white distance runners, throwers, and vaulters. Entering the Olympic Stadium, he was suddenly presented with a vision of man's potential to truly live in brotherhood. People of all shades and colors, speaking different languages, were all together in one place, united by the same purpose.

For Rodney, that was a very big deal. He never believed that politics and sport should mix, and he never believed that sports should be used to push an agenda. To Rodney, sports should be pure. Running as fast as you can, jumping as far as you can, doing the best you can against other competitors—that's pure. Ironically, Rodney's Olympic vision paralleled that of Avery Brundage. But that's where the comparison ends. Where Brundage was a major power player who used his "sanctity of the Games" stance as a means to wield his power, Rodney was a simple man with no power who wanted track to stay fun.

Around the times the Games began, Rodney was growing increasingly frustrated with all of the hypocrisy in track. It was undermining his enjoyment of the sport. As Frank Litsky wrote in his interview of Milburn prior to the Olympics, "Rod Milburn is more than a sports champion and world record-holder. He is a human being, a vulnerable human being who suffers because the world he lives in is not always perfect."[28] At the root of Rodney's frustration were the financial difficulties he had to endure even though he was one of the greatest athletes in the world.

With track being an amateur sport, it was impossible to run track professionally. Yet there was plenty of money being made by meet promoters and the sports governing bodies, particularly the AAU. Athletes were regularly being paid under the table, but the small pittances they were making didn't compare to the big money athletes in other sports were making. So Rodney was planning for these Olympic Games to be his swan song before retiring from track and taking a shot at professional football. No, he wasn't a football player, and he hadn't played since his senior year at J. S. Clark, but he was tired of being broke while athletes of similar abilities in other sports were making as much as six-figure salaries. Also, plenty of track stars had successfully made the transition from track to pro football, most notably sprinter Bob Hayes, who was now a star receiver for the Dallas Cowboys. There were also hurdlers Earl McCullough and Richmond Flowers, along with several others.

"Track is nothing but hassles," Rodney had said at the Olympic Trials two months earlier. "You run for your country and what do you get? Nobody says, 'Thanks, Rod.' They don't care. We have to pay our own way to this meet. Man, look at all the people in the stands. Where's all the money going? This is it for me. Hassles, hassles, hassles. I'm getting out of track after the Olympics. I'm going to play football."[29]

The financial situation for track athletes was "pretty tough," Tom Hill said in 2005. Just to afford travel expenses and pay for meals on the road, they had to use various unconventional (and illegal) methods to get by. "We used to shake down meet promoters," Hill said. "You'd get a little appearance money, maybe $300 or $500. You'd talk about getting a first-class plane ticket, then exchange it for a coach ticket and pocket the change. You'd get enough meal money for three days at the site, then only stay one day. You'd get money for the hotel, and then stay with relatives. Those were the kinds of things you'd have to do."[30]

Dwight Stones, television commentator for track meets in the U.S., was a high-jumper during the 1970s. He made the 1972 Olympic team and earned a bronze medal in Munich as an eighteen-year-old, going on to win a gold medal in 1976. He said in 2006 that track athletes hoping to make a career out of it were fighting a losing battle. "You couldn't possibly support yourself," he said. "The sacrifices become too great to sustain when trying to be a world-class athlete."[31] Stones also pointed out that,

## A Hurdler's Hurdler

because track was an amateur sport and athletes weren't supposed to get paid, receiving the under-the-table money often involved standing in line with other athletes outside a meet promoter's office into the wee hours of the night. "I was okay with lining up in hallways until 1:00 a.m. In Europe, a lot of guys didn't like the food, traveling by train. They'd get homesick and run up outrageously high phone bills. We had a whole generation of athletes disenchanted, disillusioned. They'd come back and people would ask, how was Europe? And they'd have to lie."

Rodney was making decent money from the European meet promoters, but definitely not enough to make him feel like continuing a track career would be worth the stress. His dissatisfaction was obvious. "I can't afford to be tired now," he had said prior to the trials. "Too much time and effort has gone into it. It seems like three years of my life has just disappeared. I can't seem to get away from it."[32]

Rodney's brother Jimmy estimates that Rodney was making somewhere in the neighborhood of six hundred to eight hundred dollars per meet in Europe, in addition to watches and medals for winning. "Those things meant nothing to him," Jimmy said. "He gave us all of the watches and stuff like that. And the little money he was getting, he'd come back home and give each family member some. He'd be like, 'Here's fifty for you, here's fifty for you, here's a hundred for you, momma.' Then he'd say 'Okay I got my hundred.' He did that a lot. He just gave it away."[33]

For Rodney, the money itself wasn't the issue, but the inequities regarding who got how much. It seemed that white athletes were making more than black athletes, and that, in America, the AAU was taking in the major haul, totally exploiting the athletes—white and black alike. As for the racial inequities, Tom Hill observed that the marquee event was the mile, featuring star Kansas middle-distance runner Jim Ryun. Also, America had many talented distance runners, including Steve Prefontaine, Frank Shorter, and Kenny Moore. Such athletes received higher under-the-table payments from meet promoters than hurdlers like Rodney, Hill, and Davenport, and even more than well-known sprinters like 100 meter world record-holder Eddie Hart. "It may not have been blatant," Hill said, "so you didn't get too caught up in it. You just reminded yourself that this is what being black in American is all about."

As for the AAU, it was an organization that was despised by the athletes for its greed, corruption, and self-indulgent practices. Its leader, Ollan Cassell, was looked upon by the athletes as the dictator of an evil empire. A gold medalist in the 4 × 400 meter relay in the 1964 Olympics, Cassell went on to serve as executive director of the AAU from 1970 to 1980.[34] Stones referred to Cassell as "the Saddam Hussein of amateur athletics. He was the most corrupt person ever. He had a stranglehold on track and field. For the athletes, it was like indentured servitude."

Former hurdling great Renaldo Nehemiah, who currently represents several track athletes as a sports agent and financial advisor, added, "Back then, the athletes were totally being taken advantage of. The Ollan Cassells of the world were making a ton of money from the athletes."[35]

Throughout the late '60s and early '70s, CBS Sports Spectacular televised track meets every weekend throughout the indoor season and outdoor season. The athletes saw none of that money. The AAU was also known to make deals with European meet promoters, promising to deliver certain athletes in exchange for money. Athletes' competition schedules therefore were largely dictated by the AAU. So, no matter how much the athletes were making under the table, the AAU was making a whole lot more. The athletes knew this, and they were bitter. Even mild-mannered Rodney Milburn had had enough.

As the opening ceremonies began to wind down, the reality of his purpose for being there began to sink in. Rodney found himself shaking out his legs and looking in the general direction of the 110 meter hurdles starting line, eager to get the competition started.

He hoped that all the sacrifices he had made over the past three years would be worth it.

* * *

The first round of the 110 meter high hurdles was scheduled for Sunday, September 3rd. There would be five heats, with the top three in each heat (plus the next-fastest overall finisher) moving on to the semi-finals. Rodney breezed to an easy victory in the third heat in a time of 13.57 into a 0.7 meters per second headwind. All the other major contenders—Davenport, Hill, Drut, and Frank Siebeck of East Germany—also qualified for the semis. The only potential medalist to fall out was young Cuban Alejandro Casanas, who did not finish his race in the fourth heat after hitting a hurdle. Rodney had the fastest prelim time, followed by Hill's 13.62 in the second heat and Drut's 13.78 in the fifth heat.[36]

The semis took place the following afternoon. Rodney ran in the second of two heats. The top four finishers in each heat would move on

## A Hurdler's Hurdler

to the finals, set to go off two days later. Again, Rodney won his heat without much of a challenge. His winning time of 13.44 was the fastest semi time overall, as Siebeck followed behind in 13.58. In the first heat, Hill defeated Drut, 13.47 to 13.49. Davenport, who ran in Rodney's heat, also made the final in a sluggish 13.73.[37]

In both of the first two rounds, Rodney got out of the blocks slowly, then came on strong in the last half of the race. He knew that with Hill and Drut only a few hundredths off his mark in the semis, he couldn't afford to have a slow start in the finals. Plus, Davenport was always a threat, as was Siebeck. But Rodney wasn't the only one having trouble with his start: it seemed that most hurdlers were. The reason for this was that electronic starting blocks were being used for the time ever. So it was now a lot riskier to try to anticipate the gun and gain an advantage on opponents. The new technology was scaring everybody. As Hill would say in 2006, "You didn't want to make it all the way over to Germany and then get kicked out by the electronic starting blocks."

Heading into the rest day of September 5th, there was pressure on the American hurdlers, especially Milburn, to produce a gold medal. Disaster had already struck in the 100 meter dash and the pole vault—two events that Americans had dominated in past Olympics and were expected to dominate again. In the 100, Eddie Hart, who had tied the world record of 9.9 at the Olympic Trials, was the favorite to capture gold. The stiffest competition was expected to come from teammate Rey Robinson and Russia's Valeriy Borzov. In Munich, Hart and Robinson had both matched the 9.9 of the Trials—an amazingly fast time for a preliminary round. In the quarter-finals later that day, Hart and Robinson failed to show up on time for their races. Coach Wright, going by an older schedule that had since been revised, thought that the quarter-finals wouldn't go off until 7:00 p.m. But the revised schedule had them running at 4:30.

Seeing the rounds taking place on television on their way to the stadium from the Olympic village, the reality of what they were watching didn't register with the two athletes at first. They thought they were watching a replay of the morning rounds. When informed that what they were watching was happening now, they sped to the track, desperately hoping to get there on time. But they were too late. The third American, Robert Taylor, arrived just in time for his heat and qualified for the next round. In the finals the next day, Borzov won in 10.1, and Taylor captured the silver. Surely, Robinson and the popular Hart, who was known as "9.9"

## Six—Hurdle Five

among the athletes in the village, would have challenged Borzov for the gold. That the blunder enabled the victory to go to a member of the despised Russian team made it a particularly bitter pill for the Americans to swallow.[38]

In the pole vault, which took place on September 2nd—one day after the 100 final—American Bob Seagren was the favorite to defend the Olympic championship that he won in the 1968 Games. But Seagren's carbon pole, called a "Cata-Pole," which he had been using in international competitions, was ruled illegal. That more than a dozen competitors were using the same type of pole didn't matter. Every athlete using a Cata-Pole was required to use a different pole. Seagren had brought nine poles with him to Munich, and all were ruled illegal: he was forced to compete with a practice pole. He struggled. Though he had vaulted 18–5¾ earlier that year, he only cleared 17–8½, good enough for a silver, but still very disappointing. The gold medalist was Wolfgang Nordwig of East Germany—another communist country.[39]

It would be up to the hurdlers to restore American pride.

\* \* \*

But they would have to wait.

At 4:30 a.m. on September 5th, terrorism entered the Olympic village and threatened to put an end to the 20th Olympiad. A group of eight Palestinian militants, disguised as athletes, snuck into the village. They carried guns, rifles, and grenades in their gym bags. The group, which called itself Black September, broke into two apartments where the Israeli National Team was housed. Two Israelis—wrestling coach Moshe Weinberg and weightlifter Yossef Romano—were killed trying to ward off the attackers. Nine other members of the Israeli team were taken hostage.[40]

"The Happy Games," as the Munich Olympics were officially called, were over. When athletes in the village woke up that morning, they were alerted to the events that were continuing to unfold. The vacation atmosphere was gone. Recalling the events in 2000, Tom Hill said that he, Rodney, and Davenport were coming down the stairs to eat breakfast when they were greeted by a man with a machine gun slung over his shoulder. When the three hurdlers tried to walk past him, "he mumbled something in a foreign language, cocked his gun and motioned us back to where we had just come from."[41]

## A Hurdler's Hurdler

When they got back to their rooms, the coaches informed them of the hostage situation.

There would be no simple resolution to the crisis, which lingered into the afternoon and evening, and deep into the night. Rumors were flying and the conflicting reports only added to the chaos. One rumor, which turned out to be tragically wrong, stated that the terrorists had all been killed and the hostages had all been rescued. The truth was that the terrorists were demanding transportation to Cairo, and that the German authorities were pretending to comply. They helicoptered the terrorists and the hostages to nearby Fürstenfeldbruck airbase, where a jet-plane awaited. Here, the German authorities planned to kill the terrorists with sharpshooters.[42]

But it didn't work out that way. The events that unfolded between 10:30 p.m. and 1:30 a.m. have been documented many times in many places. For here, suffice it to say that the rescue operation turned cataclysmic. All nine hostages were killed in the mayhem that ensued, and Germany's apolitical Games were shattered beyond hope.[43]

For the American athletes, who lived in a country where terrorism basically didn't exist, the seemingly random violence was beyond comprehension. "You don't expect it from a sporting event," Hill said in 2000. "You think that everyone is there to watch sports. What we didn't realize is that politics are woven through everything."[44] Rodney was shocked, probably even more than others because he was such an idealist.

One of the most telling photos of Rodney is one in which he is standing outside an apartment in the Olympic village with an athlete from India and another from Pakistan. The three are enjoying a light-hearted moment. The Indian runner, laughing and smiling at the camera, is pointing to Rodney's famous mutton-chop sideburns. The Pakistani runner, his head wrapped in a turban, is looking at Rodney and smiling as well. Rodney appears to be thoroughly enjoying the moment. The photo speaks volumes of Rodney's natural magnetism. "The thing I actually enjoyed most about the Olympics," Rodney said a couple weeks after the Games had ended, "was the sharing of the harmony for peace. I learned a whole lot about people at the Olympic village."[45]

That's why the terrorist act upset Rodney so much. Without warning, the Happy Games had been blown to bits by the Munich Massacre. "That morning," Rodney recalled in 1988, "after athletes had been killed the previous night, I noticed guards and Army tanks in the Olympic village. At that time I didn't know what terrorism meant. Out of a million thoughts, that tragedy would have been the last thing I would have thought could happen. I think that event caused a major political change in the Olympics."[46]

There was much uncertainty as to whether the Games would continue. The decision was in the hands of the International Olympic Committee, which meant it was in the hands of Avery Brundage. Many athletes, officials, and spectators felt that the Games should end. They felt it would be horribly insensitive to continue with sporting events after such an enormous tragedy. Grief-stricken, bewildered, and enraged, they hoped that the usually stubborn Brundage would show some compassion and officially close the Games. But there were others who viewed the catastrophe as nothing more than a minor inconvenience that didn't involve them. Those who held this opinion were eager for the competition to resume. Some even expressed anger at the Israelis and Palestinians for bringing their blood feud to a world stage instead of keeping it in their own backyard.[47]

A memorial service was held in the Olympic Stadium on the morning of September 6th. The stadium was filled to capacity. Brundage stood up to speak, holding the emotions of the entire world in his hands. He did not say a word about the slain Israeli team members. He chose instead to boast of the strength of the Olympic Movement. He even referenced the threatened anti–Rhodesia boycott, which he labeled "naked political blackmail."[48] That he mentioned Rhodesia at all showed that he couldn't care less about the Israeli victims. It seemed quite evident that, for all of his disdain for all things political in the Olympic Games, Brundage was using the deaths of the Israeli athletes in a political manner—as an opportunity to promote the sanctity of the Games and the pristine integrity of the IOC. To all 80,000 in the stadium that day, it was obvious that Brundage had no intention of canceling his beloved Games. He ended his speech with the following words:

> I am sure that the public will agree that we cannot allow a handful of terrorists to destroy this nucleus of international cooperation and good will we have in the Olympic Movement. The Games must go on and we must continue our efforts to keep them clean, pure and honest and try to extend the sportsmanship of the athletic field into other areas. We declare today a day of mourning and will continue all the events one day later than originally scheduled.[49]

Even other members of the IOC were upset with Brundage's decision, especially because he had refused to meet with them about it beforehand.[50]

## A Hurdler's Hurdler

Like Brundage, Rodney did not feel that politics should enter the athletic arena. But Rodney was sincerely idealistic, and quite naïve in his understanding of how the world works. Brundage was a politician.

For the hurdlers who qualified for the finals, the good news was that their dream was still alive. The bad news was that they'd have to mentally re-focus only one day after the most horrific calamity in sports history. Tom Hill made the following observations in 2006:

> You had planned to run on a particular day, but you understood what was going on and put it in its proper perspective. You think it through and you rationalize it. You say to yourself, "I'm not the only one going through a delay; everybody in my event is going through the same thing." I think we were all anxious to run, because that's what we were there for. But that was nothing compared to losing lives.

Rodney felt relieved that his gold medal hopes hadn't been obliterated by the terrorist attack. Earlier in the year he had had almost $300 stolen from his wallet while showering at the AAU meet. And he returned to his dorm from that meet to discover that a fire in his room had destroyed many of his belongings. Then at the Olympic Trials he messed around and almost failed to make the team. On top of that, participating in a sport that offered no opportunity to earn a livelihood was wearing him down. To have lost his chance for Olympic gold would've broken his heart.

Yet at the same time he felt genuine sympathy for the Israelis and their plight. Unlike Brundage, Rodney didn't take the stance that the Games could simply "go on." The damage had been done. The terrorist attack, Rodney said in an interview a few hours after the high hurdle final, "destroyed the entire Olympic Games. I knew my mother would be concerned, wondering if I was safe, so I called my sister Lillie in Houston last night and told her to call home. This morning the Israel incident was still on my mind."[51]

But capturing the gold medal he craved would require complete concentration. The Trials had taught him that. Any lapse in concentration could prove costly. He was determined not to let a similar letdown happen again. "There were rumors," Rodney said in a 1996 interview, "that they were going to blow up the stadium, all kinds of rumors. I blocked it out. 'This is the ultimate,' I said. 'This is it.'"[52]

In the finals, he was given lane five, in the middle of the track, where he would be able to see everybody with his peripheral vision. Next to Rodney in lane six was Siebeck. Hill was in seven, and Drut in eight. Davenport,

## Six—Hurdle Five

who had struggled in the first two rounds, was stuck in lane one, far from Rodney and the other top competitors. Rodney's performances in the prelims and semis had made him the clear favorite. Most expected Hill to gain the silver, or maybe Drut, with Davenport battling for the bronze, and Siebeck having an outside chance for a medal.

But as Hill said in 2006, "No matter what, you *always* had to worry about Willie. And Drut was always a formidable opponent. Then you had the other European athletes. You got to a point where, at that stage of the game, you didn't discount anybody."

Rodney understood that being the favorite didn't matter. Especially in a hurdle race, where there are ten chances to fall flat on your face. "I knew," he reflected in 1996, "there were three strong competitors in Davenport, Tom Hill, and the Frenchman. I knew all these guys were very tough. I couldn't make a mistake. With world competition, you have to be focused. The other athletes are just as competitive. If you make a mistake, if you hit one hurdle, you lose."[53]

In the 100, Hart and Robinson had been favorites to medal, but they didn't even show up on time for their race. So nothing was guaranteed. When asked later if he worried about missing the start time of the hurdles, Rodney dead-panned, "I was paying attention to what I was doing. I wasn't going to be late."[54]

The cold air and overcast sky set a grim tone on this first day of competition after the terrorist attack. Tensions were high as the hurdlers warmed up. Anxieties about the electronic starting blocks were even greater than they had been in the early rounds. "In previous years," Hill explained in 2006, "you could gamble a little bit. But they put the fear of God in our hearts with this thing. It could detect the slightest pressure. The timing system was linked to the block. The fully electronic timing eliminated the human element."

Adding to the tension was the fact that this was the finals. For a hurdler or sprinter, stepping into the starting blocks creates the same feeling that stepping into the ring creates for a boxer, or stepping into the batter's box creates for a baseball player. The feeling that you're all alone, that no one can help you, that you must rise to the occasion of the moment. It can be the scariest, most intimidating moment an athlete faces. As Hill recalled in 2000, "It was similar to waiting for an execution. You either do it or you don't, no in-between."[55]

The start of the race was only minutes away. Rodney stood behind his blocks, breathing slowly, shaking out his legs. His mind was clear, his senses sharp, his limbs alive and tingling. He noticed everything around him, but focused only on the rhythm of his breaths. In, out. In, out, In, out. Slowly. Rhythm, rhythm, rhythm.

The stadium was filled to its capacity of 80,000 spectators. Rodney marveled at how beautifully manicured the infield was. He looked down his lane of hurdles, observed the precise alignment. The whole straightaway, all eight lanes. Eighty 42-inch hurdles lined up neatly, perfectly spaced. So much care had been taken to set things up just right.

"Auf die platze."

The stadium turned quiet. Rodney tucked in the edges of his USA singlet, shook out his legs one more time and settled his spiked shoes firmly into the blocks. He placed both hands behind the starting line, touched his right knee to the track, and breathed.

In, out. In, out. In, out.

"Fertig."

He rolled his shoulders forward and raised his buttocks. His eyes looked straight down. In, out. In—

Boom!

For the first time in his three races in Munich, Rodney got off to a good start. He exploded out of the blocks, got his first step down quickly, and powered to the first hurdle. Steadily he rose to full height, picking up speed with each stride.

His clearance of the first hurdle was clean and efficient. His lead leg barely grazed it, then he snapped the leg back to the track with thunderous authority. This was Rodney Milburn at his best—fluid and graceful, aggressive and confident, violent yet controlled.

Coming off the first obstacle, he already had a lead on the pack. Tom Hill's recollections of the start of the race are as follows:

> Rodney was gone. From the very beginning. When you can see somebody in your peripheral vision, they really have to be in front of you. Otherwise you just have a feel for them. You can always feel the person next to you. But if I could see him, that meant he was out there. And I could see him.

Over the next four hurdles, Rodney increased his lead. By hurdle five it was looking like the race for gold was already over. Drut, Hill, and Davenport were battling it out for silver and bronze.

Rodney's sprint between the hurdles was smooth and fast. With a remarkable ease of motion he was eating up ground, pulling further away

## Six—Hurdle Five

with each stride. Over the hurdles he was employing Paxton's dime method to perfection. Skimming the hurdles but not touching them.

At hurdle six Drut made a move. With a tight, forceful trail leg action, the Frenchman was building momentum off each barrier, separating himself from the long-legged Hill and defending champion Davenport. He was also gaining ground on Rodney.

By the eighth hurdle Rodney was losing balance. He always tended to raise his left elbow very high as he drove his right leg at the crossbar. Late in races, as fatigue set in, the high left elbow caused him to tilt toward the right side of the lane. That was happening now.

Drut, meanwhile, continued to close the gap.

But Rodney was not going to be denied. Even with the balance issues, he was maintaining his speed between the hurdles. He cleared the last one and only the finish line loomed ahead. With a gleam in his eye he dashed toward it.

Drut trailed closely behind, but there would be no catching Rodney on this day. He dove at the finish line and crossed it in first place, smiling and raising his arms in victory. The gray sky no longer seemed so dark and dreary. Rodney Milburn of Opelousas, Louisiana, who had trained over wooden hurdles on a grass track, was the Olympic champion.

\* \* \*

Rodney set a new Olympic and world record with his winning time of 13.24. Drut won the silver in 13.34, and Hill edged out Davenport in a photo finish for the bronze.[56] For Rodney, the triumph was gratifying on many levels.

"I can still remember coming over that final hurdle," he said in 1988. "'What a relief,' I thought to myself. It was like when I stood on that stand to get the gold medal, I thought of all the hard work, the dedication, the people who had helped me, all the trial and error. It was a beautiful feeling. I knew I probably would never feel like that again."[57]

Next came the medal ceremony. A half hour after the race, Rodney, Drut, and Hill took their places on the medal stand. Rodney's afro was well-trimmed, shaped in a nice, tight circle, with a part down the middle. He and Hill proudly wore their USA warm-up jackets. The three athletes received their medals and stood in silent respect as the United States national anthem played in the Olympic Stadium.

Crossing the finish line had been emotional, but standing on the gold

## A Hurdler's Hurdler

medal platform, hearing the national anthem of his country being played over the loudspeakers for something *he* had accomplished led to an overwhelming flood of memories for Rodney:

> When I stood on that stand to get the gold medal, I thought of all the hard work, the dedication, the people who had helped me, all the trial and error, the number of defeats as well as the victories. It's an experience that very few people can relate to. I knew I was the first Olympian to come from Opelousas and I felt very fortunate for that, but to be able to say I put forth the effort and discipline required to reach the level I did is even more special. Unless you're on that stand, you can't know the pride that comes from winning something for America.[58]

In another telling photo, Rodney is standing between Drut and Hill on the gold medal platform after the medal ceremony, their medals draped around their necks. All three are smiling, laughing, basking in the joy of their achievement. Similarly, right after the race had ended, Rodney and Drut had embraced each other in congratulations.

Shortly after, another medal ceremony took place. This one stood in stark contrast to the hurdlers' love-fest and shoved politics back into the forefront. Americans Vince Matthews and Wayne Collett finished 1–2 in the 400 meter dash, giving the U.S. its second gold medal of the day and further re-establishing U.S. track dominance. But Matthews and Collett had no intention of standing at attention during the playing of the national anthem.

Approaching the medal stand, Collett shuffled forward nonchalantly, seemingly bored by the proceedings. Matthews did a Brooklyn-style bop as if he were walking on the streets back home. Both of them were wearing their USA warm-up jackets, but unlike Rodney and Hill, neither zipped it up. Collett wasn't wearing his warm-up pants. He wasn't even wearing shoes. As the national anthem began, Collett hopped onto the gold medal platform along with Matthews. Throughout the playing of the national anthem, neither of them once turned in the direction of the flag. They chatted, joked. Collett stood with his hands on hips, Matthews scratched his goatee. All the while, in stark contrast to the two Americans, bronze medalist Julius Sang of Kenya stood at attention.

It looked like Matthews and Collett were trying to pick up where Smith and Carlos had left off four years earlier. Except this protest didn't look nearly as organized as the '68 one. As Matthews explained later, it wasn't planned at all. He and Collett hadn't spoken about what they would do on the medal stand. The only thing Matthews knew for certain was that he was not going to stand at attention. In his autobiography, he stated that he had no desire to display a false patriotism for a country that didn't address its social injustices.[59]

Boos rained down on the two athletes as they stepped from the platform and left the stadium. Staying defiant, Collett gave a raised-fist black-power salute to his friends in the bleachers, while Matthews twirled his medal and looked into the crowd, as if to say: To hell with all of you.

When Matthews met his wife and mother afterward, they were both visibly upset, and they chastised him for not standing at attention. "You were on top of the world," his mother said to him. "Now you've knocked yourself down."[60]

When she pressed him for an explanation, he finally said, "Maybe you don't understand, mom. It's not one thing that does it, but a hundred things that you can be thinking about, and they all come together at once."[61]

For Matthews those "hundred things" included the lack of respect he had received prior to the Games as one of the world's best quarter-milers. Even though he had won a silver medal in Mexico City, and had earned a spot on the '72 team by finishing third at the Trials, many experts didn't regard him as highly as Collett, '68 gold medalist Lee Evans, and UCLA stud John Smith. Evans finished fourth at the Trials, yet Coach Bowerman desperately wanted Evans on the team, believing Evans would have a much better chance of earning a medal at the Games. He even had the two athletes do a run-off a week before the Games, which Matthews won. Matthews was bitter; he had made the team at the Trials, so why were they trying to railroad him?[62]

In its Olympic preview issue, *Track & Field News* had its panel of experts predict the medalists in each event. In the 400, only one of their experts had Matthews finishing as high as third. Most predicted he would finish fifth.[63]

After the '68 Games, Matthews had trouble finding a coach and a place to train. To get to practice every day, he had to climb the fence at Boys High School in Brooklyn. He often had to train in the dark, after work. And most big meets in the U.S. were held on the West Coast. He had to pay his own way to get to those meets. Of all the things that embittered him, climbing a fence just to train was the one that really got inside of him. Being an Olympic athlete who had represented his country in international competition, and then to have to hop a fence just to practice, hoping not to get caught by the police, was humiliating and infuriating.

## A Hurdler's Hurdler

Then the other slights and injustices just added to it, and made him more aware of how similar injustices were taking place every day in America, to the point where he questioned, "What has my race, the black race, won? Has it won the same freedom, sense of independence and equality that I felt on the track, where it was simply a matter of who was the strongest and best quarter-miler on that day?"[64]

And it all boiled over on the medal stand.

The next day, the IOC banned Matthews and Collett from any further participation in the Olympic Games. In 1968, the IOC had waited to hear what the USOC's punishment would be before taking any action. This time, the organization acted swiftly. Between the threatened '68 boycott, the '68 protest by Smith and Carlos, and the threatened '72 anti–Rhodesia boycott, Brundage had had his fill of black American athletes politicizing his Games. Matthews and Collett were done. For life. They would not even get to run in the 4 × 400 relay, which the U.S. was favored to win.[65]

Rodney had no desire to get caught up in the mayhem. When repeatedly asked his opinion on the quarter-milers' protest and subsequent expulsion, he refused to comment. Three weeks later, he did address the issue, but offered no opinion on whether Matthews and Collett were justified in their behavior.

"I was at the press hut at the time," he said, "and it was quite a while before I was aware of it. Man, I have to worry about Milburn and what he has to do. It's near impossible for me to have comments about something which didn't involve me at all."[66]

Rodney's brother Jimmy added in 2006 that Rodney was not asked to do any kind of protest on the victory stand, and wouldn't have done so anyway. "All he wanted to do," Jimmy said, "was just go over there and run his race. He didn't want any confrontation about racial things or anything like that. That wasn't even in his realm of thought."

The contrast between the Rodney/Hill and the Matthews/Collett medal ceremonies was not lost on observers. On one side there was Rodney, the quiet, humble, southern gentleman who was liked by all and who by his very nature avoided conflict. With him was Hill, a second lieutenant in the ROTC program at Arkansas State University. Hill was called to active duty immediately after the medal ceremony.[67]

On the other side was Matthews, the street-wise Brooklynite who represented the "angry black man" that white America feared and detested. He was not liked by all, he was not quiet, and he didn't avoid conflict.

## Six—Hurdle Five

With him was Collett, a West Coast urbanite who was close friends with Smith and Carlos.

The media was quick to portray Matthews and Collett as villains who betrayed their own country by turning their backs on the flag. Milburn and Hill were glorified as examples of loyal Americans who served as proof that being American had nothing to do with being black or white. Two days after the finals of the high hurdles and 400 meter dash, Bob Roesler, sports editor of the New Orleans *Times-Picayune*, wrote an article in which he praised Milburn and Hill while castigating Matthews and Collett, summing up the public attitude.

In the article, Roesler expressed his frustration with athletes politicizing the Games, feeling that Matthews and Collett had insulted and embarrassed their own country. Milburn and Hill, he said, deserved to be celebrated by their fellow Americans for the dignity with which they conducted themselves on the medal stand. "As for Collett and Matthews," he wrote, "let them swim home."[68]

Rodney probably wouldn't have agreed that he deserved such accolades. And he probably wouldn't have agreed that Matthews and Collett deserved to swim home. He held nothing against anyone who chose to engage in protest that wasn't violent, even if he had no desire to take part in it himself.

Rodney had come to Munich with one goal in mind: to win a gold medal in the high hurdles. He had done that. That was all that mattered. For the rest of his life, he would think back to that moment when he crossed the finish line, when he stood on the victory stand. For the rest of his life, he would remember.

# Seven

# Hurdle Six
## *From College to the Pros*

> "You can't run around a track and make a living."
> —Rodney Milburn[1]

Rodney liked Munich but was homesick. Instead of sticking around for the closing ceremonies, he "booked passage on the first thing heading home," as he told a reporter shortly after the end of the Games.[2] Throughout his stay in the Olympic village, he had been sending postcards to his mother Mary and sister Mary Ann.

His mother didn't see the race on TV. Mary Milburn was working as a housekeeper when the gun sounded for the 110 meter hurdles. Even if she had been home, she couldn't have viewed the race. "I wouldn't have been able to watch him run since the set's broken," she said the day after the race. She found out that Rod won while at work, when she received a phone call from her employer at the other household she worked for.[3]

While proud of her son and happy for him, she wasn't nearly as excited as other Opelousans. "I was more concerned about Rod's safety than whether or not he had won," she said, referring to the terrorist attack. "I'm just glad he's coming home," she added.[4]

Rodney's brother Jimmy did see the race, but not in his own house. Jimmy was in a patient's room in a Houston hospital, where he worked as a respiratory therapist. "Right when his race came on," Jimmy recalled, "I said, 'Hold up, my brother's gonna run in this race. Can you let me watch your TV for a minute?' The guy was like, 'Your brother?' I said, 'Yeah, he's about to run this race right here.' And sure enough he said, 'Aw, that's not your brother.' I said, 'Yeah it is.' He said, 'Your *real* brother?' I said, 'Yeah.' And *boom*, there goes the race. *Boom* he won a gold medal. It happened that quick. I had wanted to take the day off to watch the race, but I had to work."[5]

Rodney also had to work as soon as he got back to the States from Germany. He arrived in Baton Rouge on September 10th after landing at JFK Airport in New York earlier in the day. Even in the glow of victory, Rodney's plan of leaving track for football hadn't changed. If anything, he felt even more certain that he was done with track. "This is my last Olympics," he said to reporters at JFK, wearing his gold medal around his neck. "There are too many political hands reaching into your pockets."[6]

The political hands he was referring to were those of meet directors, shoe company executives, and the AAU. These were the groups making money off the athletes' efforts and performances. Rodney was not taking a shot at Collett and Matthews for their "political" statement on the victory stand, as some journalists tried to claim. The local papers in Louisiana, especially, painted Milburn as the heroic, patriotic antidote to the poison of the treacherous quarter-milers.

Rodney did not receive a hero's welcome upon his return. Family members, friends, and a few schoolmates greeted him when he stepped off the plane in Baton Rouge. Among them was the Rev. Dr. Charles Bryant, pastor of Little Zion Church in Opelousas. Years later, the Reverend Bryant reflected on the occasion: "I remember when he came back from Germany. He made everybody so proud. But there was no band at the airport, no celebrities waiting at the airport to greet him. He came back humble."[7]

The day after his arrival, Rodney, along with Coach Paxton, was called to the governor's mansion, where the governor planned to declare a holiday in Louisiana in Rodney's honor and to give Rodney an honorary medal. At the governor's mansion, Rodney, according to the Reverend Bryant, "thanked America for giving a poor boy, whose mother took in washing in order to put clothes on his back, a chance to make it. He represented this city and the world with so much dignity."[8]

Once Rodney got himself settled again on the Southern U. campus, he began classes and joined the football team as a wide-out. Now that one dream had been fulfilled, it was time to make good on another. A senior, he didn't have much time to show his talents before hoping to latch on with a professional organization. Yes, other track stars had made the transition before him, but most of them had played football throughout college. Still, Rodney was not lacking in confidence.

## A Hurdler's Hurdler

"I played three years in high school and was pretty good at it," he said the day after the Olympic final. "I scored most of my touchdowns on defense. I was a wide receiver and a defensive back. I feel my experience in track will help me. I can play. I got good hands and moves."[9]

That football involved contact and collisions didn't faze Rodney either. "I'm not worried about getting hit," he said. "I just want to get to the football—the hitting will take care of itself.... If you want to be something you can. And I want to be a great football player."[10]

But he didn't want to be a great football player. He knew track was his better sport. Or else he would've played football his first three years of college. His desire to step onto the gridiron was at least partially based on ego. He had no realistic reason to believe he could transform himself into a professional wide receiver when he hadn't done so much as play two-hand touch for three years.

But America in those days was no different than it is now: football was the "real man's" sport. Track was entertaining and could even be exciting, but if you wanted to prove yourself as an elite athlete, you had to play football. While Rodney may have been quiet and modest compared to others, he had complete confidence in his physical abilities.

Dwight Stones commented in 2006 that for sprinters and hurdlers, cockiness and bravado are basic job requirements. "You can believe," Stones said, "that every one of those eight guys in the final of a sprint or hurdle race believes he can win. As for football, there had been examples of people who could do both well. Bob Hayes, Earl McCollough, O. J. Simpson. There were just enough successful examples that Rodney probably felt like he could do it too."[11]

Rodney also felt that track offered him no more challenges. Willie Davenport had been the king of the hurdles when Rodney first came to Southern, but Rodney had bumped him down to second-best hurdler in Baton Rouge. Hill and Drut had been worthy opponents, but Rodney had proven himself better than them, too. No one else was out there.

Three weeks after his return home, while relaxing on the Southern campus, Rodney made it clear he was bored with track. "I've won the NCAA, NAIA, AAU and Olympic championships," he said, "in addition to setting a new world record, getting the Track and Field Athlete of the Year award and the James Corbett Award here at home in Louisiana. What else is there for me in track?"[12]

But he did plan on running one more indoor season before hanging up the spikes for good. After that he'd graduate with a Physical Education degree and get ready for pro football. "It's time for me to look out for Rodney Milburn now," he said.[13]

On Wednesday September 20th, Rodney left football practice early to attend a banquet in his honor in Opelousas. The "Rodney Milburn Banquet," held at the Downtowner Inn, was attended by over two hundred people. For the occasion, Rodney trimmed his beard and combed the part out of the middle of his afro. He wore his white U.S. Olympics team jacket over a blue button-down shirt and striped tie.[14]

Guest speaker Lieutenant Governor James E. Fitzmorris gave him two scrolls—one declaring him a Colonel on the governor's staff, and one making him an honorary member of the Louisiana Senate.[15]

Mayor Wilfred Cortez presented Rodney with a plaque recognizing his achievement as the first gold medalist from Opelousas. "When you stepped into the blocks on that track in Munich," Cortez said in his speech, "we were with you. We rose as one, we shared as one your moment of glory." He went on to describe Rodney as "a man of the world and a symbol of the potential of black people everywhere."[16]

Fitzmorris agreed. In his speech, he said that he had come to the banquet

> to represent all 3.7 million people of Louisiana in a salute to a fine young American. This is the typically American story. Rodney comes from a poor family, did not have the advantages many others have. He experienced failures, but he never stopped. He has the kind of determination and drive and desire of the kind of man who may lose, but will never be beaten. He is a young man who can contribute much to the world, and there is much more to be done. He can lead the way with his desire and determination.[17]

Never in Opelousas had such glowing words been spoken about a black citizen. "To see him breaking all those records at J. S. Clark," raved long-time Opelousas resident Gil Deville in 2005, "it was simply amazing. Then he went to Southern and it was the exact same thing—breaking one record after another, winning all kinds of trophies and medals. Then he went to the Olympics, and there he was on TV!"[18] By winning the Olympic gold, Rodney had transcended race.

Now the only question was whether he could transfer the success to the football field.

\* \* \*

## A Hurdler's Hurdler

A reserve wide receiver for Southern in the fall of '72, Rodney caught some passes and scored a few touchdowns, but did nothing to make anyone believe he could make it in the NFL. Then, just prior to the start of his last indoor season as a collegian, a new curiosity was brought to his attention: the ITA.

On November 13th, at a press conference in a posh New York City restaurant, several of track and field's best athletes announced that they were leaving the amateur ranks to join the International Track Association—a fledgling professional track circuit that would begin its competitions in March of 1973. Among the big names were quarter-miler Lee Evans, pole vaulter Bob Seagren, hurdler Richmond Flowers, shot-putter Randy Matson, and middle-distance runner Jim Ryun. These were some of the most recognizable figures in the sport. Their commitment to the new league gave it instant credibility. Other pro track ventures had failed in the past, but this one might be for real.[19]

The president of the ITA, Mike O'Hara, was known for establishing start-up, anti-establishment professional sports leagues. Most notable of these was the American Basketball Association, which featured a freewheeling, entertaining style of play that contrasted the more conservative, structured style of the teams in the National Basketball Association. O'Hara was big on gimmickry, such as odd, elaborate half-time shows, scantily-clad cheerleaders, and quirky innovations such as a red-white-and-blue ball and a three-point shot.[20]

O'Hara saw the destitution of America's track athletes and decided to do something about it. Whether or not his intentions were honorable is open to debate, but the ITA offered athletes a welcome alternative to being crushed by the tyranny of the AAU. Like the ABA, O'Hara wanted the ITA to be fan-friendly, so most meets would take place indoors, and only twelve events would be contested, with no more than six athletes in each. The indoor setting would provide a more intimate feel, and the limited number of athletes would allow fans to follow the circuit closely.[21]

Gimmicks would include races for throwers, celebrity races, man vs. woman races, and pacer lights for the mile and 2-mile. Long-time *Track & Field News* writer Bob Hersh pointed out in 2005 that "the ITA had more indoor meets than outdoor meets because they emphasized the entertainment value of the meets. The pacer lights were set up along the infield to set a four-minute pace. The lights were set to go off one by one. If you reached the lights before they went off, you knew you were ahead of the pace. They had a number of showbiz type things that were more effective indoors than outdoors."[22] Also, distance legend Marty Liquori would serve as the emcee for the meets while retaining his amateur status.[23]

At the press conference, the athletes gushed about finally having the opportunity to make legal, over-the-table money, just like their peers in other sports. They would now be motivated by more than just the pride of competing for their country and striving to win a gold medal. They'd be training and competing to support themselves and their families. They would be free to work out more regularly without seeking full-time employment outside of the sport. And if they wanted to take on endorsements and sponsors, they could supplement their income that way.

As Seagren said at the press conference, "When I was an amateur I always had to worry about accepting certain kinds of work involving the publicizing of my name. Now I'll be able to accept that kind of work."[24]

Evans, the 1968 gold medalist in the 400 meters, had missed out on a chance for another gold in '72 after finishing fourth at the Trials. Then, in Munich, the ejection of Collett and Matthews ruined Evans' chance for a gold in the 4×400 relay. He felt that the new league had come at just the right time to rejuvenate his career. "Now [running] is my job," he said, "and that gives me the incentive when I'm training."[25]

For Rodney, the new pro league had the potential to be a viable option if his football hopes were to fall through. But first he still had an indoor season to complete. He started off lethargically, finishing fourth in his first meet, losing to Jamaica's Godfrey Murray, LSU freshman Larry Shipp, and Davenport.[26] He then won three races in a row before finding out on February 1st that the Los Angeles Rams had picked him in the 13th round of the NFL draft.[27]

Despite the odds that such a low draft choice could make the cut, Rodney believed he could do it if he just put forth the effort. "If you want to excel in another sport, it's up to you to make it," he said. "Some track guys don't want to badly enough. I figure I can be as good at pro football as anybody else if I work at it. I feel like I can hit someone else just as hard as they can hit me."[28]

But could he catch passes? Could he run routes? "The first thing I've got to do is work on fundamentals," he said. "I haven't learned all the techniques yet. I try to concentrate on using fluidness instead of just speed."[29]

Rodney's brother Jimmy said in 2005 that Rodney was serious about

## A Hurdler's Hurdler

trying to make it big in football. According to Jimmy, Rodney prepared by traveling to Houston one weekend to work out with Houston Oilers' all-pro quarterback Dan Pastorini. "They hooked up at one of the local colleges," Jimmy said. "Pastorini threw him some passes. That was the first time I had ever seen a professional quarterback throw the ball. Those passes were like, whew! So naturally, Rodney wasn't used to anybody throwing a straight bullet to him, so he just dropped them. Then he finally started catching a few of them. But he was dropping them, dropping them. About every fourth ball, he would catch one."[30]

Meanwhile, the indoor season rolled on, and Rodney, back in his familiar domain, continued to roll over his opponents. On February 11th at the Houston Astrodome, he set a new world indoor record in the 120-yard high hurdles with a time of 13.3.[31] A week later in New York, he equaled the world indoor record in the 55 meter hurdles with a 7.0.[32] Then on March 12th he won the NCAA championships in the 60 yard hurdles with a 6.9.[33]

After the NCAAs, Rodney had a decision to make: take a shot with the Rams, sign an ITA contract, or finish out his final year of collegiate eligibility?

The situation with the Rams was looking bleak. They weren't offering him much, which was to be expected. A Ram spokesman remarked that Rodney had great physical tools, but "the chances of any 13th-round draft choice making our club are slim."[34]

Rodney, for his part, was beginning to see the writing on the wall. "I won't play football unless it's worth my while financially," he said. "I have to feel I can make it this year. If I didn't there would be no reason for even trying football."[35]

The ITA seemed more fitting. There was no doubt he had the skills to stay at the top in the hurdles. The gold medal he brought home from Munich said all that needed to be said on that subject. But making the leap to pro track would mean forfeiting his chance for another gold medal in '76. "I want to make sure," he said, "that the ITA lasts more than just one year before I commit myself and lose my amateur status."[36]

Besides, it wasn't like the ITA was begging him to join. "I've gotten one letter and that's all," he said. "Anyway, I think it's a little too risky. I think it would be taking a chance with nothing to fall back on. If it was a sure thing, I definitely would be there right now."[37]

So the safest thing to do was stay in school and run outdoors for

Southern. If the Rams or the ITA came knocking at the door with an offer he couldn't refuse, he could always abort his senior season and follow the money trail.

For sure, Rodney was discovering what other Olympic heroes had found out before him: gold medals didn't translate into dollar bills. It was proving a tough lesson to learn. Black athletes in particular were finding post–Olympic life to be a struggle. In that context, Rodney was far from alone.

Leon Coleman, fourth-place finisher in the 110s at the Mexico City Olympics, said in 2005 that race had a lot to do with why many former Olympians weren't getting a fair shake:

> "They blackballed a lot of the black '68 athletes," he said. "Tommie [Smith], John [Carlos], myself. A lot of athletes didn't get anything. Carlos had to be a plumber, and Tommie had to be what he was—coach at Santa Monica. Was it because they put their fist up? Because people didn't understand *why* they put their fist up? I ended up teachin' in California, and then in Africa. You gotta feed your family. Even Larry James, [the quarter-miler] out of Villanova—real good guy, real intelligent guy—he ended up working as a manager for Burger King. That's not bad, you know, but you figure someone like him can do better than that."[38]

But it wasn't just the '68 Olympians. In a *Washington Post* article from March of 1973, coach Brooks Johnson observed that plenty of black Americans over the years had achieved Olympic glory and then returned home to a country that did not care about them. Brooks pointed out Charley Jenkins, 1956 400-meter Olympic champion; Charlie Dumas, the first 7–0 high jumper; Wilma Rudolph, winner of three gold medals in the 1960 Olympics; and Rafer Johnson, the decathlon winner in 1960. All of these athletes, he said, did not do as well financially after the Games as their white counterparts who made similar achievements or even lesser achievements. Jenkins, he said, "was working on a garbage truck" after returning home from the 1956 Games.[39]

Ironically, Willie Davenport, who ended up working locally in Baton Rouge after winning his '68 gold medal, felt sure that Rodney would have more opportunities available to him. "Rodney Milburn will never have the trouble I had," he said in the *Washington Post* article. "I think more things will come his way than I ever dreamed of. The tradition is there. The idea of a black man doing well has been implanted. Society accepts it.... What I think he needs is an agent, somebody working for him. I think he can get endorsements, I think he can be successful on a national basis, but he needs somebody to push it."[40]

## A Hurdler's Hurdler

**Milburn playfully practices his block start as onlookers watch, circa 1973.**

But Rodney was still an amateur. Only by joining the ITA or NFL could he endorse any products or accept any sponsorship. And he didn't have the type of personality that was marketable anyway. Though friendly and good-natured, he valued his privacy and lacked the charisma required of pitchmen.

Even white athletes, if they lacked charisma, couldn't count on cashing in on Olympic gold. Mark Spitz won an unprecedented seven gold medals in swimming in Munich, but he too struggled after returning to the States. "If you're white," Leon Coleman said, "and you speak well, that's great. But if you don't speak well, then they gonna kick your ass out. Mark Spitz was a good swimmer, but he had a stuttering problem, so he wasn't marketable because he couldn't speak the way they wanted him to."

Renaldo Nehemiah, who works as an agent for several elite track athletes, said in 2006 that marketing opportunities don't happen for everyone. "There has to be an attraction or uniqueness about the athlete," he said. "Just winning doesn't guarantee anything. Personality and presence play a large role. Not every athlete is marketable. What athletes are really saying is 'pay me.' But they have to offer more than just being a great athlete. They have to represent an increase in consumer sales based on their association with a particular brand in order for the company to buy into them."[41]

So on to the outdoor season it was, wearing the yellow and blue of Southern University. Rodney breezed through the early season relay meets, his fastest race coming at the Drake Relays in Iowa, where he ran 13.3 into a 2.4 headwind.[42] In May he won his third straight NAIA championship, and then prepared for his last NCAA meet, which would be held on June 7th and 8th in Baton Rouge, at LSU.[43]

This meet held intrigue for Rodney for a couple reasons. Firstly, though LSU was located in the same town as Southern, Rodney had never run on the tartan track at Bernie Moore Stadium. Southern and LSU represented contrasting sides of the shifting times. Southern was the traditional black college, competing in the SWAC, which was comprised exclusively of historically black colleges and universities. LSU, competing in the Southeastern Conference, was one of the major universities that was beginning to lure prized black recruits away from black colleges to their more prestigious institutions with larger campuses and lavish facilities.

One recruit that LSU landed was the new kid on the hurdling block, Larry Shipp from Washington, D.C. Shipp decided to enroll at LSU mainly because "I wanted to get away from D.C.," he said in 2006. "I wanted to go somewhere the weather was warm. A decent place where I could run. Plus I wanted to study criminology, which LSU had. What topped it off was I knew I could work out with Rodney and Willie. Attending Southern wasn't an option. At that time, in the early 70s, we were still integrating schools. If there was an opportunity to go to a white school, why not go to a white school? Take advantage of the Civil Rights movement, which gave us the opportunity to be at a large school. I could use what LSU had

## A Hurdler's Hurdler

to offer, and Southern was only fifteen minutes away. So I could kill two birds with one stone."[44]

Shipp had already defeated Rodney once indoors, though Rodney admittedly had run a sloppy race. But Shipp was no slouch. Heading into the NCAAs, the hype was that the wunderkind freshman might be able to knock off the Olympic champion. Shipp's mentor, who first taught him how to hurdle, had been none other than the brash legendary hurdling guru Wilbur Ross. While coaching at Winston Salem Teachers College in North Carolina in the late 1950s, Ross made a name for himself when protégés Fran Washington and Elias Gilbert dominated the hurdles at the collegiate and national level from 1957–59. In 1966 Ross wrote the first edition of *The Hurdler's Bible*—the primary text for all hurdlers and hurdle coaches to this day.

Shipp first met Ross at a youth track meet when Shipp was still a little boy with a big afro in D.C. "He offered to teach me to high jump," Shipp recalled, "but he had a kid there with him hurdling. I was like, 'I wanna try that.'"

So their relationship began. What stood out about Ross was his attention to technical details and his complete confidence in his abilities to make good hurdlers into champion hurdlers. "Wilbur was, by far, the best coach I ever had," Shipp said. "His knowledge of hurdling, his ability to motivate. For him, it wasn't just about beating guys. It was about putting together all the parts of the race. Each step of the training was geared toward mastering the race. His thing was, you were gonna be the most technically sound, in the best shape, and the most mentally prepared to go out there and kill the bear. It wasn't about winning. That was pretty much incidental. He felt that if you had the consciousness to be able to correct mistakes at full speed, you didn't have to worry about anyone else. When it came time to race, Wilbur had you ready."

Rodney was ready, too. In Claude Paxton and Dick Hill, he also had great coaches. And Shipp knew that defeating Rodney in a major championship meet was would be a monumental task, despite Rodney's laid-back demeanor. "Rodney wouldn't talk [trash] at all," Shipp reflected. "He wasn't a braggart. He was more shy than anything else. He let his accolades speak for themselves. He could walk into a room and people'd say, 'he's here.' He wouldn't announce himself. He wouldn't say, 'I'm gonna beat you.' He'd just go out there and beat you."

Besides Rodney and Shipp, the other top contenders in the high hurdles were Charles Foster of North Carolina Central and Ricky Stubbs of Louisiana Tech. Both had already run 13.4 earlier in the year—Foster at the Penn Relays and the Martin Luther King Games, and Stubbs at the Texas Relays and USTFF championships.[45]

For the young Shipp, the focus was on Rodney. Not because he wanted it that way, but because the LSU fans were putting it to him that way. This race was to be a match between the big white school and the small black school. But for Shipp, "it was more nerve-wracking to be running the NCAAs at LSU, my home track. The interesting thing was, at that point, running against Rodney wasn't a big deal. It was my first NCAAs, so I just wanted to see what I could do. The LSU people were saying 'you gotta beat this guy from Southern.' But I had already beaten him indoors, and to beat Rodney after he won the Olympic gold, that was great. The only thing I was afraid of was him setting a track record that I couldn't break. My motivation to win was because I was home. His motivation was the same. But something you didn't want to do was piss Rodney off."

Too late. Rodney was already pissed off. So much so that he almost opted not to compete in the meet at all. Though a world record holder and Olympic champion, he had never been invited to race at Bernie Moore Stadium. And LSU had never been open to the idea of a dual meet against Southern, even though Southern had been a nationally recognized track power since Coach Hill had first arrived there from Florida A&M in the mid-sixties. In no way was Rodney trying to organize a boycott of the meet or raise anyone's social consciousness. On a simple, personal level, he didn't want to run at a school less than an hour away from his hometown that had refused to recruit him. He didn't want to run at a school that refused to acknowledge the existence of his own. Having done everything there was to do in the sport, he had nothing to lose by refusing to run. In the days leading up to it, he had made up his mind not to attend.

But others convinced him otherwise. Friends and teammates, including trusted training partner Willie Davenport, urged him to compete in hopes that his presence could help to improve future relations between the two schools. Rodney also had a heart-to-heart with Coach Hill, whose perspective as a veteran in the sport enabled Rodney to see that he could make a difference socially through athletics.[46]

So he decided to run.

Distracted by inner turmoil, uncertain about his athletic future, he took out all his anger and frustration on the 42-inch barriers, laying waste to the field in a new NCAA record 13.1. He dominated from the sound of the gun and his lead was never threatened. From a purely aesthetic point of view, this race was even more awe-inspiring than the Olympic final. Rodney looked like a varsity athlete running against a bunch of JV kids. The nearest competitor, Charles Foster, finished a full three tenths behind, in 13.4. Stubbs finished third in the same time, Charles Rich of UCLA was fourth in 13.5, and Shipp ended up fifth in 13.6.[47]

Crossing the finish line, Rodney raised both arms and then swung them down thunderously as he ripped through the tape. It's like he was saying, "Take that, LSU!"

Despite thoroughly destroying the competition, he wasn't all that impressed with his performance. "I didn't feel as much as acceleration as I normally do out of the blocks," he said after the race. "I came out a little wobbly, clipped the seventh hurdle with my right heel, slowed up after the last hurdle and just ran to the tape. If I knew I was on that pace, I could have run 12.8."[48] None of these flaws were visible to the naked eye.

Rodney indirectly acknowledged that racing at LSU gave him all the motivation he needed. "I think it helped that I was performing before the people of Baton Rouge. Most of them had never seen me run except on television. I was mentally and psychologically ready to run a good race."[49]

The following week, at the AAU championships in Bakersfield, California, he was not so ready. With the collegiate season over and the dog days of summer looming ahead, maybe his mind was more on football than track. He ran his worst race of the year, and suffered his only loss of the season, finishing fifth in 13.6. First went to Tom Hill in 13.2. Also ahead of Rodney were Tommy Lee White, Foster, and Stubbs. Rodney was in the thick of things until he smashed into the ninth hurdle and fell behind the others.[50] After the race, he told reporters he was thinking about retiring from amateur track and signing with the Rams. But, he added, he would join the ITA if negotiations with the Rams didn't start to improve soon. Negotiations with the Rams were going nowhere.[51]

On the track, he bounced back a week later at the Hayward Field Restoration Meet in Eugene, Oregon, tying his world record of 13.0 on the same track where he had set the record a year earlier. The crowd gave him a long standing ovation afterwards, perhaps aware that they may have seen this great hurdler run in their home state as an amateur for the last time.[52]

## Seven—Hurdle Six

Rodney went on to have an outstanding summer on the European circuit. On July 6 in Zurich, Switzerland, he broke Martin Lauer's fourteen-year-old world record in the 110s, slashing through the tape in 13.1, a tenth faster than Lauer's time. In the process, he defeated Munich silver medalist Guy Drut once again, and received another standing ovation from the appreciative audience.[53] With modern conversion methods, Rodney's hand-timed 13.1 would translate into a 13.34 with automatic timing. But no such conversions existed yet, so his 13.1 in Zurich was judged faster than the automatic 13.24 he had run in the Olympics. On July 22 in Siena, Italy, he tied his world record[54] and finished the season with his third consecutive #1 ranking in the high hurdles.[55]

It had been a glorious three-year stretch for Rodney. From 1971–73, he had lost a total of two races, had earned an Olympic Gold medal, had broken the world record, and had won numerous national and international titles along the way. He had taken the event into a new era. The only remaining question was, where we would he go from here?

Maybe to a football career. If the Rams didn't want him, there was another new league forming—the World Football League—that might be willing to take a chance on someone with his athletic skills. Then there was the option of the pro track circuit. Or he could always follow in Willie Davenport's footsteps—find a job in the local community that would allow him to use his Physical Education degree, and train in the meantime for a shot at another gold medal.

All options were risky. He didn't know what to do.

# Eight

## Hurdle Seven
### *The ITA Blues*

"Running track was a hustle for us. It was our employment."
—Leon Coleman[1]

In its March 1974 issue, *Track & Field News* reported that Rodney Milburn had signed a contract to join the International Track Association.[2] After much oscillation, and not without reservation, Rodney had made the decision to become a professional track athlete. With a physical education degree, a wife to support, and the prospect of continued poverty if he remained amateur, he didn't have much choice.

"I've paid my dues as an amateur," *T&FN* quoted Milburn as saying. "I'm grateful to track and field—it did a lot for me. It enabled me to win an Olympic championship for the US and for myself."[3]

By signing the ITA contract, Rodney forfeited his chances of ever defending his Olympic title—something he would later come to regret. Even at the time, losing his amateur eligibility was the biggest reason he hadn't signed with the ITA sooner. But now he had finally made the leap. Though no one knows for sure, he probably received somewhere in the neighborhood of $8,000–$10,000 for signing, considering that he was an Olympic champion and world record holder. Also, since he was the only major name to sign in 1974, he was a big catch for the new pro league, adding to its credibility in its continuing attempts to attract more fans.

From the beginning, Rodney wasn't naïve enough to believe that running track professionally would be enough to pay the bills. Besides doing the ITA circuit, he planned to find a job "working with youth or the police community relations department" in Baton Rouge.[4] There seems to be no indication that he was happy, or even comfortable, with his decision. The real money was in football, but the rams weren't offering him a contract, and the new WFL was more of a risk than the ITA.

Like many of his peers, Rodney had grown tired of the hypocrisy that corrupted amateur track. He especially hated taking part in the hypocrisy himself. Leon Coleman, who joined the ITA a year before Rodney, in 1973, said in December of 2005 that life in amateur track was miserable, especially for black athletes. "A lot of meet directors," he said, "would try to slick you. You'd run and they'd pay you on a different scale [than the white athletes]. They had their prima donnas—the pole vaulters, distance runners. The athletes themselves were cool, but not the meet directors. They'd line you up against somebody else and tell you how much [money] you gonna get. Then they giving somebody else a lot more and a plane ticket to California. They'd give you $300 while they giving them $1,000. Stuff like that went on all the time. Running track was a hustle for us. It was our employment."[5]

The 1972 bronze medalist Tom Hill said in January of 2006, "As an amateur you had to be a hypocrite. Rod's personality was such that he didn't like shaking people down."[6]

Hill too was asked to join the new professional circuit, but turned down the offer. "I've always had a healthy opinion of myself," he explained. "It wasn't an arrogance. I just knew who I was, what my values and principals were. I wasn't gonna violate my principles for money. An ITA guy came up to me in Nassau, Long Island [in 1973] and said they were gonna make me 'a standard offer'—$1500 to sign. I had a family, but I was also a second lieutenant in the army. I told him I'd give *him* $1500. We agreed to end the conversation right there. He went his way, I went mine. I wasn't angry with anybody, but I realized they had given some of the other athletes more money than that."

Rodney's last race as an amateur was the Olympic Invitational at Madison Square Garden in New York, on February 8, 1974. Among his opponents were Hill, Davenport, and Shipp. Rodney won in a new world record of 6.8 for the 55 meter distance, defeating 2nd-place finisher Shipp by a full stride.[7] Shipp recalls the race vividly:

> All of us were saying this is [Rodney's] last race, so we're gonna make sure, no matter what happens, he will not win. The world record was 7-flat. I got out real well and was going for the record. Between hurdles four and five I was winning, then I shifted into all-out speed. And he went by me. I crossed the finish line and all I could do was laugh. What else could I have done? I realized that as much as we didn't want him to win on his way out, he wanted to win on his way out.[8]

## A Hurdler's Hurdler

The previous spring, Rodney and Davenport had started training fairly regularly with Shipp, either at Southern U. or LSU, and they continued to do so. They worked on different phases of the 110 meter race, but mostly on starts over the first three hurdles. Paxton, Dick Hill, and the athletes themselves felt that mastering the first three were the key to success, since that is where tempo is established. Also, when racing opponents who are equally talented, a bad start could spell doom.

The practice sessions usually drew large crowds of onlookers. "It wasn't unusual," Shipp said, "to have about 100 people out there watching us. Very good workouts." Shipp felt that they all benefited equally from the competitive atmosphere. "It allowed you to experiment," he explained. "When you experiment against the world's best, then anything you try, if it doesn't work, you throw it out real quick. You know right then and there you're wasting your time. Like the double-arm lead. I tried that and it didn't work for me, so I dropped it. One thing about running against Rodney, whether in practice or a meet, you learned the difference between running hurdles and jumping hurdles. Rodney didn't jump hurdles, he *ran* hurdles. He hit the ground running."

Training together so often did not affect their competitive edge. As Shipp said, "All of us would talk to each other while warming up. We'd help each other, give each other tips. We wanted everybody at their best. So we were the best of friends until the starter said sweats off. Then it was time to go to work."

Training with the two Olympic champions led Shipp to develop the utmost respect for both of them. While many claim that Willie did not have the work ethic of Rodney, Shipp claims that's not true. "Willie not working hard was the biggest fallacy out there. I've never known any athlete who makes it look easy actually do it easily. Willie busted his ass. I saw Willie do things that were incredible. I saw him tie a world record indoors. He basically steps off the plane, gets to the meet, sets a world record. That doesn't happen from not training."

While Shipp feels that Davenport was the best hurdler ever "pound for pound," he gives Rodney the edge "if you throw in speed and strength. Rodney's ability to get out was amazing, and once he got to the front you weren't gonna catch him from behind. The only way you could possibly beat Rodney was to be with him for seven hurdles. The problem was being with him for seven hurdles."

But now that he had joined the ITA, Rodney would no longer be a concern of Shipp's. And because most of the ITA races were indoors, there wouldn't even be a seventh hurdle. Just five hurdles and the finish line. Rodney's main competition in the ITA would come from Leon Coleman, Paul Gibson, and the Californian Lance Babb. Rodney quickly developed a close friendship with Coleman, who served as a sort of mentor for the younger athlete in his first year out of school. Rodney was agonizing over the fact that he had forfeited his amateur eligibility, and Coleman helped him understand that he had only done what he had to do as a man with a family to look after. "The way it's set up," Coleman said in 2005, "for all intents and purposes, you're a professional athlete, but you're not getting paid for it. So why wouldn't you try football, or the ITA, when you saw athletes in other sports making all that money?"

But the ITA turned out to be a disaster. After 1976 it would fold.[9] And Rodney's professional status would force him to forfeit an opportunity to participate in the 1976 Olympic Games in Montreal. Whether he would regain amateur eligibility in time for the 1980 Games in Moscow was questionable. And he didn't make any money of consequence.

Still, he did run well.

His first ITA race took place at Nassau Coliseum in Uniondale, NY on February 16, 1974. In the 60-yard hurdles, he narrowly won with a 7.0 over Coleman, who ran the same time.[10] A week later, at the Salt Palace in Salt Lake City, Utah, he broke his own world record in the 60-yard hurdles with a dominant 6.7 victory. He received a huge ovation from the crowd for his efforts.[11] Of course, the performance wasn't officially recognized as a world record because it occurred in a professional meet. On March 23rd in Oklahoma City, he won again in 6.8.[12]

The outdoor ITA circuit took him to Los Angeles, where he stayed and trained with Coleman, who now lived on the West Coast, where he competed for the Southern California Striders. During this time is when Coleman and Rodney formed a close bond. "We'd work out all the time together," Coleman said in 2005. "When you're working out with somebody, you get to know the guy." Despite their friendship, they were rivals. And in pro track, it wasn't just a matter of medals at stake, but livelihood.

"We'd tease each other," Coleman recalls, "call each other names. We were buddies. But when that gun goes off, that's it. You're running for like a thousand dollars, two thousand dollars a race, so you had to be on the case, man. In '73, I beat Lance Babb about nineteen times in a row. Then Rod came along. And he'd run *wild*, so I'd teach him how to get over the hurdle. Rod had technique, but he had to learn how to control it. So he comes along and beats my ass. Then I was like, I'm teaching this motherfucker how to beat me? I said, 'Rod, man, I want some of my money back.' But we had a good time. It wasn't just about the money, you know, it was about the friendships."

Even before turning pro, Rodney had trained with Coleman whenever he traveled to California for a meet. Coleman had moved out there shortly after the 1968 Olympics. Among athletes from small Southern black schools, there was an unspoken understanding that they stuck together and looked out for each other. They knew that not much was expected of them, and they resented how whites, and even blacks from larger universities, looked down on them. Coleman recalls an incident that took place prior to an ITA meet in 1974:

> We're in the lobby one day, going to a track meet. Lance Babb is down in the hallway talking crap 'cause he's from USC. He's down there with some guys from UCLA, in the lobby talking about all these races they ran, how fast they ran. They trying to psyche us out. So we didn't say nothing. We went downstairs and waited for the bus to pull up to take us to the meet. Milburn comes down, and he never used to say much, 'cause it's race time. He's ready to go, he's getting his head together. So he comes down, sits in the lobby, puts his leg up on the table and says, 'Everybody ready to see who's gonna get second place? I got a can of AW Ass-Whoop in here, and I'm gonna open it up,' and that closed up everybody's mouth.

There were only three outdoor meets on the ITA schedule in Rodney's first year, all of them in April. Two were in Tokyo and one was in El Paso. Rodney won all three, but the times were pedestrian—13.9, 13.9, and 13.7.[13]

Though undefeated for the entire season, Rodney only made somewhere around $10,000 in 1974, not counting money given to him for travel expenses. Not much for someone of superstar status, and not nearly as much as the distance runners and pole vaulters were making. The prize money offered in those marquee events was higher than it was in the hurdles. But even leading money winner Ben Jipcho only made a little under $17,000, and that was with running both the mile and the two-mile at many meets.[14] Rodney was finding that professional track, like amateur track, was a hustle. As Coleman said, "You'd get a thousand for winning, maybe eight hundred if you didn't win. They'd give you plane tickets, room and board, a per diem. Running track with a per diem, you had to make your money worthwhile."

Sadly, many athletes who still ran as "amateurs" were making more than Rodney. In an article that appeared in the Fall 2001 issue of *The*

*Journal of Sport History*, Joseph M. Turrini of Catholic University wrote that illegal appearance fees were rampant throughout the 1970's, as European meet directors were willing to pay significant sums for athletes who were well-known and/or who could potentially break world records. As a result, the money that could be made in Europe during the summer was vastly greater than the amount that could be made on the indoor circuit of the ITA. Turrini quotes distance great Frank Shorter, who stated that he had probably broken all the rules of amateurism, and that if those rules were enforced strictly, there would be no eligible athletes left to compete.[15]

One athlete the ITA desperately wanted to reel in was Oregon distance runner Steve Prefontaine. "Pre," as he was popularly called, had finished fourth in the 5000 meter run in Munich and was quickly becoming a legendary figure. Unlike many distance runners who preferred to run tactical races in big meets, Pre made a habit of going out hard and grabbing the lead from the opening gun, daring all competitors to come and try to pass him. On the track and off of it, he was not one to follow the rules or settle for the conventional. He was an innovator, a daredevil, and that's why people loved him. And arguably more than any other athlete of his era, Pre despised the AAU.

In the biography of Prefontaine entitled *Pre: The Story of America's Greatest Running Legend*, Tom Jordan notes that Pre had an ongoing feud with the AAU, which demanded strict adherence to its rules. Even prior to the '72 Olympics, Pre was outspoken about the hypocrisy and ludicrous expectations of the AAU. In the biography, Jordan references a *Sport* Magazine article in which Pre states, "Amateurism is a thing that should have been kicked out in 1920, you know. The true amateurs, by the standards that were set up in the 1890s, were the elite, who were already well-established and set up in clubs and didn't need money to compete."[16]

The AAU also liked to tell athletes which meets they could and could not run in. Because many athletes were abandoning traditional competitions like the USA vs. the USSR meet in favor of European meets that promised better competition and potential for under-the-table appearance money and prize money, the AAU did not allow athletes to compete anywhere ten days prior to the national championships, and five days before international meets. For Pre, the tip of the iceberg came when he received a letter from the AAU stating that if he continued to wear a sweat suit with the word NIKE on it, he could lose his amateur status.[17]

According to Jordan, this insult was the one that almost pushed Pre

## A Hurdler's Hurdler

over the edge in deciding whether to join the ITA. The league had done okay financially in its first year of existence, but it needed him, needed his star power, if it was going to sustain itself for the long haul. So the ITA was offering him quite the handsome amount to make the leap. In 1974, its offer was in the neighborhood of $100,000—an astronomical sum that exceeded any income earned under the table or otherwise on the European circuit.[18]

Despite the lure of the big sum the ITA was willing to give him, Pre ultimately decided against turning pro, mainly because he wanted to remain eligible for the '76 Olympics and have a shot at the gold medal that had eluded him in '72.[19] Tragically, he died in a car accident in May of 1975, putting an end to a brilliant life and career.

Another factor that might have influenced Pre to stay in the amateur ranks was the newness and inherent instability of the ITA. The average attendance in '74 was 9,648, and there was no reason to assume that number would increase significantly, Pre or no Pre.[20] A big stumbling block was that the same athletes competed against each other every meet. In the hurdles, for example, it was always Milburn, Coleman, Babb, and Gibson. That amateurs could not compete against pros without losing their amateur status made for built-in monotony, regardless of the athletes' performance level. Pre's decision to stay amateur, despite the huge sum he was offered to turn pro, proved that the majority of athletes weren't willing to take the risk. Many ITA members, like Coleman, long jumper Bob Beamon, and sprinter Wyomia Tyus, were on the downside of their careers, and probably wouldn't have a legitimate shot at making the Olympic team in '76 anyway. Those who did have a shot, like Pre, Shorter, and Powell, opted to continue receiving illegal under-the-table payments and still retain their amateur status.

Rodney was obviously in the unfortunate position of still being on the upside of his career, making less money legally than others were making illegally, but being ineligible to showcase his talents on the world's greatest stage.

Despite not landing Prefontaine, ITA president Mike O'Hara felt confident about the pro league's future. Heading into 1975, he planned to up the prize money, add some televised meets, find more sponsors, and increase attendance. All of this happened, but still the situation was grim. The first three meets brought in an average of 9,000 spectators, definitely an improvement over the previous year, but not a cause for celebration.

## Eight—Hurdle Seven

The prize money did go up, but traveling money was reduced, putting even more pressure on athletes to win. Four meets were aired by television networks, but none were shown live. They were shown tape-delayed from 10:30–12 midnight, when most of America was getting ready to go to bed. Instead of just three outdoor meets, there would be six. And with the '76 Olympics right around the corner, it would be hard to lure more athletes to the professional ranks. In '74, the only new names had been Rodney and 800 meter star Dave Wottle, who had also won a gold medal in Munich. In '75 there were no new names.[21]

Rodney had another outstanding campaign in 1975. He won five of six indoor races, and five of six outdoor races. The highlight of the season came on May 10 in El Paso, Texas, where he ran 13.0 over the 120-yard distance, tying his own world record for the fourth time.[22] In the same meet, thrower Brian Oldfield demolished Al Feuerbach's world record of 71–7 in the shot-put. On his fifth throw, Oldfield tossed the 16-pound ball 73–¼ before finishing the competition with a monstrous 75–0 effort on his sixth and final attempt. But Oldfield's stunning performance would count officially only as an ITA record, not a world record. The International Amateur Athletic Federation, which sanctioned world records, refused to recognize the achievement of professional athletes.[23]

The Oldfield situation served as a sobering example of the power held by the governing bodies of amateur track and field. The IAAF, and the AAU in the United States, did not want professional track to exist because it undermined their authority and threatened their ability to control the athletes. Charles Foster, who didn't turn pro, said this in 2005 of the governing bodies:

> [They] ran a political power play because they were still hell-bent on keeping the sport amateur. The amateur movement was so strong that no one else from a political standpoint could compete against them. [Professional track] wasn't gonna work. Those athletes like Rod were pioneers of professionalism in track, and the modern athletes are benefiting from the sacrifices they made. But the IAAF, the AAU, the IOC, they didn't want professionalism in track.[24]

By not recognizing records set by pros, disallowing pros from competing in the Olympics, and prohibiting amateurs from competing at all against pros, the governing bodies ensured that upstart pro organizations like the ITA could not endure but for so long. Caught in the middle of the imbroglio was *Track &Field News*, the magazine that annually ranked the top ten athletes in the world in each event. Certainly, many ITA athletes,

## A Hurdler's Hurdler

including Rodney, were consistently competing at a level higher than or equal to many amateurs that they never faced head-to-head. But *T&FN* did not include pros in its annual rankings.

*T&FN* claimed at first that they excluded pros from their rankings because most ITA meets took place indoors. But with six outdoor meets in '75, that claim was no longer justified. They then said they didn't rank pros because they didn't compete against anyone else, and it would've been difficult to create a criteria for a separate set of athletes.[25] Regardless, the end result was that ITA members competed in a vacuum. To the world outside, it was like they didn't even exist. With the year Rodney had in '75, he unquestionably would've been ranked #1 in the high hurdles had he not been a pro. On its 110 meter hurdles rankings page in the January 1976 issue, *T&FN* ranked France's Guy Drut, who Rodney defeated in the '72 Olympics, as the #1 hurdler. But in the paragraphs explaining the listings, there is a qualifying sentence that reads, "Rod Milburn lost only one of six outdoor races against quality competitors and might have vied for first had he not been a pro."[26]

Rodney's earnings for '75 were again in the $10,000 range. To supplement his income, he tried out the following fall for the Shreveport Steamer of the fledgling World Football League. But he didn't make it.[27] As another Olympic year loomed on the horizon, the reality that he would not have the opportunity to represent his country again hit pretty hard.

In December of 1975, while visiting his brother Clary in Galveston, Texas, he did an interview with the *Galveston Daily News* in which he asserted that American pros should be allowed to compete in the Games. "I think a system similar to the one the Russians use would benefit us in international track and field competition," he told the paper. "The Russians make a profession of athletics. If we used such a system, our athletes could concentrate on being athletes on a full-time basis rather than part-time."[28]

What Rodney didn't acknowledge was that the state-run system in Russia at the time allowed its athletes to run professionally without really being professionals. Technically, they were still amateurs because they didn't earn any individual income for competing. What he did correctly point out, though, is that the American system actually hindered the best athletes from focusing on training to make the team. They had to worry too much about how they would get there if they did make it.

He recalled that, heading into the Munich Games, he had to pay his own way to the trials. "It was simply a matter of if you couldn't afford it,

## Eight—Hurdle Seven

you couldn't go to the Olympics. That's bad because it discriminates against a lot of top-flight athletes." The Russians, he observed, were catching up to America because they had found a way to work around the rules of amateurism. "They're not catching up to us in raw talent, but they are in training techniques and analysis of performances. That might make a big difference someday."[29]

Already, in 1972, Russia's Valeriy Borzov had dominated the sprints. And being a loyal American who loved his country despite its flaws, Rodney hated the thought that Russia was catching up to America athletically. Mainly though, he was bitterly disappointed that he would not be going to Montreal while professionals from other countries would. When, he wondered, would the U.S. wake up to the necessity of professionalism in track and field? When would it put the welfare of its athletes above the sanctity of its political agendas? Apparently, not anytime soon.

Rodney's brother Jimmy said in 2006 that Rodney expressed regret over being ineligible for the '76 Olympics every time they talked about it. "He used to say they had professionals running for all the foreign countries, so why can't we have our professionals running? He did make a big issue out of it, and he was wondering why [the governing bodies] couldn't get that straight before the Olympics, 'cause naturally he would've been favored to win the gold in '76."[30]

Another problem Rodney noted was that, by excluding professionals, America was relying too much on athletes who lacked international experience. Only two Americans—Charles Foster and Jerry Wilson—were ranked in the top ten in the high hurdles in 1975. Internationally, there was Drut to contend with, and Thomas Munkelt and Frank Siebeck of East Germany, and Alejandro Casanas of Cuba. Foster and Drut raced five times in 1975, with Drut winning three of the contests. Foster undoubtedly represented America's best chance for a gold medal. Wilson was unproven beyond collegiate competition, Davenport was nearing his 33rd birthday, and Tom Hill was busy trying to fit in training time while fulfilling Army obligations and raising a family. If the U.S. was to continue the dominance in the hurdles that had become routine throughout the modern history of the Olympic Games, then Rodney needed to run. But he couldn't.

Ironically, the 1976 Olympic Trials took place on Rodney's favorite track—Hayward Stadium in Eugene, Oregon, from June 22–24. Rodney didn't attend. It would've been torture for him to watch athletes he had beaten regularly earn spots on the team running times that were much

## A Hurdler's Hurdler

slower than his personal best. Plus he was busy with the ITA schedule and his job in the Baton Rouge Recreation Department.

Charles Foster emerged as the Olympic Trials victor. He ran a very respectable 13.44 in the final with the help of a 2.2 tailwind. The old master Willie Davenport made his fourth Olympic team by getting second in 13.52, and James Owens of UCLA surprised everyone by earning the third spot with a 13.57. Shipp finished sixth and Hill eighth.[31]

Hill had run the fastest semi-final time of the whole bunch, crushing Davenport—13.46 to 13.58—in the second semi-final heat. "My nightmare occurred," Hill explained in 2006. "It was a windy day, and with my long legs, I don't run well in tail winds. I over-ran the sixth hurdle." He went on to smack three of the next four hurdles, effectively knocking himself out of contention. "I finished the race," he said, "but that's about all I did. That was a real disappointment. That ended it for me. I couldn't put my life on hold another four years. I had two young sons, I needed to devote time to them. You really can't do that when you're working a job and seriously training."

As for Shipp, he, like Foster, was struggling with hamstring problems. After recovering from a broken hand earlier in the year, and then from food poisoning while in Leningrad, he had pulled a hamstring three weeks prior to the start of the trials. "Had the trials been a week later," he said in 2006, "I would've been fine." As it turns out, he ran well through the rounds. After a cautious 14.05 in the first round, just barely qualifying for the quarter-finals, he dropped down to 13.77, and then 13.82 in the semis. "In the finals," he said, "I'm like all right, let's go for it. I get to the seventh hurdle and bam! I feel my hamstring give out. I asked myself when I crossed the finish line, Larry, did you do the best you could? Yes I did. And that's all you can do. I didn't have any regrets. I busted my ass that year."

For Foster, the victory was a very emotional one. With the way his hamstring had been bothering him, he didn't expect to even make it to the finals. He initially strained it at the AAU Nationals at UCLA two weeks earlier. The University of Oregon medical staff was at the meet. They took him under their wing and flew him back to Oregon to try to get him ready for the Trials. "They were so diligent with me," Foster recalled. "They had an assigned trainer to go with me to breakfast and meet me at the training room. Those medical people, I still don't know what it was that led them to do what they did for me. I didn't ask for it, they just took it upon themselves to do it. I can't think of another time that anyone's been that kind. They took me through the lounge, had my leg taped up all the way through the rounds."

Still, the pain was getting worse. He finished third in his semi-final heat in 13.66—fifth overall, and probably not fast enough to earn him a trip to Montreal were he to run that slow in the final. So Foster made a decision:

> I decided it's now or never. No point in wrapping [the leg] now. I took the wrap off, said to the head trainer, "Give me the hottest stuff you got." He gave me red-hot. I said, "That's the hottest stuff you got?" Then he gave me some white lineament, and I went out there. When the starter said on your marks, that stuff lit me on fire. Just before he said set, I was about to raise my hand and get somebody to wipe it off. I shot out of there. When I hit step number eight, I saw the five Olympic rings right in front of me, and from there I wasn't even contested. Won the Olympic Trials hands down. I threw my hands up before the finish line, high stepping. The head trainer for the University of Oregon was standing there with open arms. He was the first one, I ran right into his arms. I looked beyond him and there stood my coach, Dr. Leroy Walker. That was the most special moment of my career.

But things didn't go as well in Montreal. For the first time since 1928, an American did not win the gold medal in the men's 110 meter high hurdles. This time it went to 1972 silver medalist Guy Drut of France, whose 13.30 was only .06 off Rodney's Olympic record. Cuban Alejandro Casanas won the silver in 13.33, and Davenport was the lone American medalist, capturing the bronze in 13.38.[32] It was a bitter day for American hurdling, and Davenport, who was especially perturbed, echoed many of the sentiments made by Rodney earlier in the year.

"We've been holding our own but times have changed," he said the day after the race. "There's no question the world has caught us. What we lack in the U.S. is a development program for our youth. It isn't enough just to develop athletes in college. A post-collegiate program is needed. It would be something if our country ever came up with a program where a man could hold a job, yet still be able to train properly and receive a paycheck. We in the U.S. are not developing our talent. We're not fertilizing the tree."[33]

Foster ended up fourth. He stayed in the thick of the hunt for the first half of the race, but his hamstring wouldn't allow him to shift gears like he needed to, so he faded badly over the last five hurdles.[34] Owens, the third American, finished sixth.[35]

Conspicuous by his absence was Rodney Milburn, who could quite easily have won his second consecutive gold medal had he been eligible to do so. But he had made the decision to turn pro, and he would have to live with it. By all accounts, he revealed no bitterness, except to family members. "If he had regrets," Tom Hill said in 2006, "he didn't express them openly. I think he was pretty satisfied that he had set the world record, Olympic record, and won the gold medal [in '72]."

Foster concurred: "It would be easy to say that you learn from Rodney that you shouldn't take risks, but really, you learn that you *should* take the risk. Joining the ITA was probably a calculated risk for him. But you've gotta live your dreams. You don't know what you can be until you stick your neck out there and try it."

Dwight Stones offered a somewhat different take, saying, "Rod made a mistake. He made a calculated decision, and he regretted his decision, naturally. He was going for what seemed to be the quicker money. Had he stayed at the level he was in '72, he would've been there in '76, but it was no slam dunk he would've won the gold. Bottom line is, he was the greatest hurdler in the world and he was devoting a lot of time to it, so he felt he should get paid for it."[36]

Three weeks after the Olympics, after only three outdoor meets, the ITA folded. Less than 1,000 people showed up at the last meet in Gresham, Oregon, and the financial burden of carrying on a pro track tour during an Olympic year was proving too much to bear. Three more scheduled meets were cancelled, with the hope of continuing operations in '77 if they could sign some big-name Montreal Olympians. But that didn't happen.[37] Between shoe companies and meet directors, especially in Europe, there was plenty of under-the-table money to be made that joining the pro tour would've been downright foolish at this point.

For the older ITA athletes, the end of the tour meant the end of their careers. There was nowhere else to go, nothing left to do. But for Rodney, Brian Oldfield, and others still in their prime, the folding of the league was a particularly harsh blow. Regaining amateur status would prove to be a very difficult matter, and would take a lot of time. In the meanwhile, they would have to seek employment elsewhere and try to stay in shape until they could compete again as amateurs.

Besides the waning public interest and the inability to sign new stars, another reason the ITA was forced to fold was a lack of credibility. Many believed that the records set in ITA meets weren't legitimate. Dwight Stones, for one, is adamant about it, and he expressed this in 2006:

## Eight—Hurdle Seven

What they did that led us to speak out was they were posting marks that we knew a lot of those people were not capable of. They must have been throwing shots that were underweight, using measuring tapes that were short. Guys were jumping farther and higher than we knew they were capable of jumping. In the pole vault they had pegs eight or nine inches long, the pole would rattle the bar but not fall off because it would hit the peg. Guys would jump heights that couldn't be converted into meters. Stuff like 7–4¾. There was little chance the official would have let someone jump at a height that can't be converted into meters. There's no way they would have allowed that. We sowed the seeds of discontent because we could not allow them out there doing things that weren't legit.

Foster echoed Stones's sentiments:

The ITA thought they had a can't-miss thing. You gotta have the superstars, and they had superstars. They thought it would last a long time, and there was no reason to think it wouldn't. The people are looking for rivalries, and they're looking for records. So the promoters started cheating, because 'We gotta have a world record tonight.' World records are boss. ITA thought they had a gold mine, because track and field was on television a whole lot in the early '70s. But when the NFL took over, that hurt the ITA, because the luxury dollar only goes so far.

Oldfield claims that no cheating took place. Especially not in the shot-put, something he asserted in 2006:

We went out of our way to make everything legitimate. "We had *T&FN* people there. [Co-founder and editor] Bert Nelson. People were saying there were razor blades on the pole vault. I didn't know such things were possible. I tried to keep it honest and everybody else did because they were trying to call us a three-ring circus. We were under scrutiny so we had to do it legitimate. I was throwing in the rotational style, and people were saying that's not legal. Well, just because you're stupid doesn't mean it's not legal. By saying crap like that they could get their names in the news. I'm talking about real stuff. I never thought about cheating or using a light shot. I put my heart and soul into it. If you're a cheater, you're only cheating yourself. You're not playing by the rules, and the rules, basically, are there to protect you from yourself.[38]

But the perception was that cheating was going on, which damaged the league's reputation and helped lead to its early demise. Rodney's calculated risk had proven to be a huge blunder. Financially, he was no better off than he would have been had he remained amateur. And the unkindest cut of all was that the greatest hurdler in the world now had nowhere to run.

# Nine

## Hurdle Eight
*Hero Without a Country*

> "I'm the fastest in the world and I can't run."
> —Rodney Milburn[1]

Financial troubles caused by the ITA's demise led to the divorce between Rodney and his second wife Janice. Haunted by feelings of inadequacy, he took whatever jobs he could find for the next few years.[2] Pro track, like amateur track, had been a hustle, but at least it had kept him afloat. Now he was really struggling.

Around this time, Rodney turned to his religious faith for strength. Raised in a Catholic household, he became a Baptist and began to attend church services regularly.[3] When he prayed, he prayed for reinstatement. He wanted to compete as an amateur again. He wanted to make the 1980 Olympic team. So, amidst all his worries, the breakdown of his second marriage, and the various jobs he took to make ends meet, he continued to run and stay in shape. He needed to be ready when the call came.

Naïve to the politics of the whole situation, he assumed that, with the dissipation of the pro league, the former ITA members would instantly regain their amateur status. Surely, the AAU would want its best athletes to represent the country after the disappointing U.S. medal haul in Montreal. They needed to bring back the pros to reassert American dominance. What Rodney didn't get was that the AAU and USOC adamantly wanted to keep track amateur in order to maintain their control over the sport. By showing leniency toward the pros, they would be undermining their own authority.

"At the time," said long-time *T&FN* correspondent Bob Hersh in 2005, "the prevailing attitude toward amateurism was quite different. And the

ITA guys had openly taken money, so there was a reluctance to reinstate them right away. The majority were toward the end of their careers and weren't looking to be reinstated. But for the others it wouldn't have been an automatic thing by any means. It's not like you could be pro one year and return to amateur the next."[4]

Brian Oldfield, who was caught in the same predicament as Rodney, said in 2006, "The AAU didn't want pro track to take over. If they ever reinstated us, that would give pro track the green light. That would be like saying, Go for it. They didn't want that."[5]

In an article that appeared in *The Washington Post* on August 31, 1977, staff writer Byron Rosen reported that the AAU was offering a glimmer of hope to the ITA refugees. "The Amateur Athletic Union," he wrote, "announced yesterday that U.S. track pros may apply for reinstatement as amateurs." Later in the article he points out that the AAU will review each case individually, and quotes AAU spokesman Pete Cava as saying, "It's a clear rule, if you accept money for competing, then you're a professional." Cava also noted that the IAAF, not the AAU, had ultimate authority. If the IAAF said no, then Rodney, Oldfield, and the others would be shut out of the Olympics once again.[6]

Don Pierson of *The Chicago Tribune* reported on July 14, 1978, that "many of the athletes who signed contracts with the ill-fated International Track Association pro circuit were disappointed when the world ruling body of amateur track (IAAF) refused last spring to review their cases."[7]

Bewildered and frustrated, Rodney remarked, "I'm the fastest in the world and I can't run."[8]

But he wasn't the fastest in the world anymore. And even if he did come back, he'd have to fight his way back to the top. The previous summer, Cuban Alejandro Casanas ran 13.21 over the 110 meter distance, eclipsing Rodney's world record of 13.24 that he had set at the Munich Games.[9] Then, a month before the *Tribune* article came out, UCLA sophomore Greg Foster (no relation to Charles Foster) broke Rodney's American record by running 13.22.[10] And then there was a freshman sensation at the University of Maryland named Renaldo Nehemiah who was looking like he might be even better than Foster. Rodney was losing precious time sitting around while these other guys were racing.

Around this time—in the fall of '78—Rodney moved in with his brother Jimmy, who was living in Houston. "He was going through a transition," Jimmy recalled. "He was down about the divorce with Janice. I told

## A Hurdler's Hurdler

him to get his stuff together and come on down to live with me. He did some clinics at local track meets. Worked at a local car dealership. My buddy who ran the place gave him a job because it was good public relations to say you had an Olympic gold medalist working for you. But that didn't last long—about three months—because Rodney wasn't much of a salesman."

But he was much of an athlete. And if he was to get his life back in order again, it would have to happen on the track. So, with no races to look forward to and no specific goals in mind, he began to train again. According to Jimmy:

> When he came to stay with me he was wondering if he could come back. He wasn't sure he'd be able to do it. He had serious doubts about it. I told him there's plenty of places you can train, just get out there and start training and see how you feel. So we went over to Rice University and he trained over there. During my lunch hour I'd go over there and time him in sprints. At first his times were slow, but they kept coming down, coming down, and he started to believe he could do it. And I think the only reason he didn't have the confidence to begin with was because of the transition he was going through at that time. Training again proved to be cathartic for him; it kind of helped him get back out of that transition.

In late 1979, Rodney started working for, and working out with, sprinter Bill Collins, a 100 meter finalist in the '76 Olympic Trials who now owned four sporting goods stores in Houston. Rodney worked in one of the stores. The two athletes had first met at a track meet in Houston in 1970 and developed a close friendship. Now that Rodney had fallen on hard times, Collins, who has gone on to become one of the greatest sprinters in the history of masters track and still competes at the masters level, was more than willing to help him. For the next five years Rodney would work in Collins's store: when Rodney finally did return to competition in 1980, Collins used his job as director of marketing and promotion with Asics Sporting Goods to land Rodney a contract to wear the Asics equipment on his comeback.[11]

Having more of a business sense than Rodney and being more aware of the politics involved in sport, Collins was angry at how the ITA, and the AAU and IAAF, treated Rodney and the others who joined the pro tour. "The ITA hurt a lot of athletes," he said in 2006. "Once they dropped the program, they left all these athletes out in the cold. I know Rodney wished he had never gone that route. The AAU and IAAF wanted to crush the program and send a message to all other athletes who were thinking of going in that direction. Or of joining any other program of its kind in the future. But Rodney continued to train. Because of his faith in God, he knew one day he would be able to run once again."[12]

Around this time he also met Betty, the woman who would later become his third wife. Rodney and Betty met at a church meeting at Wheeler Avenue Baptist Church in Houston. And unlike the common perception, Rodney didn't come off as quiet and reserved. "No, he wasn't shy," Betty recalled in 2005. "I knew of Rodney, but I had never met him before. The one thing that really stood out at that time was that he seemed like he had ... found Christ ... and he was really focused on his religion at the time. I think he always had it in him, but he focused more on it at that time. So I think that was a big change in his life."[13]

Cliff Wiley, who would go on to finish second in the 200 meter dash in the 1980 Olympic Trials, was living in Houston at the time when Rodney was training with Bill Collins. Currently, Wiley lives in Kansas City, where he works as a lawyer and coaches high school track at Washington High School. Every summer he returns to his hometown of Baltimore, Maryland as meet director of the annual Cliff Wiley Track Classic that has taken place every July for more than twenty years. He first met Rodney in 1978, when Milburn was just beginning to overcome his personal and financial struggles. Wiley recalled in 2005:

> He came into Bill Collins's store, and I could not believe it was him. It was kind of sad, this guy was using his name to promote a running clinic called "Jog with Rod." Very few people came. I was new on the international scene, having made the national team in 1977. I would see Rod at a local high school I trained at. It was really sad. He would be doing hurdle drills, his spikes were old, and he had no meets to prepare for. But Milburn was always upbeat, after the workouts he would tell me about the European meets, and the problems of the ITA circuit.[14]

By the end of 1979 it was looking like Rodney might, in fact, have meets to prepare for. The AAU was finally relenting a bit on its hard-line stance regarding pro tracksters. In an article that appeared in the November 30, 1979, issue of *The New York Times*, Neil Amdur wrote that former ITA members would be allowed to compete in the upcoming indoor season. They could compete against amateurs, but they could only compete in meets held on American soil, and they "would not be eligible for meets where invited foreign athletes participate."[15]

This was not a big step from a modern point of view, but at the time it was huge. For Rodney, it was the answer to his prayers. He would have the chance to prove himself against the new crop of hurdlers—Greg Foster

## A Hurdler's Hurdler

and Nehemiah in particular, but there were plenty others too, including Tonie Campbell of USC and Dedy Cooper of San Jose State.

The downside of the ruling, obviously, was that it didn't include international competition. Which meant Rodney was still not eligible to run in the Olympics, or even the Olympic Trials, since IAAF rules clearly stated that any meet serving as the qualifying meet for international competition was considered an international meet, even if it took place on domestic soil and consisted of only domestic athletes. Also, as Amdur's article pointed out, "International Olympic Committee eligibility rules ban an athlete who has signed a pro contract."[16]

Still, Rodney was elated, as were the other former pros who were young enough to resume their careers. John Smith, formerly of UCLA, had been one of the best quarter-milers in the early part of the decade, and he would've had a shot at a gold medal in Munich had he not pulled up lame in the final. Smith relished the chance to return to competition. "I've been exiled too long," Amdur quoted him as saying. "I want to run."[17]

When it was mentioned that pros returning to the amateur ranks might have to pay back the money they earned as pros, Rodney quipped, "No sweat. Little as I made, that would be no problem."[18]

An intriguing case was that of Mr. Anti-Establishment himself, high-jump ace Dwight Stones. The UCLA grad and member of the controversial Pacific Coast Club in Southern California had never competed as a professional, but he did participate in the made-for-television Superstars competition—a hokey but entertaining weekend space-filler in which athletes from various sports tried their best against each other in a series of events, including swimming, sprinting, rowing, bicycling, weightlifting, and everybody's favorite, the obstacle course. Money-wise, "I got completely screwed," Stones recalled.[19]

Stones did well enough to win $33,000, but he ended up giving it all back. He was told by an IAAF representative that he could compete as long as he didn't take part in any of the track and field events:

> The IAAF guy says, "Dwight, you may donate the money to the charity of your choice, which may include your track club." I said, "Okay, no problem." I went ahead and competed. Was second in the prelim, third in the final. After the world superstars, I was gonna donate the $33,000 to my track club. I called up the IAAF guy and said, "I need what you said to be put in writing." He said, "I can't do that." I said, "I just need you to attest to the fact that you told me that." Well, that wasn't gonna happen. I hired a lawyer who said, "It would've been nice if you'd've gotten that letter." So I had to go to court. A year and a half later, a guy from the AAU

says, "I think we can get you reinstated if you give back two-thirds of the money." I was like, "Okay, I've lost that much through not competing." It turns out I had to give back all the money. I profited mightily by getting back in. I hated forfeiting the $33,000 and losing to the AAU. But they had me by the balls, and I was a cocky 24-year-old, so I didn't realize it.

Stones's case differed from that of the former ITA stars. He had never participated professionally in Track & Field, so he could just give the money back and everything was okay. That track athletes could not participate professionally in *any* sport without losing their amateur eligibility in track was an issue that would be taken up several years later by Renaldo Nehemiah. But for Rodney, Oldfield, Smith, and the other former pros who wanted to compete again as amateurs, domestic meets would have to do.

In 1978, largely due to the conflict between Stones and the AAU, the U.S. Congress passed the Amateur Sports Act, which forced the AAU to choose which Olympic sport it wanted to remain in control of. They chose swimming. A new governing body was formed to run track. The Athletics Congress, as it was named, was run by the same people who had run the AAU.[20] Ollan Cassell ("Colin Asshole," Brian Oldfield said in 2006, "he spells his name wrong"[21]) switched from being president of the AAU to being executive director of TAC. "To many," Joseph Turrini wrote, "it seemed that TAC was the same as the AAU."[22] For all intents and purposes, it was. But that Congress had passed the ASA meant that times were changing, even if they were changing slowly. What seemed like simple common sense to Rodney—that the best athletes should get paid for what they do—was on its way to becoming a reality. Whether it would become so in time to benefit Rodney remained another issue.

* * *

Rodney's first race in his return to amateur track came in January of 1980. In what was to be his first amateur race in seven years, and his first race of any kind in almost four years, race rust would surely be a problem. He was twenty-nine years old. Gone were the days of the huge afro and headband. His hair was cut close, and an ever-growing bald spot was forming in the back of his head. He had spent the prime years of his career, 26–28, away from competition. The biggest question in his mind, one that was in the minds of his opponents and in the minds of track fans, was whether he could return to his old form.

## A Hurdler's Hurdler

"It was like Ali coming back from retirement," Cliff Wiley said in 2006. And it was. Muhammad Ali, too, lost the best years of his prime, and though he became a great champion once again, he was never the same quick-footed dancer who had mesmerized Sonny Liston with his amazing hand speed and ability to dodge out of range of blows. Fortunately, Rodney would not be like Jesse Owens, who lost the prime years of his youth and was never able to return to competition.

At 29, Rodney was young enough to salvage his career. He was fit as ever, and probably even more muscular and toned than he had been during his glory years at Southern. But as Bill Collins said, he had reason to be nervous about returning to the hurdle wars, "because training is never enough. You feel or think you are at one level, but you find out that when you just practice, practice, practice without racing, the timing is not there. Being on top for as many years as Rodney was, it was hard to view himself as not being the man. It was like Ali, he was so great and to have those years taken away really did a lot to his mind."

Rodney began his comeback, ironically enough, at the Muhammad Ali meet at the Long Beach arena in Long Beach, California on Saturday January 5, 1980. Nehemiah was still recovering from an ankle injury, so he would not be there. But Greg Foster and Dedy Cooper would. Going into the meet, Rodney was nervous, excited, and eager. After such a long lay-off, he didn't know what to expect. He did reasonably well, finishing third behind Foster and Cooper, but defeating old rival Charles Foster.[23]

After the race, Rodney reflected on the challenge:

> I thought I would have more problems than I did. I got out well, but I had a few problems with balance at the end. I can feel things are still there, the quickness and concentration, so I can't complain. I've had only about two weeks of serious work so far. No real speed or technique work. It will take me 6–7 weeks to really get in shape. I'm going to try to run enough meets this winter to get competitively ready. It felt strange to me to some degree. I hardly knew anyone. Charlie Foster is the only one still around from my era. I just want to make the Olympic team this year. I'm not out to challenge Renaldo Nehemiah, but I'll be competitive. We'll just have to see how each race turns out.[24]

Rodney's comeback was supposed to have continued at the National Invitational championship in Washington, D.C., on January 10th, but his entry was rejected by the meet director out of fear of the "contamination" rule—an IAAF rule that did not allow amateurs to compete against pros without facing the risk of being banned themselves. Ollan Cassell said at the time, "If we let these [amateurs] compete against professionals now,

I want our amateurs eligible for the Olympic Games."[25] But in 1979, two Russian athletes who had been banned for steroid use competed in domestic meets in the Soviet Union prior to the end of their ban.[26] So just how stringent the IAAF was in enforcing the rule was unclear. Many meet directors chose to play it safe until they were sure it no longer applied to the former ITA athletes.

A sign of the times came in the form of Larry Shipp's reaction when he heard that Rodney wouldn't be competing: "Yeah, I'd like to face Hot Rod again, but I'm more anxious to compete against Nehemiah. You always want to go for the top man, go for the present heroes instead of past heroes."[27]

At the Millrose Games on February 8th, Rodney didn't even make the finals.[28] The next night, at a low-key meet in Cleveland, he finished third.[29] His performances were unimpressive enough to prompt Don Pierson of the *Chicago Tribune* to write, without meaning to be critical, that Rodney was "running mainly for fun."[30]

Rodney earned his first comeback victory on March 1st, at the U.S. Indoor Track and Field Championships held at Madison Square Garden. It was his fifth meet of the indoor season. None of the young lions—Nehemiah, Greg Foster, or Dedy Cooper—were there, so Rodney's toughest competition would come from fellow former pro Lance Babb. Babb got out well and was leading for most of the race, but Rodney was gaining ground. Going into the last hurdle, Rodney pulled even with Babb, then Babb stumbled over the barrier and fell across the finish line as Rodney breezed past.[31]

After the race, Rodney was ecstatic with the win. After so many losses, it was a huge morale booster. "I'm super-satisfied," he said. "I'm at peace with myself and at peace with the other athletes. Regardless of the fact that Renaldo, Greg, and Dedy were not here, it was still a big win."[32]

His time of 7.09 was very fast, but nowhere near Nehemiah's world record of 6.89. Rodney had run 6.8 hand-timed in his last amateur meet prior to turning pro, but he was finding out that hand-timing and automatic timing were two very different animals. In 1976, heading into the 1977 season, the IAAF determined that all world records must be timed automatically. Hand-timed records would no longer be considered valid. With automatic timing, the starter's gun is linked to a camera at the finish line. The "watch" starts with the pulling of the trigger, and the camera records each athlete's crossing of the finish line. Automatic timing is

## A Hurdler's Hurdler

accurate to the hundredth of a second, and the IAAF determined that .24 should be added to a hand-time for any race 300 meters or shorter, and .14 should be added to a 400 meter race. So Rodney's 6.8 in the new vernacular would translate into a 7.04, and Nehemiah's 6.89 translated into the old vernacular would've been a 6.64, or, rounded up, a 6.7.[33]

Another change the IAAF was making was that only records set at metric distances would count as official records. Internationally, this was not a big deal. Only in America were races run at distances measured by yards instead of meters. The 100, 220, and 440 yard dashes would become a thing of the past, as would the 120 yard hurdles. Rodney was quickly discovering that the track world to which he had returned was not the track world he had left behind.[34]

But the biggest adjustment Rodney had to make was to get used to being an afterthought. In '78-'79, the rivalry between Nehemiah and Greg Foster had already reached epic proportions. Both had already run faster than Rodney ever had. In '79 Nehemiah broke the world record twice, lowering it from Casanas's 13.21 down to 13.16, then shattering his own record a week later with a 13.00. In the days of hand-timing, that would've been a 12.8. Seven months older than Nehemiah, Foster had instantly made his mark as a great hurdler in his freshman year at UCLA, when he ranked 7th world-wide and 4th in the U.S. Then at the NCAA championships the following year, he lowered the American record to 13.22. In that race he defeated Nehemiah, a freshman at the University of Maryland who had run an astounding 12.9 hand-timed as a prep in New Jersey. At the time, experts were heralding Foster as the next great American hurdler, in the tradition of Rodney, Davenport, Hayes Jones, Lee Calhoun, and Harrison Dillard. At 6–3, 190, Foster was an usually tall and powerful hurdler. What he lacked in technical proficiency he more than made up for in strength and aggression. After the Frenchman Guy Drut had won Olympic gold in '76, Foster was looking like a sure bet to bring American hurdling back into prominence heading into 1980.

Then along came Nehemiah. He was everything Foster was not. Where Foster was big and powerful, Nehemiah was small (5–11) and skinny. Where Foster relied on strength and aggression, Nehemiah relied on quickness and flexibility. Where Foster was taciturn, Nehemiah was charismatic. Where Foster was West Coast, Nehemiah was East Coast. And to top it off, their rivalry had the one ingredient every good rivalry needs: they didn't like each other.

## Nine—Hurdle Eight

To Foster, Nehemiah was a nuisance, a little whipper-snapper coming in who was trying to take over his territory. As Don Pierson wrote in the *Chicago Tribune* prior to the 1979 NCAA championships, "Foster is the guy who pitched a no-hitter the day before someone else pitched a perfect game."[35] And Nehemiah didn't appreciate the fact that the smug Foster did not respect his ability. Whenever they raced, it was war. And the other six guys were there basically just to fill up the rest of the lanes.

One of those six guys, more often than not, was Rodney. His first race against "Skeets," as the swift and sure-footed Nehemiah was called, came at the Lite Invitational in Rodney's adopted hometown of Houston on May 3rd.[36] Rodney, eager to begin his own rivalry with the new king of the hurdles, came into this meet ready to do battle. It would be his fourth outdoor meet of the season. His best automatic time thus far was 13.81.[37] Definitely not good enough to hang with Nehemiah, and not anywhere near Rod's own standards from his pre–ITA days. But training was going well: he was smoothing out his technical flaws, and he could feel himself getting faster each time out.

Rodney, who had turned 30 on March 18th, viewed the meeting between himself and Nehemiah as "a momentous occasion. Nehemiah is the number one hurdler in the world at this time, but I've never had a chance to run against him. People all across the country have been waiting to see us run against each other."[38]

That was true to an extent. Fans of Rodney's generation, who remembered his glory years, were fervently anxious to see their old-school hero show the young pup that he wasn't yet ready for the big time. But most track fans saw Nehemiah and Foster as representing the here and now, and Rodney as being a relic from the past. They didn't doubt that Nehemiah would smoke the old man.

But Rodney's confidence was unshakeable. He didn't dig himself from out of the grave just to concede defeat to a twenty-year-old hurdler. "Renaldo is fast like I am," he said. "The question comes to mind, how will he perform with me running alongside him? I'm physically as good as ever. I've matured and basically I know the things needed to get back into perfect shape competitively."[39]

Greg Foster and Tonie Campbell were not at the University of Houston that day. They were competing against each other in a classic UCLA vs. USC dual meet on the UCLA campus in Westwood. Foster ripped a blistering 13.30, leaving Campbell way behind in 13.73.[40] In Houston, besides

## A Hurdler's Hurdler

Nehemiah, Rodney would have to contend with Dedy Cooper, Charles Foster, and Briton Wilbert Greaves. Rodney lined up in lane four, with Renaldo beside him in lane five, Cooper on the other side of him in lane three, and Foster in six.

When the gun went off, Rodney bolted out of the blocks and took early command of the race. He ran a powerful but rhythmic race through eight hurdles, looking very much like the dominant hurdler who had won Olympic gold in 1972. But Nehemiah, though young and relatively inexperienced, had unwavering confidence in his abilities, and he was not one to get rattled when running from behind. Steadily, he made up ground on the ground, quickening his tempo between each hurdle, flicking his lead leg over each barrier with awe-inspiring grace and ease. By the ninth hurdle he was almost even with Rodney. They took off into the final barrier in a dead heat. Renaldo cleared it cleanly; Rodney clipped it with his trail leg. Renaldo sped past him, and Cooper also took advantage of Rodney's mistake to claim second place. Rodney had to settle for third.[41]

But it was one of Rodney's best races. His time of 13.40 was the second-fastest he had ever run with automatic timing. Only the 13.24 in Munich had been faster. Nehemiah's winning time was 13.32, and Cooper crossed the line in 13.34.[42] Rodney, though disappointed with the place, was pleased with the time and the progress he was making. "I have more work to do," he said afterward, "especially in the last part of the race. But I've proved I can run with these guys."[43]

A week later Rodney would run against Nehemiah again, this time at the Pepsi Invitational in Los Angeles. Greg Foster would be present, too, and Cooper again. The four favorites lined up in the middle of the track—Rodney in lane three, Nehemiah in four, Cooper in five, and Foster in six. Foster ran a great race and led from start to finish. Rodney ran a cleaner race than he did in Houston and didn't have the balance problems at the end of the race that had plagued him the previous week, but he was no match for Foster's incredible power over the hurdles. Foster won in 13.27, Cooper followed behind in 13.43, and Rodney came in third in 13.54.[44]

As for Nehemiah, he ran very sloppily, hitting many hurdles and zigzagging in his lane throughout the race. He wound up fourth in a slow 13.77. He blamed his poor performance on being, of all things, star-struck. The previous week he had been focused on coming back from his ankle injury. But, as he said in 2005, in this race it hit him that he was running against his idol:

## Nine—Hurdle Eight

I remember vividly that I watched Rod the whole race. He was right next to me. I was in awe of him. He beat me. That's when I realized he had the bald spot in the back of his head. I realized that I couldn't ever let that happen again. That was my first first-hand experience of being in awe of somebody. Throughout the race, I kind of re-lived everything I had admired and been taught about him. And I forgot to run the race. I consciously decided right then and there that I wouldn't lose to him anymore. And I didn't. I guess you could say that, subconsciously, I took the baton from him at that point in terms of moving the event forward.[45]

The next big meet was the TAC Championships in Walnut, California, on June 13–14. On the 13th, Rodney won his first round heat in 13.50, then finished second to Cooper in his semi-final heat in 13.59. The finals were set for the next day. The favorites were Rodney in lane three, Cooper in four, Nehemiah in five, and Campbell in six.[46]

In the final, Rodney had one of the worst technical races of his comeback. He crushed the second hurdle so hard with his trail leg that the force of the collision stood him upright. He never recovered. He hit the third hurdle just as hard the exact same way. He ran decently in the middle part of the race before clobbering the eighth hurdle, again with his trail leg. Nehemiah won in a comfortable 13.49. Cooper was second, Campbell third, and Rodney ended up a disappointing fourth in 13.76.[47]

This race revealed a basic flaw in Rodney's technique. He had always had the tendency to lock the knee of his lead leg—probably a consequence of practicing the "dime" method for so many years. It kept him safe from clearing hurdles too high, but because of this habit, the trail leg was often delayed in driving upward. Even in his Olympic final in '72, he had balance issues over the last three hurdles. Back then, his exceptional speed and power compensated for the flaw and made it barely perceptible. But now he was smacking hurdles with his trail leg, and it was killing his momentum.

The Olympic Trials were a week away. There was not much time to fix his technical problems.

The IAAF still hadn't made any formal announcement declaring the former pros eligible for international competition. Rodney desperately wanted to race at the Trials, the sport's biggest domestic stage. Hopefully he'd get the chance.

* * *

But then there was that nagging matter of the boycott. In December of 1979, the Soviet Union invaded Afghanistan, prompting U.S. President

## A Hurdler's Hurdler

Jimmy Carter to issue a threat: pull the troops or we'll boycott your Games. The 1980 Summer Olympics were to be the first ever held in a communist country. Carter, determined not to turn a blind eye to the Soviets Union's attempt to expand its evil empire, committed himself to making a stand. The Soviets were equally stubborn. They weren't going anywhere. Pull the troops by February 20th, Carter said, or else we'll boycott, and we'll ask other countries to boycott, too. The Soviets didn't pull the troops. Carter was adamant. He pressured the United States Olympic Committee to vote in favor of a boycott. I'll withhold funding if you don't, he said, I'll revoke your tax exemption. So the USOC voted in favor of a boycott. By March 21st Carter made it official. The United States, for the first time ever, was pulling out of the Olympic Games.[48]

And all the potential Olympians in every corner of America breathed a collective "Awww, damn." Years of training, planning, dreaming, and sacrificing were about to go down the toilet for political reasons out of their control. Rodney's main reason for returning to amateur competition had been to make another Olympic team. But it was now looking like there would be no Olympic team to make.

While Carter was known for his humanitarian ideals, many athletes couldn't help but feel that they were being used as pawns to fulfill his political agenda—specifically, to prevent the Soviets from monopolizing Middle East oil. "We are simply a tool, an implement," said marathoner Bill Rodgers when he heard the news. "No one cares about us at all until we can be used for their purposes."[49]

Consider the following passage from Carter's State of the Union Address on January 23, 1980:

> The region which is now threatened by Soviet troops in Afghanistan is of great strategic importance: It contains more than two-thirds of the world's exportable oil. The Soviet effort to dominate Afghanistan has brought Soviet military forces to within 300 miles of the Indian Ocean and close to the Straits of Hormuz, a waterway through which most of the world's oil must flow. The Soviet Union is now attempting to consolidate a strategic position, therefore, that poses a grave threat to the free movement of Middle East oil.[50]

Athletes who had trained all their lives for one moment couldn't give a damn about Middle East oil. Though the boycott had been announced well before the start of the Trials, the track and field athletes were still hoping that the Russian government would withdraw troops from Afghanistan at the eleventh hour. Nobody wanted to accept that they were competing for nothing. It was a dark, gloomy atmosphere in Eugene when the competition began on June 21st. Fittingly, rain fell from the overcast sky for much of the week.

Rodney's immediate troubles had nothing to do with the boycott or the rain. He had traveled all the way to Eugene from Houston without any word from the International Olympic Committee that he was eligible to run. In March, The IAAF reinstated Rodney and the other former pros for international competition, which included any and all meets except the Olympics.[51] But the IOC had yet to make any decision regarding their status for the Games. Since the United States was boycotting the Games anyway, it seemed like a moot point. But it wasn't.

If the Soviets *did* pull out at the eleventh hour and the U.S. *did* end up going to the Games, then the U.S. couldn't send pros that the IOC wouldn't permit to compete. So the logic was, if the pros *might* be ineligible for the Games, and the U.S. *might* go to the Games, then the pros had to stay out of the Trials. Just in case. TAC president Jimmy Carnes said at the time, "The [official] entry blank for the Olympic trials was approved two years ago. It says that only athletes eligible to compete for the United States in the Olympics can compete in our Olympic Trials."[52]

This rule had been put into effect to prevent foreign collegians attending American universities from competing in the U.S. Trials. It was not designed to keep out former pros. "Two years ago," Carnes explained, "we never anticipated the reinstatement of the former pros. We never anticipated an Olympic boycott. Is it fair to bar these athletes? Well, we have to look at both sides. I don't think it would be fair if they were ineligible for the Olympics and they displaced athletes who were eligible and might make the team."[53]

At the TAC championships, the former pros had been informed that they were ineligible to compete at the Trials. They immediately filed an appeal, though they knew their chances of winning the appeal were slim. As far as TAC was concerned, the decision wasn't in its hands anyway, but in the IOC's.

"I think it's a flim-flam," Brian Oldfield said at the time.[54]

John Smith agreed. "I think we are being wronged," he said. "They are promoting the meet as the Olympic trials, but we're not going to the Olympics. So why such stringent rules for the Olympic trials? How can they keep out such good people?"[55]

Only two former pros showed up in Eugene. Rodney and Oldfield.

## A Hurdler's Hurdler

The rest, including Smith and Lance Babb, didn't bother to show. Assumedly they had decided it wasn't worth the trouble.

Rodney made it to Eugene, but he never made it to the starting line. After his 13.40 at the Lite Invitational, he felt himself capable of going into the 13.30 range at the trials. Unfortunately, he would never get the chance. When he showed up on Sunday, June 22, 1980, ready to compete, he was told by meet officials that he couldn't.[56] Rodney appealed to meet director Bob Newland. They had a good relationship, going back to when Rodney set the 120-yard world record of 13.0 there back in 1971. The track at Hayward Field was Rodney's favorite in the whole world. He knew that, if given the chance at such a major meet as this one, he would rise to the level of his previous glory.

Newland wanted to help, but couldn't. "He and I both agreed he should be running here," Newland said at the time. "If I had it to choose, I would love to see Rod Milburn in this meet. We're very biased toward him in Eugene. He's run some great races here."[57] But, he added, the Oregon Track Club, which was running the meet under contract with the USOC and TAC, would have to abide by what those organizations said.[58]

TAC president Jimmy Carnes, who also happened to be the head coach of the Olympic team that would never go to the Olympics, reiterated what he had said a week earlier: because former pros aren't eligible to compete in the Olympic Games, they aren't eligible to compete in the Olympic trials.[59]

Rodney, enraged and desperate, didn't know who should be the object of his wrath. At first, he chose every athlete's favorite villain, TAC executive director Ollan Cassell. He claimed that Cassell had assured him back at the TAC indoor championships in February that he'd be allowed to compete at the trials. "I feel I've been lied to and stabbed in the back," he said. "I was told at the beginning of the year that I would be allowed to compete here."[60]

When it was brought to his attention that he and the other former pros had been told a week earlier that they wouldn't be allowed to compete for the reasons Carnes had mentioned, Rodney responded angrily. "That is a joke. We're not going to the Olympic Games so how can they use that as a reason to bar us?"[61]

Cassell liked Rodney. In 2006 he referred to Rodney as "a great athlete who came from a great school with a great coach."[62] Unlike Stones and Prefontaine, Rodney wasn't one to challenge the authority of track's governing bodies. Chances are, Cassell probably did want Rodney to run. But chances are slim that he actually told Rodney he could. "I have no memory of talking to Rod," he said in 2006, "in February of '80, about the trials. If everyone else was notified that they would not be able to compete in the trials, Rod was told the same thing regardless of who he talked with. The USOC was accepting athletes in accordance with IOC rules."[63]

Once Rodney had a chance to calm down, he too backed off his claim that Cassell was to blame. "I just can't say," he said. "I just don't know. There are so many people involved that I just can't say what person or persons did this to Brian [Oldfield] and myself."[64]

The following day, Bert Rosenthal of the Associated Press wrote a scathing article criticizing TAC for not allowing Rodney to compete. "Fortunately," Rosenthal wrote, "Milburn is not a rebel, or else he might have caused a serious ruckus Sunday when meet officials locked him out of the first round of the 110 meter high hurdles.... Instead, he went away quietly without any kicking or screaming. Naturally, he was disappointed at the developments, but he accepted them like a gentleman."[65]

Like Rodney and John Smith, Rosenthal felt that TAC didn't need to comply to the letter of the IOC law since the U.S. was not sending a team to Moscow anyway.

"TAC's contention," he wrote, "was that the United States was still choosing an Olympic team—however honorary—and the ex-pros who have not been sanctioned for the games by the IOC should not deny a bona-fide amateur of a spot on the team. However, Milburn, Oldfield and the others said they would gladly relinquish those positions to other athletes. Their main objective, they said, was just to run in the trials, the most glamorous track and field meet in the nation and an event conducted only once every four years."[66]

It was truly one of the saddest days in Rodney's life. All he wanted to do was run.

He boarded a plane back to Houston. The high hurdles went on without him. Nehemiah won in 13.26, Cooper got second in 13.39, and Campbell was third in 13.44. Foster didn't run in the final because of tonsillitis.[67] Campbell's time was .04 slower than Rodney's at the Lite Invitational. But it was raining all weekend in Eugene and the track was slick, so there's no telling if Rodney would have run fast enough to make the team.

We'll never know.

# Ten

# Hurdle Nine
## *The Quiet Champion*

> "Rod was a quiet champion, a gentle champion. It was pretty remarkable that he could be that good, yet be humble."
> —Renaldo Nehemiah[1]

Tonie Campbell danced with glee after crossing the finish line in third place at the trials. He hadn't expected to make the team. He had just competed in the NCAA national championships a week earlier. "So, at the trials," he said in 2005, "each round, I did the same thing I had done at the NCAAs. I knew I had to be in the top four to make the semi-finals, so I made sure I made the top four. I made it all the way to the finals that way. By some stroke of luck, Foster went out, I drew a good lane, right between Renaldo and Dedy Cooper. I told myself to just latch onto Renaldo and let him pull me in. I was a master at latching onto another hurdler's rhythm and technique. He pulled me through to a new personal best and a third-place finish."[2]

But when it hit that the Olympic boycott now affected him directly, he stopped dancing. "I was naïve like everyone else," he said, "thinking that sports and politics don't mix. When I was asked what I felt prior to the Games, I said, 'If the boycott will save one life, let's do it.' I'm thinking it's not gonna be me who's affected, but then I made third! That marked the spiritual and political awakening of Tonie Campbell. When I realized my dreams and career were being compromised by my government, it started hitting me hard."[3]

Determined not to let his dream die easily, Campbell became the youngest member of a group of track athletes set on defying the federal government's edict. While in Europe for a series of meets in July, members of the U.S. team got together and decided to ask the IOC if they could run under the IOC's umbrella if they couldn't run for their country. The IOC, which wasn't in favor of the boycott, or even the general principle of mixing sports and politics, agreed to let the Americans compete, but the athletes would have to get to Moscow on their own.

The athletes saw that one of their upcoming meets was in Budapest, Hungary, and made plans to take busses and trains that would lead them from Budapest to Moscow. "There were large risks involved," Campbell said in 2000. "You have to remember, this was one of the first times that American athletes were going behind the Iron Curtain."[4]

But the federal government caught wind of the plan and worked quickly to squash it. A Secret Service agent sent a memo to the group stating that any athletes who competed in Moscow would lose their passport and visa and be considered an expatriate.[5] "It was scary, very scary," Campbell said. "You're talking about some serious stuff."[6]

Most athletes backed off at this point and gave up. But a few remained defiant. "They were willing to risk their family, their friends, their country, whatever it took to make the Olympics. A lot of these guys were at the end of their careers and they were desperate. This was the last hope they had. All their dreams and hopes had been plugged into this one Olympics." Eventually, though, all the athletes gave up, "especially since we weren't 100% sure the IOC was going to let us compete anyway."[7]

For Nehemiah, who wasn't a part of the group, the boycott was a devastating blow to his rising career. He would only compete one more year before quitting track and trying his hand at professional football. The greatest hurdler in the world left the sport behind at the age of 22. The boycott, he said in 2005, is the reason why. "I didn't want to risk another four years of training for nothing. The [San Francisco] Forty-Niners came along at the right time. They helped me sustain a professional career, and I had no long-term track goals. Track was an amateur sport."[8]

Arguably, no other American athlete lost as much in terms of potential marketability than Nehemiah. Having already broken the world record twice and exhibited a level of dominance in the high hurdles not seen since Rodney's 1971–73 run, Olympic gold would've been the thing to make him a mega-star beyond the borders of track and field. Campbell pointed out that "it's hard for an athlete, a person who could have gotten a medal to look at the Olympics today and see all the endorsements and then think how their life could have been different. They could be in a

## A Hurdler's Hurdler

whole different financial bracket, with celebrity status, and now they're just a person with an asterisk by their name in a history book."[9]

Nehemiah was so bitter that he wouldn't even talk about the boycott for many years afterward. "I was twenty-one years old," he said, "and the best hurdler in the world, and then my dream of winning the gold was taken away from me just like that. I felt it was a gross injustice to the entire nation and the other nations who didn't take part."[10]

To assuage the anger of the athletic masses, Carter arranged for a pseudo-Olympics to be held in which he invited the other boycotting countries—including Canada, Kenya, West Germany, China, and Sudan—to participate. Carter's event was called, aptly enough, the Olympic Boycott Games. The track meet portion, held July 17th at Franklin Field on the campus of the University of Pennsylvania in Philadelphia, was dubbed the Liberty Bell Classic.[11] (Yes, very corny.) In the high hurdles, Nehemiah finished first in 13.31, bettering the time of 13.39 that Thomas Munkelt of East Germany ran to win the Olympic Games. Campbell finished a distant second behind Nehemiah in 13.68.[12]

Again, Rodney was left to wonder what might have been had he been given the chance to showcase his talents.

But Rodney didn't let the crushing disappointment of not being allowed to run in the trials or the subsequent Liberty Bell Classic to put an end to his comeback. He continued to compete throughout the summer of 1980, running in over twenty meets between the end of June through October. The 13.40 at the Lite Invitational in Houston ended up being his seasonal best, but he did run some good races in which he showed flashes of his past excellence. He even beat Nehemiah again, although the time (13.69) was slow and Nehemiah hit several hurdles along the way.[13] At the Coke Invitational in London on August 5th, Rodney came in second to Nehemiah—13.23 to 13.47—but he did beat Greg Foster for the first time.[14] Certainly Rodney had returned to the status of being a formidable opponent, but he had lost his previous ability to dominate a race. He was good enough to hang with Campbell and Cooper. Sometimes he'd beat them, sometimes they'd beat him. But the only way he could beat Nehemiah or Foster was if they made mistakes along the way.

Rodney finished the year ranked 5th in the world, and 4th in the U.S.. The only non–American world-ranked ahead of him was Olympic gold medalist Munkelt. Rodney finished ahead of Campbell and former world record holder Alejandro Casanas in the rankings.[15] Not bad for someone who hadn't raced in three and a half years.

More important than the rankings, maybe, was the respect he had gained from the younger generation of hurdle stars. At thirty years old, with his opponents being as young as the nineteen-year-old Campbell, Rodney played the role of mentor to them, and it came naturally. Campbell has many memories of traveling on the European circuit, conversing with the likes of Rodney, Nehemiah, sprinter Steve Williams, and middle-distance runner Steve Scott.

"The fact that we were sitting down talking culture and politics spoke volumes to me," Campbell said in 2005. "It shows we're not just jocks. Sure, we're warriors, it is our job to go out there and perform on the track, but there's much more to it. We're also responsible. We have a gift, and we have to show the world. Rod would say, 'I give it one hundred percent every time. You never know when a world record might come, when everything's gonna fall in place for you. It's all about giving glory to God's gift, plus you have to give your best to the fans.'"[16]

Campbell, who currently coaches collegiately, credits Rodney, Williams, Scott, and the young Nehemiah—who was very mature for his age—for helping him avoid the trappings of success. "Renaldo spearheaded that mode of thinking—realizing your gift. Steve Williams had his own business. My first year on the circuit, he and Rod would say to me, 'Look at those other young guys, spending money on jewelry, women, cars, but when it's all over, what do you have to look back on?' I took those lessons to heart. They're the best lessons I ever got, even more than the ones I got from my parents. Rod's philosophies, experience, and wisdom I carry with me to this day. The things he told me are the same things I tell my athletes now. His words live on through me."[17]

No hurdler was more heavily influenced by Rodney than Nehemiah. Athletically and personally, Nehemiah patterned himself after Rodney's example. Growing up as a school-boy hurdler at Scotch Plains Fanwood High School in New Jersey, Nehemiah's desire to become a great hurdler came from watching Rodney run on television. "Rod was the reason I got into hurdling," Nehemiah said in 2005. "When I saw him run in the 1972 Olympics, I knew I wanted to be a hurdler. After watching the gold medal race, I instantly went out and ran over the split rail fence in my backyard. I was hooked. I put the part in my hair. Everything but the headband."

Prior to ever running against his idol, in a 1979 interview with Jon

## A Hurdler's Hurdler

Hendershott of *Track & Field News*, Nehemiah spoke effusively of his admiration for Rodney, and of his desire to follow in his footsteps. He spoke of his own progression as a prep hurdler, and how it mirrored that of Rodney Milburn. The same for his progression collegiately and at what was then his current age of twenty-three. In the interview, Nehemiah made it clear that all of his goals were based on surpassing the accomplishments of Milburn, whom he looked upon as the standard bearer in the event. Nehemiah told Hendershott that he not only modeled his technique after that of Milburn, but his demeanor, and his will to win. "It was phenomenal," Nehemiah said, "how [Milburn] could start out even and almost at will take control of the race. That's what I looked into the most. Not just to outlean someone at the tape or outsprint somebody off the last hurdle, but was it that he could surge like that. That's what caused me to get into hurdling so deeply; I wanted to learn how to do it."[18]

Nehemiah and his high school coach Jean Poquette would spend hours analyzing Rodney's technique, trying to figure out what he did differently from Davenport, Drut, Tom Hill and the others that made him such a special hurdler. As Nehemiah said in 2005:

> Rod was the first person that Jean and I ever saw who could sprint off the top of the hurdle. We were fascinated by that. What was he doing to allow himself to do that? That's what we wanted to figure out. He was the first hurdler ever to sprint between the hurdles, not just three steps and a jump. That's all we worked on—getting the body to move continuously, making hurdling as close as possible to sprinting. I also know that the first three hurdles were the most important to him in setting up rhythm and cadence, and they became the most important for us. For anyone, the first three hurdles can define how your race is going to go, or not go. I can clearly say that Rod Milburn single-handedly is the reason I got into hurdling. Seeing a guy run that fast over hurdles and not lose his balance was incredible to me.[19]

For his part, Rodney relished the role of being a mentor to the next generation. As far back as his J.S. Clark days, he had always taken an interest in encouraging those who looked up to him. During his years at Southern, he would always go back to Opelousas as often as he could to conduct camps and clinics for the kids there, or just to attend local track meets and inspire kids with his presence. He would do the same things in Baton Rouge. Even now, he was doing the same thing in Houston. "He did quite a bit of public speaking," his wife Betty said in 2005. "He did clinics in Houston. He traveled, did speaking engagements at different places. He preferred going out, speaking to kids, motivating them, letting them know that he was a man who came from a small town that nobody knew about, and still accomplished a lot."[20]

Also, during this time in his life, Rodney was going through a spiritual awakening. During his lost years of 1977–79, he had prayed long and hard for the chance to return to competitive amateur track, and he felt grateful that God had granted him that wish. The time he spent living with Jimmy served to get him back on his feet, and the job in Bill Collins' store, which he still had, provided stable employment that helped offset the cost of being an amateur. By 1980, athletes were allowed to make money in track, but the money had to go into a trust fund and be used only for training and traveling expenses. So in effect, TAC was permitting professionalism in the sport, but under its terms, and under its control.[21]

Another key factor in Rodney's personal evolution was his relationship with Betty. They had met in '79, and would eventually get married in '82. During his comeback, she would sometimes travel with him on the European circuit, where she provided comfort and support as Rodney dealt with the difficulties of losing to these younger guys, many of whom, with the possible exceptions of Nehemiah and Foster, he most certainly would have beaten regularly in his prime.

"He and I had conversations," Betty recalled, "and he understood that there was always someone who was coming behind—who was better, younger, had more speed. But competing was something that was still in him, and he still wanted to do it."[22]

Nehemiah, who would make a similar comeback attempt in 1986 after playing professional football for three years, would come to understand how hard it was to return to competition in an individual sport after being away for so long. As he said in 2005:

> Rod wasn't the same athlete because of the inactivity. If you're not using speed, it can't sit dormant for years. When I returned [from pro football] and wasn't winning all my races, I tried to remember that the same thing had happened to a great champion I had admired. I didn't embrace it, but I understood it. Rod knew he couldn't beat me and Greg, but he was proud to be our motivation. Don't get me wrong now, he was still competitive, but we younger guys just enjoyed the camaraderie of being in the same race with Rod Milburn.[23]

For sure, Rodney was not yet ready to concede that time had passed him by. A 5th-place world ranking after such a long hiatus convinced him that he still had what it took to be the best. As the 1981 outdoor season rolled around, Rodney felt good about his chances to stay competitive

## A Hurdler's Hurdler

with the best hurdlers, including Nehemiah and Foster. In a *New York Times* article that appeared in February of '81, Frank Litsky—the same journalist who had written the revealing portrait of Rodney ten years earlier in *Boys' Life*—depicted Rodney as a man very much at peace with himself while transitioning into the latter phase of his career. No longer the "reluctant hero" who just wanted to be left alone, Rodney felt comfortable being a star among stars, and he genuinely appreciated the younger guys for looking up to him as a role model. Quite simply, being away from the sport for so long had made him realize how much he loved it.

"It's just as much fun now," Rodney told Litsky. "Before, I didn't have competition like this. Willie Davenport was the best before me and was still one of the best when I ran against him. But I was such a consistent winner that there was not too much of a competitive situation. It's competitive now. Others know that when [Nehemiah and I] are in a race, it's going to be a good race. It's impossible not to be. They know I'll be training and ready. It boils down to who can become the better technician. Renaldo is right now. He's very consistent."[24]

With his 31st birthday only a month away, Rodney was now "the old man in a young man's game," as Litsky described him.[25] Already Nehemiah had beaten him indoors three times. Rodney's only victory thus far had come in a meet in which Nehemiah did not compete. But Rodney still felt he could give Nehemiah all he could handle once it was time to go outside.

"I'm not discouraged," he said. "If I run a perfect race and don't win, I won't be discouraged. No way. It's incentive. This is long range. It's a nine-month season, and the bulk of the races are outdoors. I want to respond in the outdoor season."[26]

Still, Rodney all but allowed that the only way he could beat Nehemiah was if Nehemiah were to self-destruct. "There are areas where anyone can make mistakes," he said. "Renaldo can and does. He can hit a hurdle and recover quickly. But if you hit a hurdle with the center of your foot, it can almost bring you to a dead stop."[27]

Nehemiah, with his upright posture, was prone to hitting hurdles with the foot and knee of his trail leg. Plus, his exceptional speed between the hurdles was causing him all kinds of balance issues as he was still trying to figure out how to adjust his speed to the distance between the hurdles. For his part, Nehemiah understood the role that technical mistakes play in a hurdle race, and his goal was to eliminate all such mistakes, not just by prepping his body through rigorous training, but also by maximizing the level of his mental focus when it came to race preparation. Never had he lost a race in which he felt he wasn't in control at some point. In the '79 interview with *T&FN's* Hendershott, Nehemiah discussed his rivalry with Greg Foster, and bouncing back from his '78 loss to Foster in the NCAAs:

> I learned a lot from those losses. I was never convinced he could beat me. The thing that always kept me confident was that, at some point in both of those races, I was winning. Then I made a technical error and lost to him. I think if he had beaten me head up, no mistakes, then it might have been a different ball game. But I knew I was winning and he had to come get me and that helped keep me stable.[28]

Nehemiah and Milburn were both making the same basic point that all hurdlers eventually come to understand and accept: in a hurdle race, anything can happen, because, as Tonie Campbell would say many years later, "if you're not ready to fall, you're not ready to hurdle."[29]

But Rodney knew that time was not on his side. And training in Houston with the likes of super-sprinters Carl Lewis and Stanley Floyd, he recognized that the younger guys were much better athletes than the heroes of his generation. "I ran against guys like Willie Davenport and Tom Hill, who were just hurdlers," he said. "The hurdlers now are much quicker. Guys like Renaldo, Dedy Cooper, and Greg Foster run 200s in 20.3 and 400s in 45."[30] But he remembered that Davenport had won an Olympic medal at age 33. And he believed that practicing his start against Lewis and Floyd would give him the speed and quickness he needed to keep up. "They're the fastest in the world," he said, "and I'm coming out of the blocks with them."[31]

But once the outdoor season arrived, it became increasingly clear that Rodney was past his prime. Not hopelessly so, not embarrassingly so. But that extra gear, that ability to surge and pull away from the pack at the fourth hurdle, was missing. Only the great ones have it. And the great ones are great for just a small window of time. For Rodney, it seemed that window had closed.

The truth is, Rodney wasn't more than an afterthought to Nehemiah. Just like Davenport and Tom Hill could only beat Rodney when he made mistakes—like he did at the '72 Olympic trials—Rodney's only chance of defeating Nehemiah was to hope he hit hurdles. From a competitive standpoint, Rodney was just another of the seven athletes running behind him. Only Greg Foster could be considered Nehemiah's peer.

## A Hurdler's Hurdler

In the early part of the '81 outdoor season, Foster reigned supreme. The first meeting between the two new-era super hurdlers took place at the Pepsi Invitational on May 10th in sunny California, on Foster's home track on the UCLA campus in Westwood. Rodney wasn't at the meet, but was competing at the Rice Meet of Champions in Houston, where he started off his outdoor season with a victory in a solid but unspectacular 13.63.[32]

The meeting between Foster and Nehemiah had the whole track world buzzing. The two had raised the standards of hurdling excellence to levels it had never seen before. Prior to their arrival, the high hurdles had been a fringe event in track. An interesting curiosity, but never a focal point except for those who followed the event closely. In Rodney's best years, the marquee events had been the middle-distance and distance races featuring the likes of Jim Ryun, Steve Prefontaine, Marty Liquori, and Frank Shorter. Because of Rodney's dominance, actually, the hurdles hadn't garnered much attention: back then, everybody pretty much knew Rodney was going to win. But when Foster took to the blocks against Nehemiah, the stadium grew quiet, and all eyes turned to the starting line.

At the Pepsi meet, Foster, looking sinister with his dark beard and dark, thick glasses, thumped Nehemiah soundly. For the second straight year, he crossed the line and kept on running, jubilantly waving his fists in the air as the home crowd roared its approval. His time, 13.10, only one tenth slower than Nehemiah's world record of 13.00, was the second-fastest time in history. Nehemiah finished third in 13.46, behind twenty-four-year-old Sam Turner's 13.43.[33] To Foster, this performance served as proof that he was Nehemiah's equal, not merely one of the many guys running for second place. The 13.10 served notice that Nehemiah *needed* to run his best to beat him. The rivalry was a rivalry again. Nehemiah had won most of their meetings, but Foster was winning often enough to keep him honest.

But Nehemiah got hurt, and the two adversaries wouldn't race each other again until late July. During Nehemiah's absence, Foster took over. He followed up his 13.10 with a 13.18 one week later at the Modesto Relays.[34] On June 20th, he won the TAC Championships, which was now the national championship meet, in 13.39. With no Nehemiah to worry about, Foster's closest opponent was twenty-year-old NCAA champ Larry Cowling, who came in second in 13.66, almost a full three tenths behind the winner. Rodney finished a distant 5th in 13.71.[35]

## Ten—Hurdle Nine

Rodney was struggling. He had yet to come close to his 1980 seasonal best of 13.40, and he was losing regularly to Campbell, Cooper, and some of the other youngsters. In the modern era, 13.60s and 13.70s, automatically timed, weren't going to get it done. Rodney had pushed the event forward in the early '70s, but Nehemiah and Foster were now pushing it even further. Nehemiah had knocked the world record down .21 since his arrival on the world scene, and he still hadn't reached his twenty-second birthday. With everyone else trying to catch up to him and Foster, more and more athletes were passing Rodney by. His automatic 13.60s would've been hand-timed 13.4s and 13.3s back in the day, which then would've been good enough to win almost every time out. Now, such times were good for thirds, fourths, and fifths. Rodney would have to at least get back into the 13.40 range to move ahead of Campbell and the others. And he would have to get back to his Olympic level of 13.24 to even have a chance against Nehemiah and Foster.

Nehemiah returned to competition on July 14th in Lausanne, where he made a big statement with an easy victory in 13.26. With no Foster, Campbell took second in 13.54, Turner took third in 13.65, and Rodney was fourth in 13.76.[36] At the Sports Festival two weeks later, Nehemiah and Foster did battle for the first time since the Pepsi meet. In a tightly-contested battle, Nehemiah ran a scintillating 13.00, tying his world record, but the wind reading was above the allowable legal limit. Foster finished right behind in 13.22.[37] No one else was even close. Rodney didn't run this meet.

With August on the horizon, it was looking like either Nehemiah or Foster, or maybe even both, might break the current world record at one of the big meets on the European circuit. All these 13-lows hinted at the possibility that one of them might finally break the magical 13.00 barrier, which was the only unchartered territory left in the high hurdles.

After his Sports Festival victory, Nehemiah continued to run electrifying races. A 13.39 in Budapest, 13.31 in Italy, 13.17 in London.[38] With his lightning-quick lead leg and extraordinary flexibility (he was capable of doing Russian splits), he had actually improved on Rodney's dime method. Unlike Rodney, Nehemiah's lead leg never locked at any time during hurdle clearance. It looked like he was literally running over each hurdle. Despite his balance problems and occasional trail leg issues, he was quite obviously the most fluid, graceful hurdler in history.

August 19th was the date for the Weltklasse meet in Zurich, Switzerland.

## A Hurdler's Hurdler

In 1973, Rodney had run a 13.1 there, a world record at the 110 meter distance in the prehistoric days when hand-times were still verifiable. Most American athletes seemed to compete well in Europe for the simple fact that the crowds were more knowledgeable and enthusiastic. On this cool evening, the atmosphere was electric. The high hurdlers were divided into two heats—a slow heat and a fast heat. Rodney, unfortunately, was in the slow heat. He hadn't run fast enough up to this point in the year to earn a lane in the fast heat.

Rodney won his race in a ho-hum 13.78, then u-turned back to the starting line area to put his sweats back on and watch the second heat.[39] The Zurich spectators restlessly whispered to each other as they eagerly anticipated the next race. Nehemiah, dressed in a red Puma singlet with white lettering, stood in lane four, looking like the sleek, swift cat that the name of his sponsor suggested. Beside him in lane five stood Foster, wearing a blue and gold singlet—the colors of his alma mater. Fittingly, the two combatants had been assigned their rightful places in the middle of the track, where it would be easy for the audience to key in on them over every hurdle. They both shook out their legs and arms, staring directly ahead. Other notables included Turner in lane two, Cooper in three, Campbell in seven, and former world record holder Casanas in eight.

The gun went off and Nehemiah exploded out of the blocks. He touched down off the first hurdle slightly ahead of Foster. But by the second hurdle the two were even, and by the third Foster had gained the slightest advantage. Nehemiah then made a move of his own and the two were dead even for hurdles four, five, and six. By the seventh hurdle it seemed that the long legs of the 6–3 Foster couldn't turn over fast enough to keep up with Nehemiah. Nehemiah pulled ahead by a little less than a meter. He held that lead through the finish line, crossing in a new world record time of 12.93. Foster too ran a personal best, 13.03, which he would never surpass though he would go on to be the world's best hurdler for the next decade.[40]

It was a beautiful race. Neither superstar hit a hurdle. And both of them were absolutely flying.

Nehemiah pumped his fist in the air and ran a joyous victory lap, slapping hands with anyone who came into his path. At the end of it all, when he returned to the starting line to retrieve his things, one of the athletes there to greet him was Rodney.

To the casual observer, Rodney was just one in a long line of people who wanted to get close to the new world record holder and offer congratulations. But when Rodney grabbed Renaldo's shoulder and gave him a firm handshake, those with a sense of history would've realized they were witnessing a passing of the torch. Renaldo had idolized Rodney, and now he had surpassed him. If no one else appreciated the significance of the moment, Renaldo did.

"Rod was the cornerstone of the event," he would say more than twenty years later. "He did things no one else had done. He was the leader of the pack. He clearly separated himself not just in his performance, but in his stature. He was a quiet champion, a gentle champion. It was pretty remarkable that he could be that good, yet be humble. For as long as I was there, I tried to finish what he started. My thing was to continue the dominance that Rod created for all of us."[41]

But Rodney wouldn't be around much longer before he'd have to ride off into the sunset. He had acknowledged as much himself in the February *New York Times* interview with Litsky.

"Renaldo says to me, 'You're my idol.' Kids in junior high school say they model themselves after me. I like that. But there comes a time when it all ends. Soon, maybe, but not yet."[42]

# Eleven

# Hurdle Ten
*Into the Sunset*

> "Rod was still pleasant, yet at the same time still hungry."
> –Tonie Campbell[1]

Rodney ended 1981 ranked 8th in the world and 7th in the U.S. His fastest race of the year, a 13.59, came four days after the Weltklasse, and was good for third behind Nehemiah's 13.07 and Campbell's 13.54.[2] That in a down year he could still be among the world's best was encouraging. Always one who prided himself on staying in race shape, he wasn't about to hang up the spikes yet. Though the bald spot at the top of his head kept growing wider, he remained in peak condition. While more muscular than he had been in his prime, he was actually four pounds lighter than he had been in 1972.

With the 1984 Olympics still a couple years away, there were no major international competitions to train for. But the thought of still being around in '84, when the Olympics would be held in Los Angeles, did motivate Rodney to stay competitive. Having been denied the opportunity in 1980, the lingering disappointment still bothered him, even if he didn't show it. When asked about the '84 Olympics, he responded with, "It's not impossible. I'm very disciplined. I keep myself very fit."[3]

Although he'd be 34 by the LA games, there was reason for optimism. He was still among the best in the world. More and more young bucks were rising on the scene, including University of Tennessee superstar Willie Gault, but none of them were so much better than Rodney that he couldn't catch them. Foster was the only untouchable now. Gault, Campbell, Cowling, and Turner were all within reach.

And the biggest reason for optimism was Nehemiah's departure. The three-time world record holder, angered by the 1980 boycott and frustrated with the hypocrisy of amateur track both domestically and internationally, had signed a contract to play wide receiver for the San Francisco 49ers of the National Football League. With Nehemiah gone, Foster was now the irrefutable king of the high hurdles, and everyone else now held new hope that they could challenge for second-best.

Even Rodney's old compatriot Willie Davenport, never lacking in confidence, was making noise about a comeback attempt. "If I can get back to my old form," he said, "or even to 80 or 90 percent of where I was, I should be able to make the team."[4] He went on to say later, "I think I have the competitive fire and the experience some of the kids today are missing. I see some guys with some good times here and there, but nobody who has done it consistently. When I look into their eyes, I don't see the killer instinct."[5]

Davenport, who competed in the 1980 winter Olympics as a bobsledder, never made a serious comeback to the track. That he was even contemplating one at age forty speaks volumes about how wide open things were with Nehemiah gone.

The similarities between Nehemiah's exit and Rodney's in 1974 were numerous. For Nehemiah, the tipping point paralleled that of Dwight Stones back in '78. Like Stones, Nehemiah had won a big lump of money ($43,300) by winning the Superstars competition, but he wouldn't be allowed to collect it. To stay amateur, Nehemiah couldn't keep it. The money would instead go to TAC. "We will distribute it according to our procedures," Ollan Cassell said at the time. When asked what those procedures were, he replied, "We don't have any yet."[6]

The Superstars competition proved to Nehemiah beyond the shadow of a doubt that he was one of the best athletes in the world in any sport. He had finished first three years in a row, winning easily every time. Yet these guys he was beating up on were making six figure salaries, plus commercial endorsements. Here he was a better athlete than any of them but couldn't legally make a dime. So when 49ers wide receiver Dwight Clark mentioned to him during one of the Superstars competitions that he should give pro football a shot, Nehemiah saw no reason not to. Football, he said, not track, is the sport that every American male grows up wanting to play.[7]

Like Rodney, Nehemiah would go on to miss the prime years of his track career, would fight several years for reinstatement, and by the time

## A Hurdler's Hurdler

he gained it, would struggle against younger athletes he would've smoked in his prime.

Tonie Campbell noted the similarities in 2005:

> I draw so many parallels to Rod and Renaldo,. They were both at the top of their game when they forfeited their eligibility. It was like, "I'm on top, I'm beating everybody, so where's the challenge?" So with Rod, the professional league presented itself. But it hurt him. Here's an individual who was a legend, an innovator. He had that *aura* about him. A lot of times, he won the race before it even started. Other athletes were counting bodies, trying to figure out what place they could come in, already assuming Rod had first locked up. I think that in those lost years, he could've definitely taken down the world record. He had the physical gifts—the speed, the power, the flexibility, the technique, and he had the willingness to train. But it's sort of like wondering what would've happened if Renaldo hadn't left. When Rodney came back, he couldn't understand why so many people were running 13.2, 13.1, because nobody had been doing that before he left. He had raised everybody's game. He removed the veil. People went from thinking "What if" to "Why not?"[8]

The year 1982 proved to be a good year for Rodney. He was more consistent than in the previous two years of his comeback. Once he hit the European circuit in July and August, almost all of his times fell somewhere in the 13.50–13.60 range, with his seasonal best coming on August 22nd in Cologne, where he finished second behind Foster, 13.32 to 13.46. But he was getting a lot of second, third, and fourth place finishes. The younger hurdlers were continuing to improve. The only races he won were his opener at Texas Southern (13.81), the Pelican Relays at his alma mater in a hand-timed 13.1 (ah, the good old days of hand-timing), and the Milan meet in Milan, Italy, where he defeated Gault, 13.60 to 13.78.[9]

Gault would go on to gain the biggest surprise victory of the year a couple weeks later at the Sports Festival, where he beat Foster in a stunning 13.26 to 13.33.[10] It was looking like Gault might be the next big thing to come along in the hurdles. But he loved the sprints as much as he loved the hurdles, and he loved football as much as he loved track. The Sports Festival ended up being his last meet of the year. He didn't run the European Circuit in August, but chose instead to return to Knoxville for training camp. Indeed, Gault was another great hurdler that track would lose to football. He would go on to play professionally for the Chicago Bears and earn a super bowl ring on its 1985 championship team.

Though he didn't earn many first-place finishes, Rodney did cross the line ahead of one or more of the younger guys in all of the European meets in August. The only real clunker of the season came at the national championships in June, where he came in 8th with a 14.09 after running a solid 13.64 in the semis.[11]

With no Nehemiah around, Foster was an easy choice for world's best. He finished ranked #1, with the Sports Festival meet being his only loss. He and Gault were the only two hurdlers to run under 13.30. Foster ran 13.22 at Koblenz in late August.[12] To put it simply, with Nehemiah gone, there was no more drama in the event. Foster had run 13.10 and 13.03 in '81, so the 13.22 was evidence that he was just doing what he had to do to win. He seemed lonely without his rival. Victories were coming too easily for him.

For his consistency in the European meets, Rodney was rewarded with a 4th-place world ranking, behind only Foster, fellow old-timer Casanas, and Gault. But Rodney finished ranked ahead of Turner, Stewart, Cowling, and Campbell, all of whom were at least seven years younger, the latter three being ten years younger.[13] Turns out the old man still had something left after all.

Meanwhile, Rodney's personal life was as stable as it had ever been. He continued to live and train in Houston, running for the Houston Athletics Track Club, maintaining his close friendship and working relationship with Bill Collins. He also married Betty, who provided a spiritual stability and sense of family that had been missing since his divorce from his second wife Janice in 1978. That marriage had produced a six-year-old son, Rodney III, who Rodney wanted to see more often. So even in the midst of training, competing, and pushing toward another possible shot at the Olympics, he was already feeling the itch to move on to the next phase of his life.

The IAAF held its first World Championships in 1983. In many ways, making the world championship team had the potential to be as fulfilling as making an Olympic team. The World Championships would bring together all the best athletes across the globe, and, unlike the Olympics, there would be no threat of boycott since it featured only one sport.

But Rodney ran miserably at the TAC championships. Fourth in his first round heat in 13.95, then sixth in his semi-final heat in 13.98, and that was the end of that.[14]

He managed to salvage the season by running well in Europe in August and September. He ran his seasonal best of 13.61 in Rieti, Italy with the help of a 2.4 tailwind.[15] His fastest legal time was 13.65, only good for seventh at the Weltklasse meet.[16] He finished the year out of the rankings for the first time in his comeback. All of the young guys, as well as some new ones, had passed him by. Foster, Turner, and Gault earned the top three U.S. spots, and young NCAA champion Roger Kingdom from the University of Pittsburgh was sixth in the nation and eighth in the world.[17] Kingdom had surprised Gault with the NCAA victory—a sign of things to come, as he would go on to surprise Campbell at the Pan-American Games, and would go on in the next several years to develop a rivalry with Foster as competitive as the one Foster once had with Nehemiah.

The last race of Rodney Milburn's track career came on May 26, 1984, at Rice University's Meet of Champions. He finished third in 13.79.[18] "His goal," his wife Betty said in 2006, "was to make it to the '84 Olympics, but that didn't work out."[19] It was clear he had no shot of making the Olympic team, so he decided against taking a shot at the TAC championships. Neither did he go to compete in Europe that summer. He was done.

Some might say Rodney stayed in the game too long. In his comeback, he was never the same hurdler he'd been before his comeback. Yes, he had achieved high world rankings, but the question would ever linger: could he have defeated Nehemiah and Foster in his prime? Did they truly surpass him, or did they just catch him at the right time, on the downside of his career?

But he had done something unprecedented in the sport: after a three-year hiatus, he had returned and re-established himself as one of the best in the world. And his love for the sport, his appreciation for the gift, was far greater during his comeback years than it had been during his Southern U. days, when he was tired of track and resented all the headaches that came with it. He had earned his rightful place as one of the greatest track athletes in history, and Rodney could leave the sport in a peaceful frame of mind, knowing that he had given all he had—for the fans, for his opponents, and for himself—every time he stepped on the track.

Now it was time to say good-bye.

"Did he stay around too long?" Nehemiah asked in 2005. "As a runner, you want to find a means to an end as long as you can. If you're just looking at how his career ended and how he wasn't dominant, coming in fourth or fifth in most of his races, that happens to most of us. But he secured his place in his generation, in his time span. You really can't do more than that."[20]

## Eleven—Hurdle Ten

Tonie Campbell, who did make the 1984 Olympic team, concurred:

In his comeback, losing was a big adjustment for him. I always respected the fact that, at the end, Rodney was still pleasant, still humble, yet at the same time still hungry. He didn't become obsessive about losing, about trying to get back to his old form. He didn't alienate himself from the other hurdlers. One of the things I always did was congratulate my competitors after a race. I remember after I beat him for the first time, he graciously thanked me, but I remember him walking off looking a little forlorn. The reality had set in that he had just lost to someone who never would've beaten him in his prime. The whole time we were in Europe, he was still looking for that 13.2 to come back. And he'd say stuff like, "All I need is a few more races, all I need is a few more races." Before a big race, Rod would be like, "It might be my day today." After it was over, if he didn't win, he would say "It was your day." He was just a good guy like that.[21]

Betty recalls how popular Rodney was overseas. "I traveled with him to Brussels, several places in Germany. But it was nothing at all like it was [in the US]. The reception in Europe was *so* different. Here we have football, basketball, baseball. There it's soccer and track. So even the little kids knew who Rodney was. It was amazing just to see, compared to how any track athlete is treated here."[22]

Rodney himself didn't regret making a comeback, or for sticking with it for three and a half years. He felt in great condition the whole time. And when you feel fit, it's hard to accept, or even realize, that you've gotten slower. But as he said in an interview in 1993, "I don't dwell on the past. I realized a long time ago this wouldn't last forever."[23]

If he had any regrets, it would be going pro. He mentioned to Bill Collins on numerous occasions that joining the ITA was a big mistake. He also wished he had had a true rival during the early '70s. "I really think a 12.8 or 12.7 was possible for me during those days," he said in 1988. "I mean, lots of times I'd come over that last hurdle relaxed because there was nobody pressing me. I think I learned to relax too much. Maybe if I had had some stiff competition, something like the Renaldo Nehemiah–Greg Foster duels, I could have run that 12.7."[24]

Some believe he held on so long because he needed the money. There may be something to that, because it seems that, to some degree or another, Rodney was always struggling financially. But as long as he held a spot among the best in the world, there was no reason to quit. Once he dropped off from that level, he hung up the spikes, and left the sport with his legacy, and his dignity, intact.

\* \* \*

## A Hurdler's Hurdler

Even as Rodney's track career was winding to a close, the next phase of his life was beginning. Another reason he didn't run at the TAC championships and on the European tour was because he had found a new job. His old coach Dick Hill, now the athletic director at Southern University, hired Rodney as his new head track and field coach. Throughout Rodney's pro years and his return to amateur track, he and Coach Hill had remained close, and Hill even traveled to Europe with him a few times. Hill had always held a deep respect for Rodney's humility, work ethic, and determination to make a difference in the lives of young people. "When he was hired by Dick Hill," Betty recalled, "Hill recognized the champion in him, and felt Rodney would be good for the program."[25] Rodney, Hill felt sure, would make a great coach.

For Rodney, coaching presented an interesting challenge. Though he had always enjoyed doing camps and clinics, being a formal head coach with all the duties and tasks that came with it was something he had never seriously considered. But because of his loyalty to Hill, and because this was an opportunity to turn around the struggling program at his beloved alma mater, he decided to go for it. After all, he'd once been a poor boy living in Opelousas, needing to attend summer school classes at the end of his senior year of high school just to get into college. Southern had given him a chance when most schools wouldn't have, regardless of his athletic abilities. Now Coach Hill was giving him the chance to give back.

Surely, much had changed for historically black colleges and universities since Rodney's days as a student athlete. The changes had begun as far back as the early '70s, when blacks started reaping the benefits of the Civil Rights movement of the '60s. Across the country, doors were opening for black students who wanted a top-notch education. In the South, segregation was now a thing of the past, so black students had more options than just the HBCU's they had to choose from in the '50s and '60s. The major universities that had been shutting blacks out were now letting them in. Better yet (or worse yet, depending on one's perspective), they were gobbling up athletes right and left. Now that there was no longer any segregation in the professional sports leagues, the myth that blacks were inferior athletically had been fully exposed for the lie that it was. As a result, historically racist colleges that wouldn't even have given thought to recruiting or offering a scholarship to a black athlete were fielding predominantly black teams in major sports.

For HBCUs, this meant trouble. And since most of the nation's

HBCUs were in the South, this region of the country was hit hardest. Rodney the athlete, as it turns out, was one of the last of a dying breed. Since his days as a hurdler at Southern, more and more elite black athletes began matriculating at major universities, and the programs at HBCUs were suffering. The transition had begun during his time. Larry Shipp had gone to LSU, not even considering Southern as a viable option. On the West Coast, quarter-miler John Smith had gone to UCLA.

In the '50s and '60s, HBCUs ruled. There was two-time Olympic champion Lee Calhoun at North Carolina Central. Davenport and Rodney, both Olympic champions, were at Southern. Bob Hayes at Florida A&M was an Olympic champion. Vince Matthews at Johnson C. Smith was an Olympic champion. Charles Foster at NC Central was NCAA champion and Olympic finalist. Leon Coleman at Winston Salem State was an Olympic finalist. The list goes on and on. Southern's program was dominant during the '60s, even before Rodney ever got there. Texas Southern also had a dominant program. Major institutions were afraid to run against them.

But that had all changed. Almost all of the athletes Rodney competed against in his comeback represented major universities. Greg Foster, UCLA. Nehemiah, Maryland. Campbell, USC. Gault, Tennessee. Kingdom, Pittsburgh.

The only notable exception to the trend was Edwin Moses. The tall, lean 400 meter hurdler, who won the 1976 Olympic Games, dominated the event for over a decade, and went on to win another gold in Los Angeles in 1984, hailed from Morehouse College in Atlanta.

By the time Rodney the athlete had transformed into Rodney the coach, Southern's program was struggling in the same ways that most HBCUs were struggling. Funds were low, resources were limited, and the enticement of big-college facilities, programs, and limelight were luring away the best athletes who twenty years earlier wouldn't have thought of attending a predominantly white university. So Rodney was going to have to be diligent, patient, and creative if he was going to rebuild the program.

It turns out that he enjoyed coaching much more than he thought he would. Interacting with kids was something he had loved to do his whole adult life, and now he was getting a chance to do it on a daily basis. Some former star athletes have had difficulty making the transition into coaching because they grow impatient with athletes who can't do it the way they used to do it. But that wasn't the case with Rodney. Because he'd grown up poor, he saw coaching as a new opportunity to help those who came from where he had come from. And he could do so in the context of his field of expertise.

Rodney also believed strongly in the role that HBCUs played in the black community. While Southern now attracted students from all over the country and many foreign countries, there were still many students who came from small Louisiana towns like Opelousas. Many of these students, like himself fifteen years earlier, couldn't meet the admissions requirements of the state colleges. But now many of the major universities were recruiting such students anyway if they could contribute to the athletic programs and bring more income and name recognition to the school.

Long-time Southern professor Dr. George Whitfield, who started teaching in the speech and drama department in 1963, observed in 2005 that "once the schools with black athletes started beating up on the other schools, other schools would start getting black athletes too. Whatever it took to win, and you couldn't win without black athletes."[26]

In reference to Nehemiah, Campbell, Greg Foster, and others, Dr. Whitfield said:

> There was a time when all of those black athletes would've been at HBCUs. For kids in [Louisiana], you went to either Southern or Grambling. Now you got the starting five of LSU [women's basketball team] all black. Last year there was a high school girl who lived in Baton Rouge, but there was never even a consideration she would go to Southern. And she could walk to Southern from her house. That's the way it is with the top athletes. From all over the state, if LSU wants them, they're competing with other big-time schools around the country—Oklahoma, Tennessee, Alabama—not with Southern.[27]

Rodney believed in HBCUs, and Southern in particular, because they didn't exploit black student athletes like the big schools did. But even at Southern, he was finding that the culture had changed since his time there. Dr. Whitfield, who never taught Rodney but remembered him as an "indifferent" student who "made the effort and went to class," lamented the cultural change:

> When I first started teaching, the students were competitive, they wanted to show they knew as much as me. It was just like competing on the athletic field. But it reached a point where they became not learners, but grade collectors. There was no interest in learning anything, but in getting grades. By the easiest, cheapest way possible. Not by reading, studying, discussing, debating. The majority seemed to see no correlation between learning something and earning a grade. Right now, everything is correlated with jobs. Trade in the grade for a degree, trade in the

degree for a job, and you still haven't learned a damn thing. When I first started, if you didn't go to class and do your work, you didn't compete.[28]

The academic climate had changed, the athletic climate had changed, and the social climate had changed. By 1984, the civil rights movement was a distant memory, and college-aged students were too young to even remember it. Martin Luther King and Rosa Parks were names in history books. Money and material wealth mattered more than dreams or activism. In this new climate, for better or for worse, Rodney would try to make an impact.

He did. By all accounts, Rodney was loved by his athletes and was dedicated to his job. Dr. Raymond Lockett, who had taught in Southern's history department for over thirty-five years, and also served as an assistant track coach from 1973–85, recalled that Rodney's strengths as a coach were many. "He could deal with students," Lockett said, "he could deal with people. And he had a tendency to let his assistant coaches coach. He didn't try to force his will on people. When he [first] came in [as head coach] we had lost quite a few athletes, so he had to rebuild a team."[29]

And he did a good job of it. His name recognition gave instant credibility to the program. Though Southern hadn't produced an NCAA champion since Rodney won the hurdles in 1973, by 1986 he had a good group of sprinters and hurdlers who were competitive on a national level. In April of that year, Milburn stated that he felt both the 4 × 100 and the 4 × 400 were capable of qualifying for NCAA nationals, in addition to hurdler Kevin Savoie, another native Opelousan, in the 110s.[30]

But there were problems. And most of them had to do with money. The track budget wasn't much to begin with, and it was decreasing every year. Also, Rodney's easygoing, trusting nature might not have been what was always needed from a head coach. In 1985, an assistant was late entering the team for the prestigious Texas Relays, so Southern didn't go. It wasn't Rodney's mistake, but as head of the program, he bore the brunt of the blame.[31]

The following year was when the major budget cuts came. Not just in track, but across the board. Both the Texas Relays and the Drake Relays—another prestigious April meet that all the big schools used to prepare for their respective conference championships and then the NCAAs—were cut out of the budget. Southern was forced instead to compete at low-key small-school meets locally. The $40,000 allotted for the track team's travel expenses the previous year was cut in half.[32] "That's

## A Hurdler's Hurdler

pretty hard on the program," Rodney lamented at the time, "when we have kids aspiring to greatness like we do. [The Texas Relays and Drake Relays] are like going to the Olympics or Olympic trials. You really look forward to the big meets and competing against the best in the nation. It culminates your season."[33]

Ironically, Rodney didn't find out about the budget cuts until after he had already entered the team in the meets, trying to ensure that his assistant's blunder from the previous year wouldn't happen again. "When I was an athlete," he said, "I always looked forward to the Texas and Drake Relays. They were always two of my better meets because of the caliber of the athletes and the fans there. I don't think there's any coach who could operate under these conditions. As a coach, it's hard for me not to be able to get these kids competing in the manner they should be."[34]

While Rodney enjoyed recruiting and his enthusiasm for working with the kids did not wane, he was growing tired of the other aspects of the job. The politics, the budget issues, scrambling to find quality meets. Having big-time goals in a small-time program was proving to be a higher hurdle than any he had cleared throughout his athletic career. In the modern landscape, the Willie Davenports and Rodney Milburns of the world no longer attended schools like Southern. Rodney worked well with what he had, moving the program along to where it was much more competitive than when he had arrived, but he had no potential NCAA champions on his roster, no one who could turn out the type of performances that would let the world know that big things are happening at Southern.

That in itself didn't frustrate Rodney. He held no ambitions, he wasn't looking to move up in the coaching ranks, and he wasn't looking to land a job with a bigger school. He just wanted to do what he could to put Southern back on the map, and it seemed to him that the Southern administration, with its budget cuts and overall indifferent attitude toward athletics, wasn't making any effort to help him in that regard.

When Dick Hill resigned as athletic director in the spring of 1986—that marked the beginning of the end of Rodney's tenure as head coach of the Southern University track and field program.[35] A new sheriff came to town with guns blazing, hell-bent on making wholesale changes to the entire athletic department.

Marino Casem was a football guy. He arrived at Southern after twenty-two years at SWAC rival Alcorn State, where he had compiled a record of 139 wins, 70 losses, and 8 ties. In 1984, the Alcorn State football team went undefeated and became the first black college ever to finish the regular football season with the number one D I-AA ranking.[36]

As an administrator, he was a bottom-line guy. And the bottom line wasn't just wins, but money. When he stepped down as AD in 1999, he stated in his retirement speech, "One of the things that I'd like to be most remembered by is the fact that we ran a program that was fiscally sound. At the end of every fiscal period we were in the black."[37] He also took pride in having revitalized what he viewed to be a dying athletic department. "We came in 1986 and the goal here was to restore the program back to the luster and prominence that it enjoyed in years previous. The program needed a major overhaul, a real boost, and that's what we provided."[38]

Rodney had been a key part of that luster and prominence. He and Davenport were the only Olympic champions the school had ever produced. And both had given back to the university—Willie as coach of the women's team in the early to mid '70s, and Rodney now as head coach of both the men's and women's teams.

And the track program, for all of its budget problems, was making noticeable progress. Rodney first heard that his contract wasn't going to be renewed just two weeks after four members of the men's team had competed at NCAAs. "That's the most we've had in an NCAA meet since I've been here," Rodney said that the time, "and the way things are going, I would almost expect to have more in the future. We have a young team and it's only going to get better."[39]

So lack of results couldn't have been why Rodney was being fired. Most people think that Casem simply wanted to hire his own people. That Rodney was a hero at Southern didn't matter to him. "From what I heard," Rodney's brother Jimmy said in 2006, "the new director said, 'If I'm coming I'm bringing all my coaches with me,' and that's what he did."[40]

To Jimmy and other family members, the firing was a cruel act of betrayal on the part of the university. Rodney's sister Alice, when discussing the firing in 2005, bemoaned the fact that Rodney's tenure as coach was so brief:

> [It] went by so fast. It wasn't long enough to develop another Rodney Milburn or Willie Davenport. He put a lot of time into the job. He took a lot of time talking to the kids, mentoring them, working with them. When he first took the job, he was at a time in his life when he had opportunities to work at larger companies, where they had fitness centers. He ended up going to Southern to take this coaching job because it was like going home. He jumped at the chance because he was going back to where he was born, so to speak.[41]

## A Hurdler's Hurdler

Rodney's wife Betty agreed:

> There may have been one kid (Kevin Savoie) who really showed the kind of talent that Rodney could work with. The new AD, I guess, expected Rodney, because of his talent, to produce something that wasn't there, and that's just too much to ask. When Dick Hill was coaching at Southern, he had a Rodney Milburn, a Willie Davenport. He had natural talent. Rodney didn't have natural talent to work with. It takes years to produce something that can compete on a higher level.[42]

Rodney wasn't the only one who fell victim to the grim reaper. Heads were rolling all over the campus of Southern University. The men's basketball coach, the women's basketball coach, the football coach, and two of Rodney's assistants were all unceremoniously axed from their positions.[43]

Rodney's emotions ran the gamut from anger to bitterness to sadness to indignancy to utter bewilderment. Though he claimed to be as shocked by the news as everyone else, as early as April 14th he had received a letter from Casem informing him of his recommendation that Rodney's contract not be renewed. "But," Rodney explained in a July 8th news conference at his home, "I haven't received anything from the chancellor or president with regards to the recommendation."[44]

But surely Rodney understood that very rarely would a university's administration veto the recommendation of its athletic director.

In the news conference, he failed to provide any clear reason why he'd been fired. In typical Rodney fashion, he did his best to remain diplomatic and avoid conflict. "I don't want to get into a discussion of that," he said. "It was more or less a real surprise in a sense that [the track team] did quite well and I really hadn't expected to not be a part of Southern University coming into a fourth year. I do understand that with the new administration of the athletic director, that there were several things that would take place. Casem was given full power to run the program, which I have no problem with and no objections to."[45]

While acknowledging that he wished the matter had been handled more professionally, Rodney further added to its ambiguity when he admitted that Casem had mentioned the reason for his dismissal in the April letter. But Rodney wouldn't elaborate on what the reason was. According to Casem, it was "a personal matter," but he too refused to elaborate. "If [Rodney] wants to tell you," he said, "he'll tell you."[46]

It's hard to imagine what the "personal matter" could've been. By all accounts, it seems that Casem had no faith in the current coaching staff and just wanted to start all over again.

## Eleven—Hurdle Ten

Though Rodney put up a good public front, didn't disparage Casem or vent any frustration, the truth was he was heart-broken. Arguably, losing this coaching job in such a humiliating manner was a blow to his spirit that he never fully recovered from for the rest of his life.

Sue Deville, director of the Interpretive Center and Museum in Opelousas that houses an exhibit honoring Rodney, said in 2006 that "Rodney was very much devastated when he lost that coaching job at Southern."[47]

Indeed he was. Rodney's brother Jimmy said in 2006 that recovering from the firing was an even more difficult transition than the one Rodney had gone through in 1978. While some people close to Rodney, including his wife Betty, claim that Rodney had no intention of making a career out of coaching anyway, Jimmy sees it differently. "He was really upset about that because he really wanted to prove his point that he wanted to be a good track coach. So it did affect him. Now he had to go out and look for another job."[48]

So why not search for another coaching job? He had done well enough at Southern to generate interest, and LSU was already expressing interest in hiring him at least in an assistant's role. "He felt Southern had betrayed him," Jimmy explained, "so he was turned off from the whole politics of campus life. Big time."[49]

Rodney would go on to take a job with the Georgia Pacific Paper Plant in nearby Port Hudson. Though it's unclear exactly what his duties were, it was a tough, manual labor job, representing a return to his roots of working with his father building houses in Galveston. Though it seemed sad that a former Olympic champion would be reduced to manual labor in a paper mill, the move made sense. The pay was good and steady (he was making $37,000 a year, $10,000 more than he'd been making at Southern), so he could better support his family.[50] At no point in his life did he ever feel that he was above manual labor. College life, with all its uncertainties and political maneuverings, wasn't worth the risks.

Though he moved on with his life, Rodney's resentment lasted a good while. Prior to being inducted into the Louisiana Sports Hall of Fame in June of 1988, he admitted that Casem's decision not to renew his contract "really hurt me. It was like somebody coming into your house and slapping your wife. Although I never planned to retire as a head track coach, I thought I had done a lot for Southern University. And I don't consider that I failed as a coach. I've never failed in anything I've

## A Hurdler's Hurdler

ever done in sports. I brought this university and this state a lot of recognition."[51]

By 1993, Rodney had settled into his new lifestyle as a hard-working family man. His son Rodney III, from his second marriage, was playing football for Southern. Rodney and Betty also had two kids, nine-year-old Felicia and seven-year-old Russell. Rodney stayed fit and regularly worked out, and he even entertained thoughts of competing in masters meets, though it never happened. Besides working at the paper mill and spending time with his wife and kids, he also kept himself busy by speaking at many coaching clinics around the country.[52] And he seemed to have finally put the emotions of his firing by Casem behind him.

"I'm not bitter about it," he told the *Times-Picayune*. "It was time for me to start smelling the roses."[53]

And for the time being, anyway, the roses smelled sweet.

## Twelve

# Across the Finish Line
## *The Final Transition*

"It's not what the world sees, but what God sees in your heart that counts."
—Rodney Milburn[1]

Though he was no longer involved in track in any official capacity, Rodney kept in contact with the sport. He continued to work out and train. Most people who knew him agreed that if he still wanted to race he would probably still be competitive against world-class athletes, and could most likely dominate at the masters' level. For Rodney, staying fit was an ingrained part of life, whether he chose to compete or not. No one close to him can remember a time when he was ever out of shape.

He never did run another race or coach another athlete, but he often attended high school and college meets in the Baton Rouge area, and in Opelousas when he was in town visiting his mother. And he continued to volunteer his time by working with any kid who sought his help and by giving instructions at various track clinics. For Rodney, finding time to impart his knowledge to the youth was never an issue. He made time for that. He liked kids because they were genuine. They wanted to learn and they wanted to get better. Working with kids brought him back to the roots of his own passion for the sport, before he ever knew anything about traveling expenses, professionalism, politics, and all the other side issues that compromise the sport's purity. He wanted the kids to know that they could do what he had done, that he had come from nothing and become an Olympic champion, and that they could do the same.

"He did that a lot," Rodney's brother Jimmy said in 2006. "He would go to schools, church functions, to talk to kids. He'd go out of his way to

## A Hurdler's Hurdler

do it, and he did it a lot. He would never ask for any compensation. He just liked saving kids. That's how he looked at it."[2]

"We once had a kid here who was a problem child," recalled longtime Opelousas native Sue Deville. "Then someone gave him a hat that had been worn by Rodney. That kid was never a problem again. He wanted to be like Rodney Milburn."[3]

For the most part, Rodney continued to play the role of the family man, working long hours at the paper mill and helping his wife Betty to raise their two kids. Meanwhile, the accolades continued to trickle in. Occasionally someone would recognize Rodney as the former Olympic champion and would heap praise upon him, but he never let the praise get to his head, and he refused to live in the past, as glorious as it may have been.

"He had accomplished that great path, you know," his sister Alice said in 2005, "holding the world record, winning the gold medal, but you never felt like he felt he was better than you. He was always humble, even though people were crowding around him telling him how great he was. That's one thing I always admired about him. This is why when I see people today and they know how good they are, they brag and brag, it gets on my nerves. Because he never acted that way. He'd never let on how great he was. Unless somebody else would point it out, you'd never know."[4]

In July of 1992 a stretch of road on the traditionally black side of town in Opelousas was renamed Rodney Milburn Boulevard. Present at the ceremony were Mayor John Joseph, several city council members, many family members, and Rodney's old coach from J. S. Clark and Southern, Claude Paxton.[5]

In October of 1995, Rodney suffered a major heartbreak when Coach Paxton, his original hurdling mentor who used to mow the grass track at J. S. Clark all by himself, passed away at the age of 76.[6] Paxton had become nothing less than a legend in Southern Louisiana over the years, mainly for his work at J. S. Clark. Dedicated to track, he was always beating down the door of *Opelousas Daily World* sports editor Herman Fuselier, urging him to print more track articles and add more meet results to his sports page. When Rodney was fired from the coaching job at Southern, Paxton was the one who told Marino Casem he didn't need a new track coach because he already had a good one. When Casem said he didn't like the one he had, Paxton walked out of the athletic director's office and never stepped foot in there again.[7]

## Twelve—Across the Finish Line

The death of Paxton hit Rodney hard. With his father living in Galveston throughout his childhood, Paxton had served as the hands-on, visible father he would not have had. As different as they were in demeanor, they shared a passion for the hurdles, and a passion for kids. Both loved to attend high school meets and talk to athletes after their races. Both offered free advice and tips whenever asked. Over the years, after Paxton retired from coaching, Rodney visited his beloved coach whenever he was in Opelousas, and Paxton always visited Rodney when passing through Baton Rouge. Usually when they talked track, they didn't talk so much about their old days together, but about the current crop of high school and collegiate athletes in whom they saw potential.[8]

At Paxton's funeral, Rodney "fell apart," his wife Betty said. "Paxton genuinely loved Rodney, and Rodney loved him just as much. Paxton kept Rodney straight."[9]

Rodney's brother Jimmy agrees that Paxton's death devastated Rodney, even though he did see it coming. "Paxton had been sick [with diabetes] for about a year," Jimmy said. "Rodney got a chance to talk with him before he died, so I think he got some closure. But yeah, he was upset."[10]

Life went on for Rodney. He continued working at the paper mill, kept himself physically fit, and settled into family life. He was a regular at cookouts, picnics, fishing trips, and reunions. He also did some traveling for Georgia Pacific—speaking engagements, and even a commercial. "Once they realized they had an Olympian working for them," long-time rival Charles Foster said in 2005, "they started using him. They put him up front. They put him in a suit, put him in a position of prominence, and that's when he and I became real close again. I was working with the Atlanta Committee for the Olympic Games in '96, and every time he'd come to Atlanta, we'd go out and hang out together."[11]

All of this made it seem that Rodney's life was pretty stable. But the speaking engagements and Rodney's cool exterior belied the fact that the long hours at the plant were wearing him down.

Then in 1996, Betty filed for divorce. Not because they weren't getting along, but because she wanted to move somewhere that would offer more financial opportunities. Rodney wanted to stay in Baton Rouge. "We were still friends," Betty said in 2005. "I saw a need to change our lives, and in order for me to do that with my background in sales, a more lucrative place was Houston. I encouraged him to come, but I guess he was committed to the paper mill because he had been there a while. When I left,

## A Hurdler's Hurdler

I asked Rodney to come along, he said maybe he'd join us later, which never ended up happening. But I did go and I found a much better-paying job, and a better support network for the kids. I have a lot of relatives here [in Houston]. When the kids and I left, Rodney helped us pack. We cried together."[12]

So began another transition, another period of uncertainty, loneliness, and financial woes. His paycheck was being stretched to its limits. He was paying child support for Russell and Felicia on top of keeping up with his own bills.[13] He started working twelve-hour shifts at the paper mill, from 6:00 p.m. to 6:00 a.m., four days a week.[14]

He was falling behind on his rent. He missed his kids. He struggled to understand why, for the third time, a marriage of his was falling apart. The stress was getting to him, but he never let on how much. To family, friends, and the public, he was still the same Rodney. He continued doing speaking engagements and clinics, even if he had to pay his own way to get there. He still stopped by Southern on occasion to speak to coaches and athletes. He still attended local high school track meets. He still granted interviews to reporters who wanted to know more about his Olympic experience. In July of 1996, he carried the Olympic torch for a good stretch when it passed through Louisiana on the way to Atlanta. During the Games, when a pipe bomb exploded in a mall in the Olympic village, Rodney spoke to reporters and compared the event to the terrorist attack in Munich. He remained visible, never craving the spotlight, but never shying away from it if asked.[15]

None of Rodney's former hurdling rivals had a clue he was struggling. "Every time I saw him he was clean as the board of health," Charles Foster said in 2005. "When we'd go out to lunch, he was quick to offer to pay. I'd think to myself, He must be the vice-president of the company. But if you base it on what I know now, I was the one with the fat pockets."[16]

Tom Hill, who also kept in touch with Rodney long after their competitive days, recalls seeing Rodney a few times in '96 and '97. "I'll tell you something," Hill said in 2006, "I always think about this. I had seen him before his death a time or two. As far as I knew, things were going great. He was always a very neat dresser. Really paid attention to his appearance. Always looked well-kept. He never looked like he was on the edge or anything."[17]

But he was very close to the edge. Unable to keep up with the rent, he moved out of his home and moved in with his cousin Jonia in June of

'97. He put most of his belongings in storage, including many of the medals he had won throughout his track career. By this time, with the garnishment of his wages for child support, he was making $36 per paycheck after all the bills were paid. The move-in with Jonia was meant to be temporary, but it lasted five months. In November of '97, Jonia moved into a new home, further away from the paper mill. Rodney, who was having car troubles, decided to move into the Bishop Ott homeless shelter on Plank Road, closer to the plant.[18]

"He was broke," Rodney's brother Jimmy recalled in 2006. "He was going through another transition similar to the one after the divorce with Janice. He was planning to come back to Houston and live with me there, the same as he did back in '78. He was gonna quit the job at the paper plant because he was having problems there. He had been demoted, and it was a racial thing."[19]

Rodney never moved back in with Jimmy. His sister Mary Ann begged him to move in with family instead of staying in the shelter, but Rodney refused, citing that he didn't want to be a burden to anyone. Constantly though, he spoke of quitting his job, of getting involved in track again. Of coming back as a masters' athlete. Of starting his own coaching clinic. Fourteen dollars an hour at the paper mill wasn't worth it. The money didn't make up for the fact that he missed being around kids. And the money wasn't enough anyway. Jonia mentioned in December of '97 that she and Rodney often spoke of how all his medals couldn't pay his bills.[20]

\* \* \*

Rodney Milburn, former Olympic champion and world record holder, was working the night shift at the Georgia Pacific paper plant. He worked on the bleach crew. His job was to monitor the tanks of chemicals used to bleach the paper. He did this for twelve hours at a time. On November 11th, 1997, with his car broken down and having no way to get to work, he walked to a blood center in downtown Baton Rouge and sold plasma so he could have enough money to take a taxi to work.

Before going to work, he went to church. There, he prayed. "This is between me and the Lord right now," he quietly told his cousin Jonia. "No one else can help me."[21]

Those were the last words anyone ever heard him say.

At work later that night, he had a bad accident. What happened exactly isn't clear, but around 10:45 p.m., a supervisor, checking on Rodney

## A Hurdler's Hurdler

after he had failed to answer a page, found him submerged in a ninety-foot rail car full of a bleach solution.[22] Dice, as he was known to the many he grew up with in Opelousas, or Hot Rod, as he was known to the many admirers of his accomplishments on the track, or Rodney, as he was known to members of his family, was dead at the age of forty-seven.

\* \* \*

The death was ruled an accident. According to police reports, there were no signs of foul play. In an article by Julie Cart of the *Los Angeles Times*, she explained that Milburn, who was working alone at the time, "was unloading a hopper car filled with crystallized sodium chlorate, an oxidizing agent used in the bleaching process" of converting "brown wood fiber into white pulp."[23] Milburn's job was to connect a pipe to pump hot water into the car's chambers, and then drain the sodium chlorate into a holding tank. From there, "he had to visually check the filling of the tank by climbing on top of the car, negotiating a metal catwalk and opening each hatch."[24]

Most likely, this is when Milburn slipped and fell into the tank. According to Cart's article, Milburn was found later that night by a supervisor who noticed that the hatch on the tank had been opened. Peering in, he saw Milburn's orange jacket. Milburn himself was floating face down in the tank.[25]

Cart states that the coroner found that Milburn "had suffered third-degree burns over 100% of his body," and that burns to his trachea and lungs indicated he had inhaled the sodium chlorate.[26]

Thirty-six hours later, the assistant coroner inspected the hopper car, and found that he could still feel the intense heat coming out of the hatch. In re-enacting the scene in his mind, he "speculated that Milburn had been kneeling to open the hatch, was hit in the face with a blast of steam from the tank, lost his balance and fell into the 9-foot-deep chamber."[27]

\* \* \*

Other possible explanations are that Rodney was pushed into the chamber, or that he committed suicide by jumping in. That he was working alone pretty much nullifies the first one. But according to Jimmy, there were a couple of guys on the job who had been "giving him trouble." Jimmy also points out that initial reports were conflicting, and that a thorough check was never done on the body. But the family never pursued the matter, feeling that a long, drawn-out investigation would be too emotionally exhausting.[28]

As for suicide, he had obvious reasons to be depressed. With the divorce separating him from his children, with the lack of a permanent residence, and working a job he had grown to despise, but seeing no way out of it, killing himself would've been an easy way out. His final words to Jonia—"This is between me and the Lord right now"—imply that he knew he didn't have much longer to live.

But Rodney Milburn had never been one to take the easy way out. He had been down this dark path several times before, and each time he had made it through. Plus he did have hope for the future. He and Mary Ann had been discussing a possible joint business venture, and, according to Mary Ann, he was actively searching for an apartment. And as Jonia said, "I wouldn't say he completely hit rock bottom. It wasn't like he failed. He still had a job; it's not like he was a bum or did anything bad or committed crimes to get money. He was just down, working his way back up."[29]

There's no reason to believe that Rodney's death was anything but an accident. He wasn't doing anything that night that he hadn't done hundreds of times. But this time, after giving blood earlier that morning, his alertness and reflexes weren't sharp. So when he lost his balance, he fell. When most of us fall, we land on the ground, we skin our knees and elbows. But in Rodney's job, slipping and falling meant landing in a vat of burning chemicals. It may not have been fair, but tragedy never is.

\* \* \*

The funeral took place on Saturday, November 15, 1997, at 1:00 p.m., at the Little Zion Baptist Church in Opelousas. The church was filled to capacity. Family members, old friends, old classmates and teammates from J. S. Clark and Southern, and many people in the track world had come to pay their last respects to a man they had all grown to love. Willie Davenport was there. Tom Hill was there. Guy Drut sent a telegram. Even president Bill Clinton sent a telegram.[30]

One of Rodney's younger cousins, Stanislars Joseph Milburn, recalled the scene in 2005. "Man, that place was packed," he said. "One of my high school buddies was talking, he was saying, man, there'll never be another one like him. And I said, man, you're probably right about that one."[31]

Tom Hill recalled that the mood at the funeral was somber. "On the one hand you mourn the loss of a good American, a competitor, but on the other hand you wanna celebrate his life. He accomplished things that most people can only dream about. I had the privilege of saying a few words at the funeral. Once of the things I told the folks was, if he walked in the door right now, in order to recognize him he'd have to turn around, because I saw his back quite a bit."[32]

For Hill, as for many others in the hurdling fraternity, the toughest pill to swallow was that they became aware of their friend's financial troubles after it was too late to help him. "When you're in the trenches with someone as many times as we were," Hill said, "there's a camaraderie there, a sense of brotherhood. Based on that fact, I had to be at the funeral. The one thing I regret, and Willie and I talked about this, is that he didn't feel comfortable coming to us and saying, Hey, I'm struggling. We would've helped him. We had enough contacts that we could've helped him. That's one of the regrets we have—that whatever, however we could've done something else just to let him know we all will have difficult times in our lives. That's what friends are for."[33]

Bill Collins of Houston, who had given Rodney a job in the late '70s and trained with him during his comeback years, found out about Rodney's death from a family member. Collins did not attend the funeral. "I was just too emotional at the time to go," he said in 2006. "And I wanted to remember Rodney the way I knew him."[34]

Tonie Campbell concurred. "His death touched me," he said in 2006. "He wasn't just someone I ran against. He was a friend of mine. Then to find out that happened, then to find out he had no money, it was really sad. Willie Davenport called me the following weekend, basically venting. He was saying that being an Olympian is like being in the military. We go out and represent our country, and bring back honor and glory to our country. He said there's no reason an Olympian shouldn't be buried in Arlington National Cemetery and have a government-funded funeral."[35]

Davenport, more than any other of Rodney's old rivals, was especially bitter about Rodney's poverty at the end of his life. He would later propose that every Olympian receive a ceremonial funeral that included an Olympic flag draped over the coffin. He had asked the Olympic Committee to send a flag to Rodney's funeral, and they had agreed to do so. But it arrived too late. When asked why he felt so strongly about this cause, he responded, "I'm doing this as a tribute to Rodney, and for all the Olympians who were forgotten when they died."[36]

For those whose relationship with Rodney had nothing to do with track, the loss was most devastating of all. Perhaps the two people closest to Rodney were his mother and his sister Mary Ann. "My mother still isn't over his death," Jimmy said in 2006. "She has taken down all the pictures of Rodney in her house. She has pictures in her home of all of her children, except Rodney. Mary Ann is just now beginning to get over it. Throughout his life, Rodney communicated with her more than anyone else. When Rod would take long trips, he'd always send her a card. In the last few weeks of his life, she was the one helping him financially. She had taken down all the pictures of Rodney in her house too, and she's just now putting them back up."[37]

For Betty, who never harbored any bitter feelings toward her former husband, the hardest part was losing the father to her children. "Rodney was a family man," she said in 2005. "We did things together. What I think about most right now, and what I miss the most, does not relate so much to that time period when he was alive. What I miss most is not having him here to raise my two children. My youngest is a boy, nineteen. Because Rodney's not around, Russell has lost some of the fatherly knowledge that he would have gained by having Rodney around, having Rodney to talk to and ask questions. That's the biggest thing that I think about in regards to missing Rodney because Russell does not have Rodney to talk to now. Because of that, he isn't growing as fast as I would like. That's what I miss the most about not having Rodney around. In the time we spent together, we had fun. We'd go fishing, visit family. We enjoyed playing cards with family, sitting around talking with family. The biggest thing I miss is the connection that was severed between him and his son."[38]

There were many other kids who would miss Rodney too. His two older sisters, Alice and Lillie, spoke of how their sons looked up to Rodney. "Alice's son was a track person," Lillie said, "and my son was a track person, and Rodney taught them more than anybody else ever had. He had a lot of knowledge he wanted to share with them and let them know. He'd say 'Let me show you this,' and 'Let me show you that.' And they treasured that. And other boys were jealous because they didn't have someone like that they could learn from."[39]

Alice adds, "My son Gene wanted to run track to compete with his uncle. I asked Rodney one time, 'Why can't he whup you?' He said, 'Because I'm a world-class runner.' But that was definitely my son's dream—to compete against Rodney. To run in the same race with him. And Rodney would say, 'Oh Alice, you must be dreamin'.'"[40]

## A Hurdler's Hurdler

Rodney Milburn was an ordinary man. Rodney Milburn was a great man. For those who knew him well, the reality of his death, and the horrors of the circumstances surrounding it, still haven't fully sunken in. "I just miss seeing him around, man," his cousin Stanislars said. "I used to see him around when he was coaching at Southern University, used to see him on campus at Southern. I just miss seeing him, man. I just miss his inspiration, and how positive he was. It's kind of hard to say what I miss about him without getting really emotional. I miss his kindness ... and thoughtfulness ... he was such a nice person, man."[41]

Perhaps former rival and friend Leon Coleman said it best, as he sat on the back porch at his home in Rocky Mount, North Carolina, and breathed a heavy sigh: "Rod, man, Rod was just a dynamite dude."[42]

# Chapter Notes

## Chapter One

1. Gunn, Billy. "Opelousas Honors Gold Medal Winner Milburn." *Opelousas Daily World*, 4 July 1992, p. 8A. print.
2. *The City of Opelousas Louisiana*. Opelousas Museum & Interpretive Center, 2000–2011, http://www.cityofopelousas.com/opelousas-museum-interpretive-center. Accessed 12 February, 2006.
3. Milburn, Jimmy. Personal Interview by author: 12 April 2006. All information in this chapter regarding Rodney Milburn's childhood and upbringing comes from interviews conducted with Jimmy Milburn from April 12–14, 2006.
4. Milburn, Jimmy. Personal Interview by author: 13 April 2006. All direct quotes from Jimmy Milburn in this chapter come from interviews conducted from April 12–14, 2006.
5. Meuillion, Harry. Personal Interview by author: 13 April 2006.
6. Deville, Gilbert. Personal Interview by author: 12 April 2006.

## Chapter Two

1. Dabney, Vont. Personal Interview by author: 13 Apr. 2006.
2. Jackson, Oliver. Personal Interview by author: 15 Nov. 2005.
3. Campbell, Bill. "'Gift from God' Meant Gold to Milburn." *The Times-Picayune* [New Orleans] 23 June 1993: D1. *NewsLibrary NewsBank InfoWeb*. Web. 23 Dec. 2005.
4. *Ibid.*
5. Milburn, Jimmy. Personal Interview by author: 12 Apr. 2006. All direct quotes from Jimmy Milburn in this chapter come from interviews conducted between 12–14 Apr. 2006.
6. Morrison, Robert. Personal Interview by author: 06 Nov. 2005.
7. Hawkins, Huey. Personal Interview by author: 06 Nov. 2005.
8. Grant, Ed. "T-and-f: A Patron Saint for the Sport?" *The Mail Archive*. N.p., 01 Oct. 2000. Web. 25 Oct. 2005. <http://www.mail-archive.com/t-and-f@lists.uoregon.edu/msg03516.html>.
9. Information in this paragraph comes from two sources: Tatum, Regina. Personal Interview by author: 14 Apr. 2006; "Paxton Hired for One Year." *Opelousas Daily World* July 1969: n. pag. Print.
10. Jackson, Oliver. Personal Interview by author: 15 Nov. 2005. All direct quotes from Oliver Jackson in this chapter come from this interview.
11. *Ibid.*
12. Spicer, Charles. "And Now He Loves It." *Opelousas Daily World* 28 May 1969. Print.
13. Litsky, Frank. "Rod Milburn: Reluctant Hero." *Boys' Life* Aug. 1972: n. pag. Print.
14. *Ibid.*
15. Gunn, Billy. "Opelousas Honors Gold Medal Winner Milburn." *Opelousas Daily World* 4 July 1992, p. 8A. print.
16. "Aaron Thompson Shines: J. S. Clark Edges Cohen of New Orleans." *Opelousas Daily World* May 1967: n. pag. Print.

# Notes—Chapter Three

17. Spicer, Charles. "And Now He Loves It." *Opelousas Daily World* 28 May 1969: n. pag. Print.
18. *Ibid.*
19. "New Orleans Carver Wins Clark Relays." *Opelousas Daily World* Mar. 1968: n. pag. Print.
20. Spicer, Charles. "Rodney Milburn." *Daily World* [Opelousas] 1971: n. pag. Print.
21. *Ibid.*
22. *Ibid.*
23. Litsky, Frank. "Rod Milburn: Reluctant Hero." *Boys' Life* Aug. 1972: n. pag. Print.
24. Spicer, Charles. "And Now He Loves It." *Opelousas Daily World* 28 May 1969: n. pag. Print.
25. Milburn, Jimmy. Personal Interview by author: 12 Apr. 2006.
26. Dabney, Vont. Personal Interview by author: 13 April 2006. All direct quotes from Dabney in this chapter come from this interview.
27. Milburn, Jimmy. Personal Interview by author: 13 Apr. 2006.
28. Morrison, Robert. Personal Interview by author: 06 Nov. 2005.
29. Spicer, Charles. "Milburn Ties Mark; Carver Takes Relays." *Opelousas Daily World* 29 Mar. 1969: n. pag. Print.
30. Spicer, Charles. "Rodney Milburn." *Daily World* [Opelousas] 1971: n. pag. Print.
31. Milburn, Stanislars. Personal Interview by author: 20 Nov. 2005.
32. "Houston Dash Star Betters Morrow Mark." *Chicago Tribune* 31 May 1969: n. pag. Print.
33. Litsky, Frank. "Rod Milburn: Reluctant Hero." *Boys' Life* Aug. 1972: n. pag. Print.
34. Spicer, Charles. "Rodney Milburn." *Daily World* [Opelousas] 1971: n. pag. Print.
35. Spicer, Charles. "A Dash of Spice." *Opelousas Daily World* 18 June 1969: n. pag. Print.
36. *Ibid.*
37. Thistlethwatite, John R. "Our Proud Gold Medalist." *Opelousas Daily World* 08 Sep. 1972: n. pag. Print.
38. *Ibid.*
39. "Paxton Hired for One Year." *Opelousas Daily World* June 1969: n. pag. Print.
40. Litsky, Frank. "Rod Milburn: Reluctant Hero." *Boys' Life* Aug. 1972: n. pag. Print.

# Chapter Three

1. Dorr, Gregory P. "Q&A: Willie Davenport." Dorrk.com. @ Dorrk, 1 Jan. 2001. Web. 22 Sept. 2005. Reprinted from *Portland Living Magazine*, 1 Jan. 1998.
2. Biography.com Editors. "Willie Davenport." Biography.com. A&E Networks Television, 05 Feb. 2016. Web. 07 July 2017.
3. Pierson, Don. "Keeping Track." *Chicago Tribune* 23 Dec. 1971: n. pag. Print.
4. *Ibid.*
5. *Ibid.*
6. "Hayes Jones." *USATF—Hall of Fame*. USATF, 1985. Web. 07 July 2017.
7. Ryan, Dennis. "Army Full Bird Is Gold Olympic Roadrunner." Dcmilitary.com. Pentagram, 17 May 2002. Web. 9 May 2006.
8. Hymans, Richard. "The History of the United States Olympic Trials—Track and Field." *USATF.org*. United States Track and Field, 2008. Web. 7 July 2017. <http://www.usatf.org/statistics/champions/OlympicTrials/HistoryOfTheOlympicTrials.pdf>.
9. This information was derived from three sources: Bannister, Nik G. "Southern U. Mourns Olympian's Death." *Southern Digest*. U-Wire, 28 June 2002. Web. 09 May 2006; "The Races of Willie Davenport." *AOL Hometown*. AOL, n.d. Web. 28 Nov. 2005; "110m Hurdles Men." *Mexico City 1968/Athletics*. International Olympic Committee, 22 June 2017. Web. 07 July 2017.
10. Haskell, Bob. "Five-time Olympian Col. Willie Davenport Remembered." *American Forces Information Service News Articles*. DefenseLINK News, June 2002. Web. 09 May 2006.
11. This information was derived from two sources: Florence, Mal. "The USC

## Notes—Chapter Three

440-Relay Team That Secured a Place in History: 20 Years Ago Today, Trojans Burned Track." Latimes.com. Los Angeles Times, 17 June 1987. Web. 07 July 2017; "Earl McCullouch Stats." Pro-Football-Reference.com. Sports Reference LLC, 2017. Web. 07 July 2017.

12. This information was derived from two sources: Nack, William. "In the Name of the Father: Richmond Flowers and His Namesakes Carry a Legacy of Accomplishment and the Burden of Unfinished Business." *Sports Illustrated* 7 July 1997: 63–69. *Sports Illustrated*. Sports Illustrated Vault, 2015. Web. 7 July 2017; "The Races of Willie Davenport." *AOL Hometown*. AOL, n.d. Web. 28 Nov. 2005.

13. "Davenport of Southern Now Is Unattached." *Chicago Tribune* 17 Apr. 1968: n. pag. Print.

14. This information was derived from two sources: Hymans, Richard. "The History of the United States Olympic Trials—Track and Field." *USATF.org*. United States Track and Field, 2008. Web. 7 July 2017. <http://www.usatf.org/statistics/champions/OlympicTrials/HistoryOfTheOlympicTrials.pdf>; Nack, William. "In the Name of the Father: Richmond Flowers and His Namesakes Carry a Legacy of Accomplishment and the Burden of Unfinished Business." *Sports Illustrated* 7 July 1997: 63–69. *Sports Illustrated*. Sports Illustrated Vault, 2015. Web. 7 July 2017.

15. Hymans, Richard. "The History of the United States Olympic Trials—Track and Field." *USATF.org*. United States Track and Field, 2008. Web. 7 July 2017. <http://www.usatf.org/statistics/champions/OlympicTrials/HistoryOfTheOlympicTrials.pdf>.

16. "Athletics at the 1968 Summer Olympics—Men's 110 Metres Hurdles." *Wikipedia*. Wikimedia Foundation, 02 July 2017. Web. 07 July 2017.

17. *1968 Olimpiadas México—Janis Lusis, Tommie Smith, Bob Seagren, Willie Davenport, Viktor Saneyev*. Perf. Willie Davenport. YouTube.com. Retroclips, 16 May 2016. Web. 07 July 2017. <https://www.youtube.com/watch?v=iuwDCT0-grc>.

18. Schiefelbein, Joseph. "SU Track Legend Willie Davenport Dies—Suffers Heart Attack in Chicago Airport." *The Advocate* [Baton Rouge] 19 June 2002: 1D. *ProQuest Historical Newspapers [ProQuest]*. Web. 02 Dec. 2005.

19. "110m Hurdles Men." *Mexico City 1968/Athletics*. International Olympic Committee, 22 June 2017. Web. 07 July 2017

20. Whitfield, George, Dr. Personal Interview by author: 20 Dec. 2005. All direct quotes from Dr. Whitfield in this chapter come from this interview.

21. Coleman, Leon. Personal Interview by author: 20 Dec. 2005. All direct quotes from Leon Coleman in this chapter come from this interview.

22. Ryan, Dennis. "Army Full Bird Is Gold Olympic Roadrunner." Dcmilitary.com. Pentagram, 17 May 2002. Web. 9 May 2006.

23. *Fists of Freedom: The Story of the '68 Summer Games*. Dir. George Roy. Perf. Tommie Smith and John Carlos. HBO Sports, 1999. Television Documentary.

24. Ibid.

25. Goldstein, Richard. "Willie Davenport, 59, Gold Medal Olympian in High Hurdles." Nytimes.com. The New York Times, 19 June 2002. Web. 09 July 2017.

26. Dorr, Gregory P. "Q&A: Willie Davenport." Dorrk.com. @ Dorrk, 1 Jan. 2001. Web. 02 Sept. 2005. Reprinted from *Portland Living Magazine*, 1 Jan. 1998.

27. Pierson, Don. "Keeping Track." *Chicago Tribune* 23 Dec. 1971: n. pag. Print.

28. Oldfield, Brian. Personal Interview by author: 10 April 2006.

29. Matthews, Vincent, and Neil Amdur. *My Race Be Won*. New York: Charterhouse, 1974. Print.

30. Foster, Charles. Personal Interview by author: 13 Oct. 2005.

31. Pierson, Don. "Keeping Track." *Chicago Tribune* 2 July 1970: n. pag. Print.

32. Hersh, Bob. "Davenport Too Good a Prophet: Milburn Fastest." *Track & Field News* July 1971: n. pag. Print.

33. Ibid.

34. "The Races of Rodney Milburn." *AOL Hometown*. AOL, n.d. Web. 28 Nov. 2005.

35. Hersh, Bob. "Davenport Too Good a Prophet: Milburn Fastest." *Track & Field News* July 1971: n. pag. Print.
36. "The Races of Rodney Milburn." *AOL Hometown*. AOL, n.d. Web. 28 Nov. 2005.
37. Information in this paragraph was dervied from two sources: "Hill Equals World Mark." *Chicago Tribune* 14 June 1970: n. pag. Print; "The Races of Rodney Milburn." *AOL Hometown*. AOL, n.d. Web. 28 Nov. 2005.
38. "120 Yard High Hurdles." *Track & Field News* August 1970: n. pag. Print.

## Chapter Four

1. Foster, Charles. Personal Interview by author: 13 Oct. 2005. All direct quotes from Charles Foster in this chapter are from this interview.
2. Spicer, Chuck. "'Old' Milburn Honored; New Career Begins." *Daily World* [Opelousas] 21 Sep. 1972: 11. Print.
3. Nelson, Bert. "Rod Milburn: No Hurdle Too High. *Track & Field News* Jan. 1972: 8. Print.
4. *Ibid.*
5. *Ibid.*
6. *Ibid.*
7. *Ibid.*
8. Litsky, Frank. "Rod Milburn: Reluctant Hero." *Boys' Life* Aug. 1972: n. pag. Print.
9. "120 Yard—110 Meter Hurdles: Milburn Dominates as No Other in 71." *Track & Field News* Jan. 1972: 35. Print.
10. Hersh, Bob. "Davenport Too Good a Prophet: Milburn Fastest." *Track & Field News* July 1971: n. pag. Print.
11. Nelson, Bert. "Rod Milburn: No Hurdle Too High. *Track & Field News* Jan. 1972: 8. Print.
12. *Ibid.*
13. This quote comes from the 1972 Southern University yearbook. Title of the article is: "Meet Rodney Milburn ... Rodney who???? Rodney Milburn, S.U's newest track sensation!!!"
14. Shipp, Larry. Personal Interview by author: 23 May 2006. All direct quotes from Larry Shipp in this chapter are from this interview.
15. "Liquori Edges Ryun in 3:54.6" *Chicago Tribune* 17 May 1971: n. pag. Print.
16. Pierson, Don. "Drake Relays Pacesetters Fall." *Chicago Tribune* 25 April 1971: n. pag. Print.
17. McGill, Steve. "Marcus Walker: Keeping the Community Together." *Hurdlesfirst.com*. Hurdles First, 2005. Web. 10 July 2017.
18. "120 Yard High Hurdles." *Track & Field News* Mar. 1971: n. pag. Print.
19. "Vets Lose in Hurdles at California." *Chicago Tribune* 30 May 1971: n. pag. Print.
20. Nelson, Bert. "Rod Milburn: No Hurdle Too High. *Track & Field News* Jan. 1972: 8. Print.
21. *Ibid.*
22. Parks, Bob. "NAIA Championships: Milburn Scoots a Best-Ever Windy 13.0 Hurdles." *Track & Field News* June 1971: n. pag. Print.
23. Nelson, Bert. "Rod Milburn: No Hurdle Too High. *Track & Field News* Jan. 1972: 8. Print.
24. *Ibid.*
25. Hill, Thomas. Personal Interview by author: 4 Jan. 2006.
26. Lockett, Raymond. Personal Interview by author: 14 Jan. 2006.
27. Nelson, Bert. "Rod Milburn: No Hurdle Too High. *Track & Field News* Jan. 1972: 8. Print.
28. Davis, O.K. "Milburn: King of the World in High Hurdles." *The Advocate* [Baton Rouge] 1971: n. pag. Print.
29. *Ibid.*
30. Nelson, Bert. "Rod Milburn: No Hurdle Too High. *Track & Field News* Jan. 1972: 8. Print.
31. Davis, O.K. "Milburn: King of the World in High Hurdles." *The Advocate* [Baton Rouge] 1971: n. pag. Print.
32. Dodge, Dick. "NCAA College Championships: Milburn Impresses, Minty Double Distance Victor." *Track & Field News* June 1971: 8. Print.
33. Information in the last part of this paragraph came from two sources: Pierson, Don. "Jackson Wins N.C.A.A. 100 in Meet's Number One Upset." *Chicago Trib-*

## Notes—Chapter Five

une 19 June 1971: n. pag. Print; "The Races of Rodney Milburn." *AOL Hometown*. AOL, n.d. Web. 28 Nov. 2005.

34. Information in this paragraph came from three sources: Pierson, Don. "Milburn Sets World Mark in Hurdles." *Chicago Tribune* 26 June 1971: n. pag. Print; "Rod Milburn Decisively the Best Hurdler and T&FN's World Athlete of 1971." *Track & Field News* Jan. 1972: 4. Print; "120 Yard—110 Meter Hurdles: Milburn Dominates as No Other in 71." *Track & Field News* Jan. 1972: 35. Print.

35. *Ibid*.

36. Pierson, Don. "Milburn Sets World Mark in Hurdles." *Chicago Tribune* 26 June 1971: n. pag. Print.

37. Pierson, Don. "Keeping Track." *Chicago Tribune* 23 Dec. 1971: n. pag. Print.

38. This quote comes from the 1972 Southern University yearbook. Title of the article is: "Meet Rodney Milburn ... Rodney who???? Rodney Milburn, S.U's newest track sensation!!!"

39. Litsky, Frank. "Rod Milburn: Reluctant Hero." *Boys' Life* Aug. 1972: n. pag. Print.

40. Mickles, Sheldon. "Milburn's Hurdles Became Second Nature." *Daily World* [Opelousas] 19 June 1988: 6+. Print.

41. Litsky, Frank. "Rod Milburn: Reluctant Hero." *Boys' Life* Aug. 1972: n. pag. Print.

42. *Ibid*.

43. Milburn, Jimmy. Personal Interview by author: 14 April 2006.

44. Litsky, Frank. "Rod Milburn: Reluctant Hero." *Boys' Life* Aug. 1972: n. pag. Print.

45. Hersh, Bob. Personal Interview by author: 6 Dec 2005.

46. Davis, O.K. "Milburn: King of the World in High Hurdles." *The Advocate* [Baton Rouge] 1971: n. pag. Print.

47. Litsky, Frank. "Rod Milburn: Reluctant Hero." *Boys' Life* Aug. 1972: n. pag. Print.

48. "120 Yard—110 Meter Hurdles: Milburn Dominates as No Other in 71." *Track & Field News* Jan. 1972: 35. Print.

49. Spicer, Charles. "Rodney Milburn." *Daily World* [Opelousas] 1971: n. pag. Print.

50. This information was derived from three sources: "Signing Autographs / Representative Congratulates Milburn." *Daily World* [Opelousas] 29 Aug. 1971: 10. Print; *The City of Opelousas Louisiana*. Opelousas Museum & Interpretive Center, 2000–2011, http://www.cityofopelousas.com/opelousas-museum-interpretive-center. Accessed 12 February, 2006; Mickles, Sheldon. "Milburn's Hurdles Became Second Nature." *Daily World* [Opelousas] 19 June 1988: 6+. Print.

51. Milburn, Lillie. Personal Interview by author: 06 Nov. 2005.

52. Deville, Gilbert. Personal Interview by author: 12 April 2006.

## Chapter Five

1. Litsky, Frank. "Rod Milburn: Reluctant Hero." *Boys' Life* Aug. 1972: n. pag. Print.

2. *Ibid*.

3. Hill, Thomas. Personal Interview by author: 4 Jan. 2006.

4. "Milburn Sets 13.4 High Hurdle Mark." *Chicago Tribune* 13 Feb. 1972: n. page. Print.

5. "Late News: Milburn 13.0w, Porter 9.2, Van Reenen 215–10." *Track & Field News* Apr. 1972: 11. Print.

6. Nelson, Bert. "El Paso: Milburn Bucks Wind to 13.3, DeBernardi Gets 68–7¾." *Track & Field News* June 1972: 6. Print.

7. This info was found on a website that no longer exists, called "AOL Hometown." This specific page, entitled "The Races of Rodney Milburn," listed every race Milburn ran throughout his collegiate and post-collegiate career.

8. Nelson, Bert. "California: Wind Aids Milburn, Hines to Top Marks, Big Wins." *Track & Field News* June 1972: n. pag. Print.

9. Foster, Charles. Personal Interview by author: 13 October 2005. All quoted material from Charles Foster in this chapter comes from this interview.

## Notes—Chapter Five

10. The information in this sentence comes from two sources: "120 Yard—110 Meter Hurdles: Milburn Dominates as No Other in 71." *Track & Field News* Jan. 1972: 35. Print; "120 Yard—110 Meter Hurdles: Milburn Nearly as Flawless as in 71." *Track & Field News* Jan. 1973: n. pag. Print.
11. "120 Yard—110 Meter Hurdles: Milburn Nearly as Flawless as in 71." *Track & Field News* Jan. 1973: n. pag. Print.
12. Ross, Wilbur L., and Hernandez De Ross Norma F. *The Hurdler's Bible 2*. Place of Publication Not Identified: Self-published, 1997. Print.
13. This information came from two sources: Milburn's time in this race was found on a website that no longer exists, called "AOL Hometown." This specific page, entitled "The Races of Rodney Milburn," listed every race Milburn ran throughout his collegiate and post-collegiate career; Foster, Charles. Personal Interview by author: 13 October 2005.
14. "120 Yard—110 Meter Hurdles: Milburn Nearly as Flawless as in 71." *Track & Field News* Jan. 1973: n. pag. Print.
15. Fachet, Robert. "Milburn Primed for Last Hurdles." *The Washington Post* 12 June 1972: D5. *ProQuest Historical Newspapers*. Web. 24 July 2017.
16. *Ibid.*
17. Pierson, Don. "Rod Milburn on 2-Year Streak." *Chicago Tribune* 17 Jun. 1972: n. pag. Print.
18. Nelson, Cordner. "110 Meter Hurdles." *Track & Field News* July 1972: 13. Print.
19. *Ibid.*
20. Fachet, Robert. "Hill's Victory: 'Greatest Thing.'" *The Washington Post* 11 July 1972: D3. *ProQuest Historical Newspapers*. Web. 21 July 2017.
21. Pierson, Don. "Milburn Wins A.A.U. Hurdles." *Chicago Tribune* 17 June 1972: n. pag. Print.
22. Nelson, Cordner. "110 Meter Hurdles." *Track & Field News* July 1972: 13. Print.
23. Fachet, Robert. "Milburn Primed for Last Hurdles." *The Washington Post* 12 June 1972: D5. *ProQuest Historical Newspapers*. Web. 24 July 2017.
24. "Olympic Status Quo." *Track & Field News* Aug. 1972. n. pag. Print.
25. Fachet, Robert. "Milburn Primed for Last Hurdles." *The Washington Post* 12 June 1972: D5. *ProQuest Historical Newspapers*. Web. 24 July 2017.
26. Litsky, Frank. "Rod Milburn: Reluctant Hero." *Boys' Life* Aug. 1972: n. pag. Print.
27. *Ibid.*
28. *Ibid.*
29. "Olympic Status Quo." *Track & Field News* August 1972: n. pag. Print.
30. Hymans, Richard. "The History of the United States Olympic Trials—Track and Field." *USATF.org*. United States Track and Field, 2008. Web. 24 July 2017. <http://www.usatf.org/statistics/champions/OlympicTrials/HistoryOfTheOlympicTrials.pdf>.
31. This information comes from two sources: Hymans, Richard. "The History of the United States Olympic Trials—Track and Field." *USATF.org*. United States Track and Field, 2008. Web. 24 July 2017. <http://www.usatf.org/statistics/champions/OlympicTrials/HistoryOfTheOlympicTrials.pdf>; Hersh, Bob. "110 Meter Hurdles." *Track & Field News* July 1972. 17. Print.
32. Hymans, Richard. "The History of the United States Olympic Trials—Track and Field." *USATF.org*. United States Track and Field, 2008. Web. 24 July 2017.
33. Fachet, Robert. "Hill's Victory: 'Greatest Thing.'" *The Washington Post* 11 July 1972: D3. *ProQuest Historical Newspapers*. Web. 21 July 2017.
34. Hill, Thomas. Personal Interview by author: 4 Jan. 2006.
35. Hersh, Bob. "110 Meter Hurdles." *Track & Field News* July 1972. 17. Print.
36. *Ibid.*
37. Campbell, Bill. "'Gift from God' Meant Gold to Milburn." *The Times-Picayune* [New Orleans] 16 Jan. 1993: D1. *NewsBank InfoWeb NewsLibrary*. Web. 23 Dec. 2005.
38. Hill, Thomas. Personal Interview by author: 4 Jan. 2006.
39. *Ibid.*
40. *Ibid.*

## Notes—Chapter Six

41. Milburn, Jimmy. Personal Interview by author: 13 Apr. 2006. All direct quotes from Jimmy Milburn in this chapter come from this interview.
42. Campbell, Bill. "'Gift from God' Meant Gold to Milburn." *The Times-Picayune* [New Orleans] 16 Jan. 1993: D1. *NewsBank InfoWeb NewsLibrary*. Web. 23 Dec. 2005.
43. Hersh, Bob. "110 Meter Hurdles." *Track & Field News* July 1972. 17. Print.
44. Campbell, Bill. "'Gift from God' Meant Gold to Milburn." *The Times-Picayune* [New Orleans] 16 Jan. 1993: D1. *NewsBank InfoWeb NewsLibrary*. Web. 23 Dec. 2005.
45. *Ibid.*
46. Fachet, Robert. "Hill's Victory: 'Greatest Thing.'" *The Washington Post* 11 July 1972: D3. *ProQuest Historical Newspapers*. Web. 21 July 2017.
47. Hill, Thomas. Personal Interview by author: 4 Jan. 2006.
48. *Ibid.*

## Chapter Six

1. Planas, Joe. "Milburn Had Good Timing***From Opelousas to Olympic Glory." *The Advocate* [Baton Rouge] 19 June 1988: 1-C. *NewsLibrary Newsbank InfoWeb*. Web. 23 Dec. 2005.
2. "Coach Predicts 10 U.S. Gold Medals." *Chicago Tribune* 13 Aug. 1972: n. pag. Print.
3. Wright, George. *Stan Wright: Track Coach ; Forty Years in the "Good Old Boy Network" as Told to George Wright*. San Francisco, CA, Pacifica Sports Research Publications, 2005.
4. Matthews, Vincent, and Neil Amdur. *My Race Be Won*. New York, Charterhouse, 1974.
5. Wright, George. *Stan Wright: Track Coach ; Forty Years in the "Good Old Boy Network" as Told to George Wright*. San Francisco, CA, Pacifica Sports Research Publications, 2005.
6. Matthews, Vincent, and Neil Amdur. *My Race Be Won*. New York, Charterhouse, 1974.
7. Rollow, Cooper. "Bill Bowerman Accepted Thankless Coaching Job." *Chicago Tribune* 9 Jul. 1972: n. pag. Print.
8. Fachet, Robert. "Milburn Primed for Last Hurdles." *The Washington Post* 12 June 1972: D5. *ProQuest Historical Newspapers*. Web. 24 July 2017.
9. Rollow, Cooper. "Bill Bowerman Accepted Thankless Coaching Job." *Chicago Tribune* 9 Jul. 1972: n. pag. Print.
10. Matthews, Vincent, and Neil Amdur. *My Race Be Won*. New York, Charterhouse, 1974.
11. Coleman, Leon. Personal Interview by author: 20 Dec. 2005.
12. "BBC ON THIS DAY | 22 | 1972: Rhodesia out of Olympics." *BBC News*. BBC, 22 Aug. 2008. Web. 27 July 2017.
13. *Ibid.*
14. Guttmann, Allen. *The Games Must Go On: Avery Brundage and the Olympic Movement*. New York: Columbia UP, 1984. Print.
15. *Ibid.*
16. McRae, Donald. *Heroes without a Country: America's Betrayal of Joe Louis and Jesse Owens*. New York, NY, Ecco, 2002.
17. *Ibid.*
18. *Ibid.*
19. Bass, Amy. *Not the Triumph but the Struggle: The 1968 Olympics and the Making of the Black Athlete*. Minneapolis: U of Minnesota, 2004. Print.
20. *Ibid.*
21. "'The Most Terrifying Night of My Life.'" *BBC News*. BBC, 02 Oct. 2008. Web. 28 July 2017.
22. Guttmann, Allen. *The Games Must Go On: Avery Brundage and the Olympic Movement*. New York: Columbia UP, 1984. Print.
23. Bass, Amy. *Not the Triumph but the Struggle: The 1968 Olympics and the Making of the Black Athlete*. Minneapolis: U of Minnesota, 2004. Print.
24. Guttmann, Allen. *The Games Must Go On: Avery Brundage and the Olympic Movement*. New York: Columbia UP, 1984. Print.
25. McRae, Donald. *Heroes without a Country: America's Betrayal of Joe Louis and Jesse Owens*. New York, NY, Ecco, 2002.

## Notes—Chapter Six

26. "Olga Connolly." *Olga Connolly*, Mt. Sac Relays, www.mtsacrelays.com/archives/HallFame/OlgaConn.htm. Accessed 14 Dec. 2006.

27. "Digitized Version of the Official Report of the Organizing Committee for the Games of the XXth Olympiad Munich 1972 (Volume 2)." *Die Spiele (Volume 2)*. Ed. Herbert Kunze. Amateur Athletics Foundation of Los Angeles, 2003. Web. 28 July 2017. <http://library.la84.org/6oic/OfficialReports/1972/1972s2pt2.pdf>.

28. Litsky, Frank. "Rod Milburn: Reluctant Hero." *Boys' Life* Aug. 1972: n. pag. Print.

29. "Olympic Personalities: The Next Hurdle." *The New York Times* 09 Sept. 1972: 19. *ProQuest Historical Newspapers*. Web. 21 Feb. 2006.

30. Hill, Thomas. Personal Interview by author: 4 Jan. 2006. Unless otherwise noted, all direct quotes from Hill in this chapter come from this interview.

31. Stones, Dwight. Personal Interview by author: 25 Mar. 2006. All direct quotes from Stones in this chapter come from this interview.

32. Fachet, Robert. "Milburn Primed for Last Hurdles." *The Washington Post* 12 June 1972: D5. *ProQuest Historical Newspapers*. Web. 24 July 2017.

33. Milburn, Jimmy. Personal Interview by author: 14 Apr. 2006. All direct quotes from Jimmy Milburn come from interviews conducted by author between Apri 12–14 2006.

34. "Ollan Cassell." *USATF—Hall of Fame*. USATF.org, 2006. Web. 28 July 2017. <http://www.usatf.org/HallOfFame/TF/showBio.asp?HOFIDs=219>.

35. Nehemiah, Renaldo. Personal Interview by author: 27 Jan. 2006.

36. "Athletics at the 1972 München Summer Games: Men's 110 Metres Hurdles Round One." *Olympics at Sports-Reference.com*. Sports-reference.com, 2000. Web. 29 July 2017. <https://www.sports-reference.com/olympics/summer/1972/ATH/mens-110-metres-hurdles-round-one.html>.

37. "Athletics at the 1972 München Summer Games: Men's 110 Metres Hurdles Semi-Finals." *Olympics at Sports-Reference.com*. Sports-reference.com, 2000. Web. 29 July 2017. <https://www.sports-reference.com/olympics/summer/1972/ATH/mens-110-metres-hurdles-semi-finals.html>.

38. Wright, George. *Stan Wright: Track Coach ; Forty Years in the "Good Old Boy Network" as Told to George Wright*. San Francisco, CA, Pacifica Sports Research Publications, 2005.

39. Ortega, John. "Seagren Clears Air in Pole Controversy." *Los Angeles Times*. Los Angeles Times, 30 Aug. 2002. Web. 29 July 2017.

40. Burton, Simon. "50 Stunning Olympic Moments No 26: The Terrorist Outrage in Munich in 1972 | Simon Burnton." *The Guardian*. Guardian News and Media, 02 May 2012. Web. 29 July 2017.

41. Grundmann, Ashley. "Thomas Hill—Memories of Bronze." *Iowa State Daily*. Iowa State University, 25 Sept. 2000. Web. 07 Feb. 2006.

42. Burton, Simon. "50 Stunning Olympic Moments No 26: The Terrorist Outrage in Munich in 1972 | Simon Burnton." *The Guardian*. Guardian News and Media, 02 May 2012. Web. 29 July 2017.

43. *Ibid*.

44. Grundmann, Ashley. "Thomas Hill—Memories of Bronze." *Iowa State Daily*. Iowa State University, 25 Sept. 2000. Web. 07 Feb. 2006.

45. Spicer, Chuck. "'Old' Milburn Honored; New Career Begins." *Opelousas Daily World* 21 Sep. 1972: 11. Print.

46. Planas, Joe. "Milburn Had Good Timing***From Opelousas to Olympic Glory." *The Advocate* [Baton Rouge] 19 June 1988: 1-C. *NewsLibrary Newsbank InfoWeb*. Web. 23 Dec. 2005.

47. Guttmann, Allen. *The Games Must Go On: Avery Brundage and the Olympic Movement*. New York: Columbia UP, 1984. Print.

48. *Ibid*.

49. *Ibid*.

50. *Ibid*.

51. Reglane, Bernie. "Opelousas' Rod Milburn Captures Olympic Gold." *The Times-Picayune* [New Orleans] 08 Sept. 1972: n. pag. Print.

52. King, Sam. "Milburn Remembers

Munich Massacre." *The Advocate*, 28 July 1996, p. 1.c. *The Advocate Archives*, Accessed 2 Dec. 2005.

53. King, Sam. "Milburn Remembers Munich Massacre." *The Advocate*, 28 July 1996, p. 1.c. *The Advocate Archives*, Accessed 2 Dec. 2005.

54. Spicer, Chuck. "'Old' Milburn Honored; New Career Begins." *Opelousas Daily World* 21 Sep. 1972: 11. Print.

55. Grundmann, Ashley. "Thomas Hill—Memories of Bronze." *Iowa State Daily*. Iowa State University, 25 Sept. 2000. Web. 07 Feb. 2006.

56. "110m Hurdles Men." *International Olympic Committee*, Olympic.org, 22 June 2017, www.olympic.org/athletics/110m-hurdles-men. Accessed 26 July 2017.

57. Planas, Joe. "Milburn Had Good Timing***From Opelousas to Olympic Glory." *The Advocate* [Baton Rouge] 19 June 1988: 1-C. *NewsLibrary Newsbank InfoWeb*. Web. 23 Dec. 2005.

58. Ibid.

59. Matthews, Vincent, and Neil Amdur. *My Race Be Won*. New York, Charterhouse, 1974.

60. Ibid.
61. Ibid.
62. Ibid.
63. Ibid.
64. Ibid.
65. Ibid.

66. Thomas, Bennie. "Olympic Star Eyes Football." *Tri-State Defender* [Memphis, Tenn.] 30 Sep. 1972: 14. *ProQuest*. Web. 15 Dec.2005.

67. Grundmann, Ashley. "Thomas Hill—Memories of Bronze." *Iowa State Daily*. Iowa State University, 25 Sept. 2000. Web. 07 Feb. 2006.

68. Roesler, Bob. "Let 'em Swim Home." *The Times-Picayune* [New Orleans] 9 Sep. 1972. n. pag. Print.

## Chapter Seven

1. "Olympic Personalities: The Next Hurdle." *The New York Times* 9 Sept. 1972: 19. *ProQuest Historical Newspapers*. Web. 11 Jan. 2006.

2. Thomas, Bennie. "Olympic Star Eyes Football." *Tri-State Defender* [Memphis] 30 Sept. 1972: 14. *ProQuest*. Web. 15 Dec. 2005.

3. "Rod's Mom Missed Win." *The Times-Picayune* [New Orleans] 8 Sept. 1972: n. pag. Print.

4. Ibid.

5. Milburn, Jimmy. Personal Interview by author: 12 Apr. 2006.

6. "Last Olympics, Says Milburn." *The Times-Picayune* [New Orleans] 9 Sept. 1972: n. pag. Print.

7. Fuselier, Herman. "Hundreds Mourn Milburn." *Opelousas Daily World* 16 Nov. 1997: 1A+. Print.

8. Ibid.

9. "Olympic Personalities: The Next Hurdle." *The New York Times* 9 Sept. 1972: 19. *ProQuest Historical Newspapers*. Web. 11 Jan. 2006.

10. Spicer, Chuck. "'Old' Milburn Honored; New Career Begins." *Opelousas Daily World* 21 Sept. 1972: 11. Print.

11. Stones, Dwight. Personal Interview by author: 25 Mar. 2006.

12. Thomas, Bennie. "Olympic Star Eyes Football." *Tri-State Defender* [Memphis] 30 Sept. 1972: 14. *ProQuest*. Web. 15 Dec. 2005.

13. Ibid.

14. Bandy, Fred. "City's Olympic Champ Is Saluted at Banquet." *Opelousas Daily World* 21 Sept. 1972: n. pag. Print.

15. Ibid.
16. Ibid.
17. Ibid.

18. Deville, Gilbert. Personal Interview by author. 12 April 2006.

19. Hersh, Bob. "Pro Track Debut Imminent." *Track & Field News* 14 Nov. 1972: n. pag. Print.

20. Fitzsimmons, Brian. "Bringing the Funk: How the ABA Changed the NBA Forever." AOL.com. AOL, 14 July 2016. Web. 30 June 2017.

21. Hersh, Bob. "Pro Track Debut Imminent." *Track & Field News* 14 Nov. 1972: n. pag. Print.

22. Hersh, Bob. Personal Interview by author: 06 December 2005.

23. Hersh, Bob. "Pro Track Debut Im-

minent." *Track & Field News* 14 Nov. 1972: n. pag. Print.
24. *Ibid.*
25. *Ibid.*
26. "Michigan Hurdler Upsets 3 Olympians." *Chicago Tribune* 14 Jan. 1973: n. pag. Print.
27. "Hurdling Star to Get Shot at Pro Football." *Chicago Tribune* 2 Feb. 1973: n. pag. Print.
28. "Milburn Feels He Can Make It in the N.F.L." *Chicago Tribune* 11 Feb. 1973: n. pag. Print.
29. *Ibid.*
30. Milburn, Jimmy. Personal Interview by author: 12 Apr. 2006.
31. "Milburn Runs High in 13.3." *Chicago Tribune* 11 Feb. 1973: n. pag. Print.
32. "Milburn Ties World Record." *Chicago Tribune* 17 Feb. 1973: n. pag. Print.
33. "Track: NCAA Meet at Detroit." *Chicago Tribune* 12 Mar. 1973: n. pag. Print.
34. "120-Yard High Hurdles." *Track & Field News* July 1973: 14. Print.
35. *Ibid.*
36. *Ibid.*
37. Gildea, William. "Blacks Find Olympic Gold No Ticket to Better Things." *The Washington Post* 28 Mar. 1973: D1. *ProQuest Historical Newspapers.* Web. 11 Jan. 2006.
38. Coleman, Leon. Personal interview by author: 20 Dec. 2005.
39. Gildea, William. "Blacks Find Olympic Gold No Ticket to Better Things." *The Washington Post* 28 Mar. 1973: D1. *ProQuest Historical Newspapers.* Web. 11 Jan. 2006.
40. *Ibid.*
41. Nehemiah, Renaldo. Email Interview by author: 26 Jan. 2006.
42. This info was found on a website that no longer exists, called "AOL Hometown." This specific page, entitled "The Races of Rodney Milburn," listed every race Milburn ran throughout his collegiate and post-collegiate career. The 13.3 came in a semi-final heat. In the final he ran 13.5.
43. *Ibid.* In the three rounds at the NAIA Championships, Milburn ran 13.4, 13.7, and 13.6, respectively.
44. Shipp, Larry. Personal Interview by author: 23 May 2006. All quoted material from Larry Shipp in this chapter comes from this interview.
45. "Spectacular Year for Hot Rod." *Track & Field News* Jan. 1974: n. pag. Print.
46. The information in this paragraph comes from two sources: "Rod Milburn Changes, Will Run NCAA." *Oakland Post* 6 June 1973: 10. *ProQuest.* Web. 11 Jan. 2006; Amdur, Neil. "Milburn's 13.1 Lowers N.C.A.A. Hurdles Record." *The New York Times* 9 June 1973: 26. Print.
47. Hill, Garry. "120 Yard High Hurdles." *Track & Field News* June 1973: 17–18. Print.
48. Amdur, Neil. "Milburn's 13.1 Lowers N.C.A.A. Hurdles Record." *The New York Times* 9 June 1973: 26. *ProQuest Historical Newspapers.* Web. 11 Jan. 2006.
49. Fachet, Robert. "Milburn Pleases Self, Home Folks With 13.1." *The Washington Post* 9 June 1973: C4. *ProQuest Historical Newspapers.* Web. 11 Jan. 2006.
50. "Milburn Stumbles, Hill Wins." *Chicago Tribune* 16 June 1973: n. pag. Print.
51. "Wottle Runs 3:53.3; Milburn: 13 Flat." *Chicago Tribune* 21 June 1973: n. pag. Print.
52. *Ibid.*
53. "From Tribune Wire Services." *Chicago Tribune* 7 July 1973: n. pag. Print.
54. "Milburn Ties 13.1 Mark for 110 Meters." *Chicago Tribune* 23 July 1973: n. pag. Print.
55. "Spectacular Year for Hot Rod." *Track & Field News* Jan. 1974: 38. Print.

## Chapter Eight

1. Coleman, Leon. Personal Interview by author: 20 Dec. 2005.
2. "U.S. Scene: Hurdles." *Track & Field News* Mar. 1974: 22. Print.
3. *Ibid.*
4. "ITA: Milburn and Wottle on the Brink." *Track & Field News* Feb. 1974: 23. Print.

## Notes—Chapter Eight

5. Coleman, Leon. Personal Interview by author: 20 Dec. 2005. All quoted material from Leon Coleman in this chapter comes from this interview.
6. Hill, Thomas. Personal Interview by author: 4 Jan. 2006. All quoted material from Thomas Hill in this chapter comes from this interview.
7. UPI. "Milburn Cracks Record." *Chicago Tribune* 9 Feb. 1974: n. pag. Print.
8. Shipp, Larry. Personal Interview by author: 23 May 2006. All quoted material from Larry Shipp in this chapter comes from this interview.
9. Rosen, Byron. "AAU Issues Halfhearted Welcome to Return of Trackmen." *The Washington Post* 31 Aug. 1977: E5. *ProQuest Historical Newspapers.* Web. 11 Jan. 2006.
10. "Rod Milburn Wins in Pro Track Debut." *Chicago Tribune* 16 Feb. 1974: n. pag. Print.
11. "Smith Vaults 18–1, Milburn Sets Mark." *Chicago Tribune* 23 Feb. 1974: n. pag. Print.
12. "Pro Track." *Chicago Tribune* 23 Mar. 1974: n. page. Print.
13. This info was found on a website that no longer exists, called "AOL Hometown." This specific page, entitled "The Races of Rodney Milburn," listed every race Milburn ran throughout his collegiate and post-collegiate career. Milburn's two 13.9's in Tokyo, on April 6 and 7 respectively, were presumably a semi-final and final. The 13.7 in El Paso took place on April 27.
14. "Late-Night TV Boosts Pro Track." *Chicago Tribune* 2 Mar. 1975: n. pag. Print.
15. Turrini, Joseph. "'It Was Communism Versus the Free World': The USA-USSR Dual Track Meet Series and the Development of Track and Field in the United States, 1958–1985." *Journal of Sports History* Fall (2001): 427–55. Print.
16. Jordan, Tom. *Pre: The Story of America's Greatest Running Legend, Steve Prefontaine.* Emmaus, PA: Rodale, 1997. Print.
17. Ibid.
18. Ibid.
19. Ibid.
20. Turrini, Joseph M. *The End of Amateurism in American Track and Field.* Urbana: U of Illinois, 2010. Print.
21. "Late-Night TV Boosts Pro Track." *Chicago Tribune* 2 Mar. 1975: n. pag. Print.
22. "Oldfield's Shot Record Not Record." *Chicago Tribune* 11 May 1975: n. pag. Print.
23. Ibid.
24. Foster, Charles. Personal Interview by author: 13 October 2005. All quoted material from Charles Foster in this chapter comes from this interview.
25. "The 110 Meter and 120 Yard Hurdles." N.p., n.d. Web. 7 June 2017. <http://personal.bgsu.edu/~jsquire/M110H.pdf>.
26. "110 Meter Hurdles: Drut Ends Long U.S. Reign." *Track & Field News* Jan. 1976: 34. Print.
27. This info comes from two sources: Milburn, Jimmy. Personal Interview by author: 12 Apr. 2006; Stone, Ed. "AAU Ban Dropped." *Chicago Tribune* 13 Jun. 1975: n. pag. Print.
28. Power, Irvin. "U.S. Needs Professionals for International Track." *The Galveston Daily News* 14 Dec. 1975: 12-C. Print.
29. Ibid.
30. Milburn, Jimmy. Personal Interview by author: 12 Apr. 2006.
31. Hymans, Richard. "The History of the United States Olympic Trials—Track and Field." *USATF.org.* United States Track and Field, 2008. Web. 29 June 2017. <http://www.usatf.org/statistics/champions/OlympicTrials/HistoryOfTheOlympicTrials.pdf>.
32. "Montreal 1976 Olympic Games." *Montreal 1976 110m Hurdles Men—Olympic Athletics.* Olympic.org, 2016. Web. 29 June 2017. <https://www.olympic.org/montreal-1976/athletics/110m-hurdles-men>.
33. "Davenport Is Lone U.S. Medalist." *Chicago Tribune* 29 July 1976: n. pag. Print.
34. Foster, Charles. Personal Interview by author: 13 October 2005.
35. "Montreal 1976 Olympic Games." *Montreal 1976 110m Hurdles Men—Olympic Athletics.* Olympic.org, 2016. Web. 29 June 2017. <https://www.olympic.org/montreal-1976/athletics/110m-hurdles-men>.

Notes—Chapter Nine

36. Stones, Dwight. Personal Interview by author: 25 Mar. 2006.
37. "Pro Track Tosses in Towel." *Chicago Tribune* 26 Aug. 1976: n. pag. Print.
38. Oldfield, Brian. Personal Interview by author: 10 Apr. 2006.

# Chapter Nine

1. Pierson, Don. "Milburn Facing Hurdles." *Chicago Tribune* 14 July 1978: n. pag. Print.
2. Milburn, Jimmy. Personal Interview by author: 12 Apr. 2006. All direct quotes from Jimmy Milburn in this chapter come from this same interview.
3. Milburn, Betty. Personal Interview by author: 06 Nov. 2005.
4. Hersh, Bob. Personal Interview by author: 06 Dec. 2005.
5. Oldfield, Brian. Personal Interview by author: 10 Apr. 2006.
6. Rosen, Byron. "AAU Issues Halfhearted Welcome to Return of Trackmen." *The Washington Post* 31 Aug. 1977: E5. *ProQuest Historical Newspapers*. Web. 11 Jan. 2006.
7. Pierson, Don. "Milburn Facing Hurdles." *Chicago Tribune* 14 July 1978: n. pag. Print.
8. *Ibid.*
9. "2 Cubans Set Records." *The New York Times* 22 Aug. 1977: 42. Print.
10. Verschoth, Anita. "Skeets Is Really Scooting." *Sports Illustrated* 22 Jan. 1979: n. pag. SI.com. Sports Illustrated, 2015. Web. 11 Aug. 2017.
11. Collins, William. Email Interview by author: 16, Jan. 2006.
12. *Ibid.* All direct quotes from Bill Collins in this chapter come from this same interview.
13. Milburn, Betty. Personal Interview by author: 06 Nov. 2005.
14. Wiley, Cliff. Email Interview by author: 08 Dec. 2005.
15. Amdur, Neil. "Former Pros Accepted in Domestic Track." *The New York Times* 30 Nov. 1979: 9. *ProQuest Historical Newspapers*. Web. 11 Jan. 2006.
16. *Ibid.*

17. *Ibid.*
18. "110 Hurdles." *Track & Field News* July 1977: 38. Print.
19. Stones, Dwight. Personal Interview by author: 25 Mar. 2006. All direct quotes from Dwight Stones in this chapter come from this same interview.
20. Turrini, Joseph. "'It Was Communism Versus the Free World': The USA-USSR Dual Track Meet Series and the Development of Track and Field in the United States, 1958–1985." *Journal of Sports History* Fall (2001): 427–55. Print.
21. Oldfield, Brian. Personal Interview by author: 10 Apr. 2006.
22. Turrini, Joseph. "'It Was Communism Versus the Free World': The USA-USSR Dual Track Meet Series and the Development of Track and Field in the United States, 1958–1985." *Journal of Sports History* Fall (2001): 427–55. Print.
23. "U.S. Scene: Milburn's Comeback." *Track & Field News* Feb. 1980: 34. Print.
24. *Ibid.*
25. Amdur, Neil. "Former Pros Accepted in Domestic Track." *The New York Times* 30 Nov. 1979: 9. *ProQuest Historical Newspapers*. Web. 11 Jan. 2006.
26. *Ibid.*
27. Fachet, Robert. "Shipp Back in Hurdle Wars." *The Washington Post* 10 Jan. 1980: F3. *NewsLibrary—NewsBank InfoWeb*. Web. 23 Dcc. 2005.
28. Pierson, Don. "Milburn, Evans Make Tracks in Return from Exile." *Chicago Tribune* 24 Feb. 1980: n. pag. Print.
29. *Ibid.*
30. *Ibid.*
31. "Win Cheers Milburn on Comeback." *The Washington Post* 2 Mar. 1980: B14. *ProQuest Historical Newspapers*. Web. 11 Jan. 2006.
32. *Ibid.*
33. Lee, Jimson. "Why 0.24 Seconds Is Added to Hand Times." *Speed Endurance: Success in Track and Field ... and Life*. Speedendurance.com, 20 Aug. 2014. Web. 27 June 2017.
34. "Propose Records by Yards Be Killed." *Chicago Tribune* 8 May 1976: n. pag. Print.
35. Pierson, Don. "Foster Still Looking

Ahead." *Chicago Tribune* 31 May 1979: n. pag. Print.

36. Hersh, Bob. "Nehemiah Meets/Beats Milburn." *Track & Field News* May 1980: 18. Print.

37. This info was found on a website that no longer exists, called "AOL Hometown." This specific page, entitled "The Races of Rodney Milburn," listed every race Milburn ran throughout his collegiate and post-collegiate career. Milburn ran the 13.81 in a semi-final heat at the Gulf Coast Invitational in Pasadena, TX, on April 26, 1980.

38. "Nehemiah, Milburn Duel." *The Washington Post* 3 May 1980: D6. *ProQuest Historical Newspapers*. Web. 11 Jan. 2006.

39. *Ibid.*

40. Davis, Scnott. "Sanford Steaming—9.88w." *Track & Field News* May 1980: 18. Print.

41. Hersh, Bob. "Nehemiah Meets/Beats Milburn." *Track & Field News* May 1980: 18. Print.

42. *Ibid.*

43. *Ibid.*

44. Nehemiah, Renaldo. Personal Interview by author: 27 Jan. 2006.

45. *Ibid.*

46. Dunaway, Jim. "110 Hurdles." *Track & Field News* July 1980: 25. Print.

47. *Ibid.*

48. "Carter Announces Olympic Boycott." History.com. A&E Television Networks, n.d. Web. 11 Aug. 2017.

49. Drehs, Wayne. "For Those Affected, Boycott Still Lingers." ESPN.com. ESPN, 19 Sept. 2000. Web. 31 July 2007.

50. Library, Jimmy Carter. "Jimmy Carter State of the Union Address 1980." *State of the Union Address 1980*. Jimmy Carter Presidential Library & Museum, 30 Mar. 2016. Web. 28 June 2017.

51. Litsky, Frank. "Ex-Pros Out of Olympic Trials." *The New York Times* 17 June 1980: C15. *ProQuest Historical Newspapers*. Web. 11 Jan. 2006.

52. *Ibid.*

53. *Ibid.*

54. *Ibid.*

55. *Ibid.*

56. Cour, Jim. "Rod Milburn Miffed over Being Tripped." *The Times-Picayune* [New Orleans] 23 June 1980, sec. 6: 6. Print.

57. *Ibid.*

58. *Ibid.*

59. *Ibid.*

60. *Ibid.*

61. *Ibid.*

62. "RE: Rod Milburn." Message to the author. 4 Apr. 2006. E-mail.

63. "RE: Rod Milburn." Message to the author. 7 Apr. 2006. E-mail.

64. Cour, Jim. "Rod Milburn Miffed over Being Tripped." *The Times-Picayune* [New Orleans] 23 June 1980, sec. 6: 6. Print.

65. Rosenthal, Bert. "Another Damaging Blow for U.S. Track and Field." *The Times-Picayune* [New Orleans] 24 June 1980: n. pag. Print.

66. *Ibid.*

67. "110 Hurdles." *Track & Field News* Aug. 1980: 14. Print.

## Chapter Ten

1. Nehemiah, Renaldo. Personal Interview by author: 28 Nov. 2005.

2. McGill, Steven. "Love at First Flight." Hurdlesfirst.com. Hurdles First, 2005. Web. 31 July 2007.

3. *Ibid.*

4. Drehs, Wayne. "Campbell, Others Nearly Defied Boycott." ESPN.com. ESPN, 22 Sept. 2000. Web. 31 July 2007.

5. *Ibid.*

6. Drehs, Wayne. "For Those Affected, Boycott Still Lingers." ESPN.com. ESPN, 19 Sept. 2000. Web. 31 July 2007.

7. Drehs, Wayne. "Campbell, Others Nearly Defied Boycott." ESPN.com. ESPN, 22 Sept. 2000. Web. 31 July 2007.

8. McGill, Steven. "Renaldo Nehemiah: Master of the Art Form." Hurdlesfirst.com. Hurdles First, 2005. 31 July 2007.

9. Drehs, Wayne. "For Those Affected, Boycott Still Lingers." ESPN.com. ESPN, 19 Sept. 2000. Web. 31 July 2007.

10. "Renaldo Nehemiah." Everything2.com. N.p., 16 Oct. 2001. Web. 31 July 2007.

## Notes—Chapter Eleven

<https://everything2.com/?node=renaldo%2Bnehemiah>.

11. "Liberty Bell Classic." *Wikipedia, the Free Encyclopedia*. Wikipedia, 8 Jan. 2017. Web. 26 June 2017. <https://en.wikipedia.org/wiki/Liberty_Bell_Classic>.

12. *Ibid.*

13. "110 Hurdles: Three for Nehemiah." *Track & Field News* Jan. 1981: 32. Print.

14. "Nehemiah Coming into Form." *Track & Field News* Sep. 1980: 46. Print.

15. "110 Hurdles: Three for Nehemiah." *Track & Field News* Jan. 1981: 32. Print.

16. Campbell, Tonie. Personal Interview by author: 30 Nov. 2005

17. *Ibid.*

18. Doherty, Ken, Ph.D. *Track and Field Omnibook*. 4th ed. Los Altos: Tafnews, 1985. Print. Page 453. Original Interview by Jon Hendershott of *Track & Field News* is embedded in the book.

19. McGill, Steven. "Renaldo Nehemiah: Master of the Art Form." Hurdlesfirst.com. Hurdles First, 2005. 31 July 2007.

20. Milburn, Betty. Personal Interview by author: 06 Nov. 2005.

21. Nehemiah, Renaldo. Personal Interview by author: 27 Jan. 2006.

22. Milburn, Betty. Personal Interview by author: 06 Nov. 2005.

23. Nehemiah, Renaldo. Personal Interview by author: 28 Nov. 2005.

24. Litsky, Frank. "Milburn Still Hoping to Defeat Nehemiah." *The New York Times* 23 Feb. 1981: n. pag. *The New York Times Archive*. Web. 26 Jan. 2006.

25. *Ibid.*

26. *Ibid.*

27. *Ibid.*

28. Doherty, Ken, Ph.D. *Track and Field Omnibook*. 4th ed. Los Altos: Tafnews, 1985. Print. Page 453. Original Interview by Jon Hendershott of *Track & Field News* is embedded in the book.

29. McGill, Steven. "Love at First Flight." Hurdlesfirst.com. Hurdles First, 2005. Web. 31 July 2007.

30. Litsky, Frank. "Milburn Still Hoping to Defeat Nehemiah." *The New York Times* 23 Feb. 1981: n. pag. *The New York Times Archive*. Web. 26 Jan. 2006.

31. *Ibid.*

32. "Houston Meet of Champions." *Track & Field News* June 1981: n. pag. Print.

33. Moore, Kenny. "Gone with the Wind, Literally." *Sports Illustrated* 18 May 1981: n. pag. SI.com. Sports Illustrated, 2015. Web. 11 Aug. 2017.

34. "No. 4 for Nehemiah." *Track & Field News* Jan. 1982: 33. Print.

35. Hendershott, Jon. "110 Hurdles." *Track & Field News* Aug. 1981: 24. Print.

36. This info comes from two sources: "No. 4 for Nehemiah." *Track & Field News* Jan. 1982: 33. Print; "The Races of Rodney Milburn." *AOL Hometown*. AOL, n.d. Web. 28 Nov. 2005.

37. "No. 4 for Nehemiah." *Track & Field News* Jan. 1982: 33. Print.

38. *Ibid.*

39. "The Races of Rodney Milburn." *AOL Hometown*. AOL, n.d. Web. 28 Nov. 2005.

40. Moore, Kenny. "Some Fine Swiss Clock Work." *Sports Illustrated* 31 Aug. 1981: 18–23.SI.com. Sports Illustrated, 13 Oct. 2015. Web. 12 Aug. 2017.

41. Nehemiah, Renaldo. Personal Interview by author: 28 Nov. 2005.

42. Litsky, Frank. "Milburn Still Hoping to Defeat Nehemiah." *The New York Times* 23 Feb. 1981: n. pag. *The New York Times Archive*. Web. 26 Jan. 2006.

## Chapter Eleven

1. Campbell, Tonie. Personal Interview by author: 30 Nov. 2005

2. "110 Hurdles: No. 4 for Nehemiah." *Track & Field News*. Jan. 1982: 33. Print.

3. "110 Hurdles." *Track & Field News*. Oct. 1980: 41. Print.

4. "Sports People; Davenport Plans Return." *The New York Times* 16 June 1983: n. pag. *The New York Times Company*. Web. 31 Jan. 2006.

5. "Sports People; Davenport is Ready." *The New York Times* 8 January 1984: n. pag. *The New York Times Company*. Web. 1 Feb. 2006.

6. "Track Notebook." *The New York Times* 24 Feb. 1981: n. pag. *The New York Times Archive*. Web. 30 Jan. 2006.

## Notes—Chapter Eleven

7. Nehemiah, Renaldo. Personal Interview by author: 28 Nov. 2005
8. Campbell, Tonie. Personal Interview by author: 30 Nov. 2005
9. "110 Hurdles: Foster Finally First." *Track & Field News.* Jan. 1983: n. pag. Print.
10. *Ibid.*
11. *Ibid.*
12. *Ibid.*
13. *Ibid.*
14. "110 Hurdles." *Track & Field News.* Jan 1984. n. page. Print.
15. *Ibid.*
16. *Ibid.*
17. *Ibid.*
18. This info was found on a website that no longer exists, called "AOL Hometown." This specific page, entitled "The Races of Rodney Milburn," listed every race Milburn ran throughout his collegiate and post-collegiate career. The author also used this page to verify the results found in the year-end rankings found in *Track & Field News* that are cited in other endnotes for this chapter.
19. Milburn, Betty. Personal Interview by author: 23 Jan. 2006
20. Nehemiah, Renaldo. Personal Interview by author: 28 Nov. 2005
21. Campbell, Tonie. Personal Interview by author: 30 Nov. 2005
22. Milburn, Betty. Personal Interview by author: 06 Nov. 2005
23. Campbell, Bill. "'Gift from God' Meant Gold to Milburn." *The Times-Picayune* [New Orleans] 23 June 1993: D1. *NewsLibrary—NewsBank InfoWeb.* Web. 23 Dec. 2005.
24. Planas, Joe. "Milburn Had Good Timing***From Opelousas to Olympic Glory." *The Advocate* [Baton Rouge] 19 June 1988: 1-C. *News Library—Newsbank InfoWeb.* Web. 23 Dec. 2005.
25. Milburn, Betty. Personal Interview by author: 06 Nov. 2005
26. Whitfield, George. Personal Interview by author: 20 Dec. 2005
27. *Ibid.*
28. *Ibid.*
29. Lockett, Raymond. Personal Interview by author: 14 Jan. 2006
30. "Budget Cuts Affect Southern." *The Advocate* [Baton Rouge] 4 Apr. 1986: 3-E. *NewsLibrary—NewsBank InfoWeb.* Web. 17 Dec. 1986.
31. Hunter, Bruce. "Jaguars Jolted by Budget Cuts." *The Advocate* [Baton Rouge] 4 Apr. 1986: 2-E. *NewsLibrary—NewsBank InfoWeb.* Web. 17 Dec. 2005.
32. *Ibid.*
33. *Ibid.*
34. *Ibid.*
35. Crosley, Roger. "Richard A. Hill Named Director of Athletics." *MIT News on Campus and Around the World.* Massachusetts Institute of Technology, 26 Aug. 1992. Web. 25 June 2006.
36. "Southern Athletic Director Marino Casem Announces Retirement." *Onnidan News: Southern Athletic Director Marino Casem Announces Retirement.* Onnidan News, 15 Apr. 1999. Web. 19 Dec. 2005.
37. *Ibid.*
38. *Ibid.*
39. Hunter, Bruce. "Jaguars Jolted by Budget Cuts." *The Advocate* [Baton Rouge] 4 Apr. 1986: 2-E. *NewsLibrary—NewsBank InfoWeb.* Web. 17 Dec. 2005.
40. Milburn, Jimmy. Personal Interview by author: 13 Apr. 2006
41. Milburn, Alice. Personal Interview by author: 06 Nov. 2005.
42. Milburn, Betty. Personal Interview by author: 06 Nov. 2005
43. "Sports Briefs." *Houston Chronicle* 3 July 1987: 8. *Houston Chronicle Archives.* Web. 2 Dec. 2005.
44. Mickles, Sheldon. "Milburn Fails in Effort to Clear Air over Firing***Ex-SU Track Coach Leaves Questions about Dismissal." *The Advocate* [Baton Rouge] 9 July 1987: 1-C. *NewsLibrary—NewsBank InfoWeb.* Web. 17 Dec. 2005.
45. *Ibid.*
46. *Ibid.*
47. Deville, Sue. Personal Interview by author: 3 Apr. 2006
48. Milburn, Jimmy. Personal Interview by author: 13 Apr. 2006
49. *Ibid.*
50. Cart, Julie. "Life's Hurdles Tragic for Olympic Medalist; Obituary: Bad Timing Curbed Rodney Milburn's Chances for

## Notes—Chapter Twelve

Success." *Los Angeles Times* 17 Nov. 1997: 1. *ProQuest*. Web. 15 Dec. 2005.

51. Planas, Joe. "Milburn Had Good Timing***From Opelousas to Olympic Glory." *The Advocate* [Baton Rouge] 19 June 1988: 1-C. *News Library—Newsbank InfoWeb*. Web. 23 Dec. 2005.

52. Campbell, Bill. "'Gift from God' Meant Gold to Milburn." *The Times-Picayune* [New Orleans] 23 June 1993: D1. *NewsLibrary—NewsBank InfoWeb*. Web. 23 Dec. 2005.

53. *Ibid.*

## Chapter Twelve

1. "Reaching for the Gold—The Rod Milburn Story." *Opelousas Museum and Interpretive Center*. N.p., 20 Aug. 2001. Web. 8 Aug. 2007. <http://www.cityofopelousas.com/opelousas-museum-interpretive-center>.

2. Milburn, Jimmy. Personal Interview by author: 14 Apr. 2006.

3. Deville, Sue. Personal Interview by author: 05 Nov. 2005.

4. Milburn, Alice. Personal Interview by author: 06 Nov. 2005.

5. "Opelousas Will Name Street in Honor of Rodney Milburn." *The Advocate* [Baton Rouge] 3 July 1992: n. pag. Web.

6. "Former Southern Track Coach Dies." *The Advocate* [Baton Rouge] 6 Oct. 1995: 9-D. Web.

7. Campbell, Bill. "'Gift from God' Meant Gold to Milburn." *The Times-Picayune* [New Orleans] 23 June 1993: D1. *NewsLibrary—NewsBank InfoWeb*. Web. 23 Dec. 2005.

8. The information in this paragraph was compiled from interviews conducted by the author with Rodney's brother Jimmy, his sisters Alice and Lillie, and his wife Betty in November 2005 and April 2006.

9. Milburn, Betty. Personal Interview by author: 06, Nov. 2005.

10. Milburn, Jimmy. Personal Interview by author: 14 Apr. 2006.

11. Foster, Charles. Personal Interview by author: 13 Oct. 2005.

12. Milburn, Betty. Personal Interview by author: 06, Nov. 2005.

13. Fuselier, Herman. "Reaching for the Gold: New Exhibit Explores Glory, Mystery, Tragedy of Olympian's Life." *The Daily Advertiser* [Acadiana] 2 Sept. 2001: n. pag. Web.

14. Cart, Julie. "Life's Hurdles Tragic for Olympic Medalist; Obituary: Bad Timing Curbed Rodney Milburn's Chances for Success." *Los Angeles Times* 17 Nov. 1997: 1. *ProQuest*. Web. 15 Dec. 2005.

15. King, Sam. "Gold Medalist Rodney Milburn Seemed Born to Hurdle." *The Advocate* [Baton Rouge] 13 Nov. 1997: n. pag. *The Advocate Archives*. Web. 2 Dec. 2005.

16. Foster, Charles. Personal Interview by author: 13 Oct. 2005.

17. Hill, Thomas. Personal Interview by author: 4 Jan. 2006.

18. Longman, Jere. "Hardship Followed Glory for a Champion." *The New York Times* 3 Dec. 1997: C.1. *ProQuest*. Web. 15 Dec. 2005.

19. Milburn, Jimmy. Personal Interview by author: 14 Apr. 2006

20. O'Neill, Helen. "The Swift Glory and Slow Decline of a Champion." *South Coast Today*. N.p., 21 Dec. 1997. Web. 19 Sept. 2005. <http://www.s-t.c0m/daily/12-97/12-21-97/b06sp084.htm>.

21. *Ibid.*

22. Herman Fuselier. "Reaching for the Gold: New Exhibit Explores Glory, Mystery, Tragedy of Olympian's Life." *The Daily Advertiser* [Acadiana] 2 Sept. 2001: n. pag. Web.

23. Cart, Julie. "Life's Hurdles Tragic for Olympic Medalist; Obituary: Bad Timing Curbed Rodney Milburn's Chances for Success." *Los Angeles Times* 17 Nov. 1997: 1. *ProQuest*. Web. 15 Dec. 2005.

24. *Ibid.*
25. *Ibid.*
26. *Ibid.*
27. *Ibid.*

28. Milburn, Jimmy. Personal Interview by author: 14 Apr. 2006

29. Longman, Jere. "Hardship Followed Glory for a Champion." *The New York Times* 3 Dec. 1997: C.1. *ProQuest*. Web. 15 Dec. 2005.

## Notes—Chapter Twelve

30. Fuselier, Herman. "Hundreds Mourn Milburn." *Daily World* [Opelousas] 16 Nov. 1997: 1a+. Print.
31. Milburn, Stanislars. Personal Interview by author: 20 Nov. 2005.
32. Hill, Thomas. Personal Interview by author: 4 Jan. 2006.
33. *Ibid.*
34. Collins, William. Email Interview by author: 16 Jan. 2006.
35. Campbell, Tonie. Personal Interview by author: 30 Nov. 2005.
36. O'Neill, Helen. "Ceremonial Funerals Proposed for Olympians: Those Who Compete in the Games Deserve Special Tributes for Service to Their Country, Former Hurdler and Bobsledder Says." *Los Angeles Times* 10 May 1998: 7. *ProQuest.* Web. 15 Nov. 2005.
37. Milburn, Jimmy. Personal Interview by author: 14 Apr. 2006
38. Milburn, Betty. Personal Interview by author: 06 Nov. 2005
39. Milburn, Lillie. Personal Interview by author: 06 Nov. 2005.
40. Milburn, Alice. Personal Interview by author: 06 Nov. 2005.
41. Milburn, Stanislars. Personal Interview by author: 20 Nov. 2005.
42. Coleman, Leon. Personal Interview by author: 20 Dec. 2005.

# Bibliography

"Aaron Thompson Shines: J. S. Clark Edges Cohen of New Orleans." *Opelousas Daily World* May 1967: n. pag. Print.
Amdur, Neil. "Former Pros Accepted in Domestic Track." *The New York Times* 30 Nov. 1979: 9. *ProQuest Historical Newspapers*. Web. 11 Jan. 2006.
———. "Milburn's 13.1 Lowers N.C.A.A. Hurdles Record." *The New York Times* 9 June 1973: 26. Print.
"Athletics at the 1968 Summer Olympics—Men's 110 Metres Hurdles." *Wikipedia*. Wikimedia Foundation, 02 July 2017. Web. 07 July 2017.
"Athletics at the 1972 München Summer Games: Men's 110 Metres Hurdles Round One." *Olympics at Sports-Reference.com*. Sports-reference.com, 2000. Web. 29 July 2017. <https://www.sports-reference.com/olympics/summer/1972/ATH/mens-110-metres-hurdles-round-one.html>.
"Athletics at the 1972 München Summer Games: Men's 110 Metres Hurdles Semi-Finals." *Olympics at Sports-Reference.com*. Sports-reference.com, 2000. Web. 29 July 2017. <https://www.sports-reference.com/olympics/summer/1972/ATH/mens-110-metres-hurdles-semi-finals.html>.
Bandy, Fred. "City's Olympic Champ Is Saluted at Banquet." *Opelousas Daily World* 21 Sept. 1972: n. pag. Print.
Bannister, Nik G. "Southern U. Mourns Olympian's Death." *Southern Digest*. U-Wire, 28 June 2002. Web. 09 May 2006.
Bass, Amy. *Not the Triumph but the Struggle: The 1968 Olympics and the Making of the Black Athlete*. Minneapolis: U of Minnesota, 2004. Print.
"BBC ON THIS DAY | 22 | 1972: Rhodesia out of Olympics." *BBC News*. BBC, 22 Aug. 2008. Web. 27 July 2017.
Biography.com Editors. "Willie Davenport." Biography.com. A&E Networks Television, 05 Feb. 2016. Web. 07 July 2017.
"Budget Cuts Affect Southern." *The Advocate* [Baton Rouge] 4 Apr. 1986: 3-E. *NewsLibrary—NewsBank InfoWeb*. Web. 17 Dec. 1986.
Burnton, Simon. "50 Stunning Olympic Moments No 26: The Terrorist Outrage in Munich in 1972 | Simon Burnton." *The Guardian*. Guardian News and Media, 02 May 2012. Web. 29 July 2017.
Campbell, Bill. "'Gift from God' Meant Gold to Milburn." *The Times-Picayune* [New Orleans] 23 June 1993: D1. *NewsLibrary NewsBank InfoWeb*. Web. 23 Dec. 2005.
Campbell, Tonie. Personal Interview by author: 30 Nov. 2005.
Cart, Julie. "Life's Hurdles Tragic for Olympic Medalist; Obituary: Bad Timing Curbed Rodney Milburn's Chances for Success." *Los Angeles Times* 17 Nov. 1997: 1. *ProQuest*. Web. 15 Dec. 2005.

## Bibliography

"Carter Announces Olympic Boycott." History.com. A&E Television Networks, n.d. Web. 11 Aug. 2017.
Cassell, Ollan. Email Interview by author: 4 Apr. 2006.
"Coach Predicts 10 U.S. Gold Medals." *Chicago Tribune* 13 Aug. 1972: n. pag. Print.
Coleman, Leon. Personal Interview by author: 20 Dec. 2005.
Collins, William. Email Interview by author: 16, Jan. 2006.
Cour, Jim. "Rod Milburn Miffed over Being Tripped." *The Times-Picayune* [New Orleans] 23 June 1980, sec. 6: 6. Print.
Crosley, Roger. "Richard A. Hill Named Director of Athletics." *MIT News on Campus and Around the World*. Massachusetts Institute of Technology, 26 Aug. 1992. Web. 25 June 2006.
Dabney, Vont. Personal Interview by author: 13 Apr. 2006.
"Davenport Is Lone U.S. Medalist." *Chicago Tribune* 29 July 1976: n. pag. Print.
"Davenport of Southern Now Is Unattached." *Chicago Tribune* 17 Apr. 1968: n. pag. Print.
Davis, O.K. "Milburn: King of the World in High Hurdles." *The Advocate* [Baton Rouge] 1971: n. pag. Print.
Davis, Scnott. "Sanford Steaming—9.88w." *Track & Field News* May 1980: 18. Print.
Deville, Gilbert. Personal Interview by author: 12 April 2006.
Deville, Sue. Personal Interview by author: 3 Apr. 2006.
"Digitized Version of the Official Report of the Organizing Committee for the Games of the XXth Olympiad Munich 1972 (Volume 2)." *Die Spiele (Volume 2)*. Ed. Herbert Kunze. Amateur Athletics Foundation of Los Angeles, 2003. Web. 28 July 2017. <http://library.la84.org/6oic/OfficialReports/1972/1972s2pt2.pdf>.
Dodge, Dick. "NCAA College Championships: Milburn Impresses, Minty Double Distance Victor." *Track & Field News* June 1971: 8. Print.
Doherty, Ken, Ph.D. *Track and Field Omnibook*. 4th ed. Los Altos: Tafnews, 1985. Print. Page 453.
Dorr, Gregory P. "Q&A: Willie Davenport." Dorrk.com. @ Dorrk, 1 Jan. 2001. Web. 22 Sept. 2005. Reprinted from *Portland Living Magazine*, 1 Jan. 1998.
Drehs, Wayne. "Campbell, Others Nearly Defied Boycott." ESPN.com. ESPN, 22 Sept. 2000. Web. 31 July 2007.
_____. "For Those Affected, Boycott Still Lingers." ESPN.com. ESPN, 19 Sept. 2000. Web. 31 July 2007.
Dunaway, Jim. "110 Hurdles." *Track & Field News* July 1980: 25. Print.
"Earl McCullouch Stats." Pro-Football-Reference.com. Sports Reference LLC, 2017. Web. 07 July 2017.
Fachet, Robert. "Hill's Victory: 'Greatest Thing.'" *The Washington Post* 11 July 1972: D3. *ProQuest Historical Newspapers*. Web. 21 July 2017.
_____. "Milburn Pleases Self, Home Folks With 13.1." *The Washington Post* 9 June 1973: C4. *ProQuest Historical Newspapers*. Web. 11 Jan. 2006.
_____. "Milburn Primed for Last Hurdles." *The Washington Post* 12 June 1972: D5. *ProQuest Historical Newspapers*. Web. 24 July 2017.
_____. "Shipp Back in Hurdle Wars." *The Washington Post* 10 Jan. 1980: F3. *NewsLibrary—NewsBank InfoWeb*. Web. 23 Dec. 2005.
*Fists of Freedom: The Story of the '68 Summer Games*. Dir. George Roy. Perf. Tommie Smith and John Carlos. HBO Sports, 1999. Television Documentary.
Fitzsimmons, Brian. "Bringing the Funk: How the ABA Changed the NBA Forever." AOL.com. AOL, 14 July 2016. Web. 30 June 2017.
Florence, Mal. "The USC 440-Relay Team That Secured a Place in History: 20 Years Ago Today, Trojans Burned Track." Latimes.com. Los Angeles Times, 17 June 1987. Web. 07 July 2017.
"Former Southern Track Coach Dies." *The Advocate* [Baton Rouge] 6 Oct. 1995: 9-D. Web.

# Bibliography

Foster, Charles. Personal Interview by author: 13 Oct. 2005.
"From Tribune Wire Services." *Chicago Tribune* 7 July 1973: n. pag. Print.
Fuselier, Herman. "Hundreds Mourn Milburn." *Opelousas Daily World* 16 Nov. 1997: 1A+. Print.
\_\_\_\_\_. "Reaching for the Gold: New Exhibit Explores Glory, Mystery, Tragedy of Olympian's Life." *The Daily Advertiser* [Acadiana] 2 Sept. 2001: n. pag. Web.
Gildea, William. "Blacks Find Olympic Gold No Ticket to Better Things." *The Washington Post* 28 Mar. 1973: D1. *ProQuest Historical Newspapers*. Web. 11 Jan. 2006.
Grant, Ed. "T-and-f: A Patron Saint for the Sport?" *The Mail Archive.* N.p., 01 Oct. 2000. Web. 25 Oct. 2005. <http://www.mail-archive.com/t-and-f@lists.uoregon.edu/msg03516.html>.
Goldstein, Richard. "Willie Davenport, 59, Gold Medal Olympian in High Hurdles." Nytimes.com. *The New York Times*, 19 June 2002. Web. 09 July 2017.
Grundmann, Ashley. "Thomas Hill—Memories of Bronze." *Iowa State Daily*. Iowa State University, 25 Sept. 2000. Web. 07 Feb. 2006.
Gunn, Billy. "Opelousas Honors Gold Medal Winner Milburn." *Opelousas Daily World* 4 July 1992, p. 8A. print.
Guttmann, Allen. *The Games Must Go On: Avery Brundage and the Olympic Movement*. New York: Columbia UP, 1984. Print.
Haskell, Bob. "Five-time Olympian Col. Willie Davenport Remembered." *American Forces Information Service News Articles*. DefenseLINK News, June 2002. Web. 09 May 2006.
Hawkins, Huey. Personal Interview by author: 06 Nov. 2005.
"Hayes Jones." *USATF - Hall of Fame*. USATF, 1985. Web. 07 July 2017.
Hersh, Bob. "110 Meter Hurdles." *Track & Field News* July 1972. 17. Print.
\_\_\_\_\_. "Davenport Too Good a Prophet: Milburn Fastest." *Track & Field News* July 1971: n. pag. Print.
\_\_\_\_\_. "Nehemiah Meets/Beats Milburn." *Track & Field News* May 1980: 18. Print.
\_\_\_\_\_. Personal Interview by author: 6 Dec 2005.
\_\_\_\_\_. "Pro Track Debut Imminent." *Track & Field News* 14 Nov. 1972: n. pag. Print.
"Hill Equals World Mark." *Chicago Tribune* 14 June 1970: n. pag. Print.
Hill, Garry. "120 Yard High Hurdles." *Track & Field News* June 1973: 17–18. Print.
Hill, Thomas. Personal Interview by author: 4 Jan. 2006.
"Houston Dash Star Betters Morrow Mark." *Chicago Tribune* 31 May 1969: n. pag. Print.
"Houston Meet of Champions." *Track & Field News* June 1981: n. pag. Print.
Hunter, Bruce. "Jaguars Jolted by Budget Cuts." *The Advocate* [Baton Rouge] 4 Apr. 1986: 2-E. *NewsLibrary—NewsBank InfoWeb*. Web. 17 Dec. 2005.
"Hurdling Star to Get Shot at Pro Football." *Chicago Tribune* 2 Feb. 1973: n. pag. Print.
Hymans, Richard. "The History of the United States Olympic Trials—Track and Field." *USATF.org*. United States Track and Field, 2008. Web. 7 July 2017.
"ITA: Milburn and Wottle on the Brink." *Track & Field News* Feb. 1974: 23. Print.
Jackson, Oliver. Personal Interview by author: 15 Nov. 2005.
Jordan, Tom. *Pre: The Story of America's Greatest Running Legend, Steve Prefontaine*. Emmaus, PA: Rodale, 1997. Print.
King, Sam. "Gold Medalist Rodney Milburn Seemed Born to Hurdle." *The Advocate* [Baton Rouge] 13 Nov. 1997: n. pag. *The Advocate Archives*. Web. 2 Dec. 2005.
\_\_\_\_\_. "Milburn Remembers Munich Massacre." *The Advocate*, 28 July 1996, p. 1.c. *The Advocate Archives*, Accessed 2 Dec. 2005.
"Last Olympics, Says Milburn." *The Times-Picayune* [New Orleans] 9 Sept. 1972: n. pag. Print.
"Late News: Milburn 13.0w, Porter 9.2, Van Reenen 215–10." *Track & Field News* Apr. 1972: 11. Print.

## Bibliography

"Late-Night TV Boosts Pro Track." *Chicago Tribune* 2 Mar. 1975: n. pag. Print.
Lee, Jimson. "Why 0.24 Seconds Is Added to Hand Times." *Speed Endurance: Success in Track and Field ... and Life*. Speedendurance.com, 20 Aug. 2014. Web. 27 June 2017.
"Liberty Bell Classic." *Wikipedia, the Free Encyclopedia*. Wikipedia, 8 Jan. 2017. Web. 26 June 2017. <https://en.wikipedia.org/wiki/Liberty_Bell_Classic>.
Library, Jimmy Carter. "Jimmy Carter State of the Union Address 1980." *State of the Union Address 1980*. Jimmy Carter Presidential Library & Museum, 30 Mar. 2016. Web. 28 June 2017.
"Liquori Edges Ryun in 3:54.6" *Chicago Tribune* 17 May 1971: n. pag. Print.
Litsky, Frank. "Ex-Pros Out of Olympic Trials." *The New York Times* 17 June 1980: C15. *ProQuest Historical Newspapers*. Web. 11 Jan. 2006.
\_\_\_\_. "Milburn Still Hoping to Defeat Nehemiah." *The New York Times* 23 Feb. 1981: n. pag. *The New York Times Archive*. Web. 26 Jan. 2006.
\_\_\_\_. "Rod Milburn: Reluctant Hero." *Boys' Life* Aug. 1972: n. pag. Print.
Lockett, Raymond. Personal Interview by author: 14 Jan. 2006.
Longman, Jere. "Hardship Followed Glory for a Champion." *The New York Times* 3 Dec. 1997: C.1. *ProQuest*. Web. 15 Dec. 2005.
Matthews, Vincent, and Neil Amdur. *My Race Be Won*. New York: Charterhouse, 1974. Print.
"Michigan Hurdler Upsets 3 Olympians." *Chicago Tribune* 14 Jan. 1973: n. pag. Print.
McGill, Steven. "Love at First Flight." Hurdlesfirst.com. Hurdles First, 2005. Web. 31 July 2007.
McGill, Steve. "Marcus Walker: Keeping the Community Together." *Hurdlesfirst.com*. Hurdles First, 2005. Web. 10 July 2017.
McGill, Steven. "Renaldo Nehemiah: Master of the Art Form." Hurdlesfirst.com. Hurdles First, 2005. 31 July 2007.
McRae, Donald. *Heroes without a Country: America's Betrayal of Joe Louis and Jesse Owens*. New York, NY, Ecco, 2002.
Meuillion, Harry. Personal Interview by author: 13 April 2006.
Mickles, Sheldon. "Milburn Fails in Effort to Clear Air over Firing\*\*\*Ex-SU Track Coach Leaves Questions about Dismissal." *The Advocate* [Baton Rouge] 9 July 1987: 1-C. *NewsLibrary—NewsBank InfoWeb*. Web. 17 Dec. 2005.
\_\_\_\_. "Milburn's Hurdles Became Second Nature." *Daily World* [Opelousas] 19 June 1988: 6+. Print.
Milburn, Alice. Personal Interview by author: 06 Nov. 2005.
Milburn, Betty. Personal Interview by author: 06 Nov. 2005.
\_\_\_\_. Personal Interview by author: 23 Jan. 2006
"Milburn Feels He Can Make It in the N.F.L." *Chicago Tribune* 11 Feb. 1973: n. pag. Print.
Milburn, Jimmy. Personal Interview by author: 12–14 April 2006.
Milburn, Lillie. Personal Interview by author: 06 Nov. 2005.
"Milburn Runs High in 13.3." *Chicago Tribune* 11 Feb. 1973: n. pag. Print.
"Milburn Sets 13.4 High Hurdle Mark." *Chicago Tribune* 13 Feb. 1972: n. page. Print.
Milburn, Stanislars. Personal Interview by author: 20 Nov. 2005.
"Milburn Stumbles, Hill Wins." *Chicago Tribune* 16 June 1973: n. pag. Print.
"Milburn Ties 13.1 Mark for 110 Meters." *Chicago Tribune* 23 July 1973: n. pag. Print.
"Milburn Ties World Record." *Chicago Tribune* 17 Feb. 1973: n. pag. Print.
"Montreal 1976 Olympic Games." *Montreal 1976 110m Hurdles Men—Olympic Athletics*. Olympic.org, 2016. Web. 29 June 2017. <https://www.olympic.org/montreal-1976/athletics/110m-hurdles-men>.
Morrison, Robert. Personal Interview by author: 06 Nov. 2005.
Moore, Kenny. "Gone with the Wind, Literally." *Sports Illustrated* 18 May 1981: n. pag. SI.com. Sports Illustrated, 2015. Web. 11 Aug. 2017.

# Bibliography

\_\_\_\_\_. "Some Fine Swiss Clock Work." *Sports Illustrated* 31 Aug. 1981: 18–23.SI.com. Sports Illustrated, 13 Oct. 2015. Web. 12 Aug. 2017.
Nack, William. "In the Name of the Father: Richmond Flowers and His Namesakes Carry a Legacy of Accomplishment and the Burden of Unfinished Business." *Sports Illustrated* 7 July 1997: 63–69. *Sports Illustrated*. Sports Illustrated Vault, 2015. Web. 7 July 2017.
"Nehemiah Coming into Form." *Track & Field News* Sep. 1980: 46. Print.
"Nehemiah, Milburn Duel." *The Washington Post* 3 May 1980: D6. *ProQuest Historical Newspapers*. Web. 11 Jan. 2006.
Nehemiah, Renaldo. Personal Interview by author: 28 Nov. 2005.
\_\_\_\_\_. Email Interview by author: 26 Jan. 2006.
\_\_\_\_\_. Personal Interview by author: 27 Jan. 2006.
Nelson, Bert. "California: Wind Aids Milburn, Hines to Top Marks, Big Wins." *Track & Field News* June 1972: n. pag. Print.
\_\_\_\_\_. "El Paso: Milburn Bucks Wind to 13.3, DeBernardi Gets 68-7 ¾." *Track & Field News* June 1972: 6. Print.
\_\_\_\_\_. "Rod Milburn: No Hurdle Too High. *Track & Field News* Jan. 1972: 8. Print.
Nelson, Cordner. "110 Meter Hurdles." *Track & Field News* July 1972: 13. Print.
"New Orleans Carver Wins Clark Relays." *Opelousas Daily World* Mar. 1968: n. pag. Print.
*1968 Olimpiadas México—Janis Lusis, Tommie Smith, Bob Seagren, Willie Davenport, Viktor Saneyev*. Perf. Willie Davenport. YouTube.com. Retroclips, 16 May 2016. Web. 07 July 2017. <https://www.youtube.com/watch?v=iuwDCT0-grc>.
Oldfield, Brian. Personal Interview by author: 10 April 2006.
"Oldfield's Shot Record Not Record." *Chicago Tribune* 11 May 1975: n. pag. Print.
"Olga Connolly." *Olga Connolly*, Mt. Sac Relays, www.mtsacrelays.com/archives/Hall Fame/OlgaConn.htm. Accessed 14 Dec. 2006.
"Ollan Cassell." *USATF—Hall of Fame*. USATF.org, 2006. Web. 28 July 2017. <http://www.usatf.org/HallOfFame/TF/showBio.asp?HOFIDs=219>.
"Olympic Personalities: The Next Hurdle." *The New York Times* 09 Sept. 1972: 19. *ProQuest Historical Newspapers*. Web. 21 Feb. 2006.
"Olympic Status Quo." *Track & Field News* Aug. 1972. n. pag. Print.
O'Neill, Helen. "Ceremonial Funerals Proposed for Olympians: Those Who Compete in the Games Deserve Special Tributes for Service to Their Country, Former Hurdler and Bobsledder Says." *Los Angeles Times* 10 May 1998: 7. *ProQuest*. Web. 15 Nov. 2005.
\_\_\_\_\_. "The Swift Glory and Slow Decline of a Champion." *South Coast Today*. N.p., 21 Dec. 1997. Web. 19 Sept. 2005. <http://www.s-t.c0m/daily/12-97/12-21-97/b06sp 084.htm>.
"110 Hurdles." *Track & Field News* July 1977: 38. Print.
"110 Hurdles." *Track & Field News* Aug. 1980: 14. Print.
"110 Hurdles." *Track & Field News*. Oct. 1980: 41. Print.
"110 Hurdles." *Track & Field News*. Jan 1984. n. page. Print.
"110 Hurdles: Foster Finally First." *Track & Field News*. Jan. 1983: n. pag. Print.
"110 Hurdles: No. 4 for Nehemiah." *Track & Field News*. Jan. 1982: 33. Print.
"110 Hurdles: Three for Nehemiah." *Track & Field News* Jan. 1981: 32. Print.
"110m Hurdles Men." *International Olympic Committee*, Olympic.org, 22 June 2017, www.olympic.org/athletics/110m-hurdles-men. Accessed 26 July 2017.
"110m Hurdles Men." *Mexico City 1968/Athletics*. International Olympic Committee, 22 June 2017. Web. 07 July 2017.
"110 Meter Hurdles: Drut Ends Long US Reign." *Track & Field News* Jan. 1976: 34. Print.
"120 Yard—110 Meter Hurdles: Milburn Dominates as No Other in 71." *Track & Field News* Jan. 1972: 35. Print.

## Bibliography

"120 Yard—110 Meter Hurdles: Milburn Nearly as Flawless as in 71." *Track & Field News* Jan. 1973: n. pag. Print.
"120 Yard High Hurdles." *Track & Field News* August 1970: n. pag. Print.
"120 Yard High Hurdles." *Track & Field News* Mar. 1971: n. pag. Print.
"120 Yard High Hurdles." *Track & Field News* July 1973: 14. Print.
"Opelousas Will Name Street in Honor of Rodney Milburn." *The Advocate* [Baton Rouge] 3 July 1992: n. pag. Web.
Ortega, John. "Seagren Clears Air in Pole Controversy." *Los Angeles Times*. Los Angeles Times, 30 Aug. 2002. Web. 29 July 2017.
Parks, Bob. "NAIA Championships: Milburn Scoots a Best-Ever Windy 13.0 Hurdles." *Track & Field News* June 1971: n. pag. Print.
"Paxton Hired for One Year." *Opelousas Daily World* July 1969: n. pag. Print.
Pierson, Don. "Drake Relays Pacesetters Fall." *Chicago Tribune* 25 April 1971: n. pag. Print.
\_\_\_\_. "Foster Still Looking Ahead." *Chicago Tribune* 31 May 1979: n. pag. Print.
\_\_\_\_. "Keeping Track." *Chicago Tribune* 2 July 1970: n. pag. Print.
\_\_\_\_. "Keeping Track." *Chicago Tribune* 23 Dec. 1971: n. pag. Print.
\_\_\_\_. "Jackson Wins N.C.A.A. 100 in Meet's Number One Upset." *Chicago Tribune* 19 June 1971: n. pag. Print.
\_\_\_\_. "Milburn, Evans Make Tracks in Return from Exile." *Chicago Tribune* 24 Feb. 1980: n. pag. Print.
\_\_\_\_. "Milburn Facing Hurdles." *Chicago Tribune* 14 July 1978: n. pag. Print.
\_\_\_\_. "Milburn Sets World Mark in Hurdles." *Chicago Tribune* 26 June 1971: n. pag. Print.
\_\_\_\_. "Milburn Wins A.A.U. Hurdles." *Chicago Tribune* 17 June 1972: n. pag. Print.
\_\_\_\_. "Rod Milburn on 2-Year Streak." *Chicago Tribune* 17 Jun. 1972: n. pag. Print.
Planas, Joe. "Milburn Had Good Timing***From Opelousas to Olympic Glory." *The Advocate* [Baton Rouge] 19 June 1988: 1-C. *NewsLibrary Newsbank InfoWeb*. Web. 23 Dec. 2005.
Power, Irvin. "U.S. Needs Professionals for International Track." *The Galveston Daily News* 14 Dec. 1975: 12-C. Print.
"Pro Track." *Chicago Tribune* 23 Mar. 1974: n. page. Print.
"Pro Track Tosses in Towel." *Chicago Tribune* 26 Aug. 1976: n. pag. Print.
"Propose Records by Yards Be Killed." *Chicago Tribune* 8 May 1976: n. pag. Print.
Reglane, Bernie. "Opelousas' Rod Milburn Captures Olympic Gold." *The Times-Picayune* [New Orleans] 08 Sept. 1972: n. pag. Print.
"Renaldo Nehemiah." Everything2.com. N.p., 16 Oct. 2001. Web. 31 July 2007. <https://everything2.com/?node=renaldo%2Bnehemiah>.
"Rod Milburn Changes, Will Run NCAA." *Oakland Post* 6 June 1973. 10. *ProQuest*. Web. 11 Jan. 2006.
"Rod Milburn Decisively the Best Hurdler and T&FN's World Athlete of 1971." *Track & Field News* Jan. 1972: 4. Print.
"Rod Milburn Wins in Pro Track Debut." *Chicago Tribune* 16 Feb. 1974: n. pag. Print.
"Rod's Mom Missed Win." *The Times-Picayune* [New Orleans] 8 Sept. 1972: n. pag. Print.
Roesler, Bob. "Let 'em Swim Home." *The Times-Picayune* [New Orleans] 9 Sep. 1972. n. pag. Print.
Rollow, Cooper. "Bill Bowerman Accepted Thankless Coaching Job." *Chicago Tribune* 9 Jul. 1972: n. pag. Print.
Rosen, Byron. "AAU Issues Half-hearted Welcome to Return of Trackmen." *The Washington Post* 31 Aug. 1977: E5. *ProQuest Historical Newspapers*. Web. 11 Jan. 2006.
Rosenthal, Bert. "Another Damaging Blow for U.S. Track and Field." *The Times-Picayune* [New Orleans] 24 June 1980: n. pag. Print.

# Bibliography

Ross, Wilbur L., and Hernandez De Ross Norma F. *The Hurdler's Bible 2*. Place of Publication Not Identified: Self-published, 1997. Print.
Ryan, Dennis. "Army Full Bird Is Gold Olympic Roadrunner." Dcmilitary.com. Pentagram, 17 May 2002. Web. 9 May 2006.
Schiefelbein, Joseph. "SU Track Legend Willie Davenport Dies—Suffers Heart Attack in Chicago Airport." *The Advocate* [Baton Rouge] 19 June 2002: 1D. *ProQuest Historical Newspapers [ProQuest]*. Web. 02 Dec. 2005.
Shipp, Larry. Personal Interview by author: 23 May 2006.
"Signing Autographs / Representative Congratulates Milburn." *Daily World* [Opelousas] 29 Aug. 1971: 10. Print.
"Smith Vaults 18–1, Milburn Sets Mark." *Chicago Tribune* 23 Feb. 1974: n. pag. Print.
"Southern Athletic Director Marino Casem Announces Retirement." *Onnidan News: Southern Athletic Director Marino Casem Announces Retirement*. Onnidan News, 15 Apr. 1999. Web. 19 Dec. 2005.
"Spectacular Year for Hot Rod." *Track & Field News* Jan. 1974: n. pag. Print.
Spicer, Charles. "A Dash of Spice." *Opelousas Daily World* 18 June 1969: n. pag. Print.
\_\_\_\_\_. "And Now He Loves It." *Opelousas Daily World* 28 May 1969. Print.
\_\_\_\_\_. "Milburn Ties Mark; Carver Takes Relays." *Opelousas Daily World* 29 Mar. 1969: n. pag. Print.
Spicer, Chuck. "'Old' Milburn Honored; New Career Begins." *Daily World* [Opelousas] 21 Sep. 1972: 11. Print.
Spicer, Charles. "Rodney Milburn." *Daily World* [Opelousas] 1971: n. pag. Print.
"Sports Briefs." *Houston Chronicle* 3 July 1987: 8. *Houston Chronicle Archives*. Web. 2 Dec. 2005.
"Sports People; Davenport is Ready." *The New York Times* 8 January 1984: n. pag. The New York Times Company. Web. 1 Feb. 2006.
"Sports People; Davenport Plans Return." *The New York Times* 16 June 1983: n. pag. The New York Times Company. Web. 31 Jan. 2006.
Stone, Ed. "AAU Ban Dropped." *Chicago Tribune* 13 Jun. 1975: n. pag. Print.
Stones, Dwight. Personal Interview by author: 25 Mar. 2006.
Tatum, Regina. Personal Interview by author: 14 Apr. 2006.
"The 110 Meter and 120 Yard Hurdles." N.p., n.d. Web. 7 June 2017. <http://personal.bgsu.edu/~jsquire/M110H.pdf>.
*The City of Opelousas Louisiana*. Opelousas Museum & Interpretive Center, 2000–2011, Accessed 12 February, 2006.
"'The Most Terrifying Night of My Life.'" *BBC News*. BBC, 02 Oct. 2008. Web. 28 July 2017.
"The Races of Rodney Milburn." *AOL Hometown*. AOL, n.d. Web. 28 Nov. 2005.
"The Races of Willie Davenport." *AOL Hometown*. AOL, n.d. Web. 28 Nov. 2005.
Thistlethwatite, John R. "Our Proud Gold Medalist." *Opelousas Daily World* 08 Sep. 1972: n. pag. Print.
Thomas, Bennie. "Olympic Star Eyes Football." *Tri-State Defender* [Memphis, Tenn.] 30 Sep. 1972: 14. *ProQuest*. Web. 15 Dec.2005.
"Track: NCAA Meet at Detroit." *Chicago Tribune* 12 Mar. 1973: n. pag. Print.
"Track Notebook." *The New York Times* 24 Feb. 1981: n. pag. *The New York Times Archive*. Web. 30 Jan. 2006.
Turrini, Joseph M. *The End of Amateurism in American Track and Field*. Urbana: U of Illinois, 2010. Print.
Turrini, Joseph. "'It Was Communism Versus the Free World': The USA-USSR Dual Track Meet Series and the Development of Track and Field in the United States, 1958–1985." *Journal of Sports History* Fall (2001): 427–55. Print.
"2 Cubans Set Records." *The New York Times* 22 Aug. 1977: 42. Print.

## Bibliography

UPI. "Milburn Cracks Record." *Chicago Tribune* 9 Feb. 1974: n. pag. Print.
US Scene: Hurdles." *Track & Field News* Mar. 1974: 22. Print.
"US Scene: Milburn's Comeback." *Track & Field News* Feb. 1980: 34. Print.
Verschoth, Anita. "Skeets Is Really Scooting." *Sports Illustrated* 22 Jan. 1979: n. pag. SI.com. Sports Illustrated, 2015. Web. 11 Aug. 2017.
"Vets Lose in Hurdles at California." *Chicago Tribune* 30 May 1971: n. pag. Print.
Whitfield, George, Dr. Personal Interview by author: 20 Dec. 2005.
Wiley, Cliff. Email Interview by author: 08 Dec. 2005.
"Wottle Runs 3:53.3; Milburn: 13 Flat." *Chicago Tribune* 21 June 1973: n. pag. Print.
"Win Cheers Milburn on Comeback." *The Washington Post* 2 Mar. 1980: B14. *ProQuest Historical Newspapers*. Web. 11 Jan. 2006.
Wright, George. *Stan Wright: Track Coach ; Forty Years in the "Good Old Boy Network" as Told to George Wright*. San Francisco, CA, Pacifica Sports Research Publications, 2005.

# Index

Afghanistan (Soviet invasion) 121
Alcindor, Lew 23
Alcorn State University 148–149
Ali, Muhammad 23, 44, 116
Amateur Athletic Union (AAU) 34, 50, 62–63, 67–69, 83, 86, 101, 103, 110–113, 115
Amateur Athletic Union Championships 28, 34–35, 40, 45, 48, 50–53, 74, 84, 94, 106
Amateur Sports Act (ASA) 115
Amdur, Neil 113–114
American Basketball Association (ABA) 86
"Aquarius" (song by The Fifth Dimension) 44
Ardoin, Bobby 7
Arkansas State University 80
Arlington National Cemetery 160
Asics Sporting Goods 112
Associated Press 125

Babb, Lance 41, 53, 99–100, 102, 117, 124
*Baton Rouge Advocate* 7, 40, 45
Baton Rouge Recreation Department 106
Bayou Teche 3–4, 6–7
Beamon, Bob 102
Bishop Ott Homeless Shelter 157
Black September 71–72
Borzov, Valeriy 70–71, 105
Bowdoin College 60
Bowerman, Bill 59–60, 79
Boys High School (Brooklyn) 79
*Boys' Life* Magazine 13, 44, 132
Brown, Jim 23
Brundage, Avery 61–66, 73–74

Bryant, Charles, Rev. 83
Bush, Jim 59

Calhoun, Lee 49, 118, 145
Campbell, Bill 11
Campbell, Tonie 1, 113, 119, 121, 125–129, 133, 135–136, 138, 140–141, 143, 145–146, 160
Canada 128
Carlos, John 30–31, 64–65, 80, 89
Carnes, Jimmy 123–124
Cart, Julie 158
Carter, Jimmy (US President) 122
Casanas, Alejandro 69, 105, 107, 111, 118, 129, 136, 141
Casem, Marino 148–151, 154
Cassell, Olan 68–69, 115–117, 124–125, 139
Catholic University 101
Cava, Pete 111
CBS Sports Spectacular 69
Chamberlain, Wilt 44
Chicago Bears 140
*Chicago Tribune* 50, 111, 117, 119
China 128
Clark, Dwight 139
Cliff Wiley Track Classic 113
Clinton, Bill (US President) 159
Coke Invitational 128
Coleman, Leon 28–30, 32, 34, 39, 43, 53, 61, 89, 90–91, 96–97, 99–100, 102, 145, 162
Collett, Wayne 78–81, 83, 87
Collins, Bill 112–113, 116, 131, 141, 143, 160
Connolly, Hal 65
Connolly, Olga 65
Cooper, Dedy 114, 116–117, 120–121, 125–126, 133, 135–136

# Index

Cornell University 17
Cortez, Wilfred 85
Cowling, Larry 134, 138, 141
CYO National Invitational (Maryland) 33

Dabney, Vont 20, 22–23
Davenport, Willie 27–39, 41–44, 46–56, 58–60, 65, 68–72, 74–77, 84, 87, 89, 91, 93, 95, 97–98, 105–107, 118, 130, 132–133, 139, 145, 148–150, 159–160
Detroit Lions 28
Deville, Gilbert 9, 46, 85
Deville, Sue 1, 151, 154
Dillard, Harrison 118
"Dime Method" of hurdling 15, 19
Dogwood Relays 28
Drake Relays 38, 48, 60, 91, 147–148
Draper, Ron 38, 41–42, 45, 48–49, 52–53, 55
Drut, Guy 32, 49–51, 70, 74–78, 84, 95, 104–105, 107, 118, 130, 159
Duke University 53
Dumas, Charlie 89

East Germany 128
East Junior High (Opelousas) 34
Edwards, Harry 30
Emerson, Lawrence 25
Ethiopia 61
Evans, Lee 30, 64, 79, 86–87

Feuerbach, Al 103
the Fifth Dimension (music group) 44
Fitzmorris, James 85
Florida A&M University 28, 93, 145
Flowers, Richmond 21, 23, 28–30, 67, 86
Floyd, Stanley 133
Foster, Charles 32, 35, 39–40, 48–50, 53, 93–94, 103, 105–109, 111, 116, 120, 145, 155–156
Foster, Greg 1, 111, 113, 116–120, 125–126, 128, 132–136, 138–143, 145–146
Fuselier, Herman 154

Gault, Willie 138, 140–142, 145
*Galveston Daily News* 104
George Washington Carver High School 15, 21
Georgia Pacific Paper Plant 151, 155–157

Gibson, Paul 34, 48, 53, 99, 102
Gilbert, Elias 92
Golden West Invitational 24–25
Grambling State University 17, 146
Greaves, Wilbert 120
Guilbeaux, Eddie 11, 14, 23, 25

Hall, Erv 28–29, 41, 53
Hall, Vincent 19
Hart, Eddie 68, 70, 75
Hawkins, Huey 12
Hayes, Bob 27–28, 67, 84, 145
Hendershott, Jon 130, 133
*Heroes Without a Country: America's Betrayal of Joe Louis and Jesse Owens* 63
Hersh, Bob 44, 86–87, 110–111
Hill, Dick (Richard) 26, 28, 35–40, 92–93, 98, 144, 148, 150
Hill, Tom (Thomas) 32–34, 38–39, 41, 47–51, 53–59, 67–72, 74–78, 80–81, 84, 94, 97, 105–108, 130, 133, 156, 159–160
Hines, Jim 60
Hitler, Adolf 62
Houston Athletics Track Club 141
Houston Oilers 88
Howland High School (Ohio) 27
Howser, Jeff 53, 55
*The Hurdler's Bible* 92

Indoor Track & Field Championships (USA) 117
International Amateur Athletic Federation (IAAF) 103, 111–112, 114, 116–117, 121, 123, 141
International Olympic Committee (IOC) 61–62, 64–65, 73, 80, 103, 123, 125–127
International Track Association (ITA) 86–88, 90, 94, 96–104, 106, 108–113, 115, 117–119, 143

Jackson, Oliver 10, 13
James, Larry 89
Jenkins, Charley 89
Jim Corbett Award 45, 84
Jipcho, Ben 100
Johnson, Brooks 89
Johnson, Rafer 89
Johnson C. Smith University 145
Jones, Hayes 27–28, 118

190

## Index

Jordan, Tom  101
Joseph, John  154
*The Journal of Sports History*  101
J.S. Clark Elementary School  4
J.S. Clark High School  6, 9–12, 16–17, 19–21, 23–25, 34, 40, 53, 67, 85, 130, 154, 159
J.S. Clark Relays  12, 17, 20, 22, 24–25

Kansas University  37
Kennedy Games (Berkeley, CA)  50
Kenya  128
the Kettle (restaurant)  6
King, Martin Luther, Jr.  147
Kingdom, Roger  142, 145

Lauer, Martin  38, 95
Lewis, Carl  133
Lewis, Fulton  10, 15
LHSAA (Louisiana High School Athletic Association)  17, 24
LIALO (Louisiana Interscholastic Athletic and Literary Organization) State Championships  17, 24
Liberty Bell Classic (128)
Lindgren, Blaine (Gerry)  28, 42
Liquori, Marty  37–38, 87, 134
Liston, Sonny  116
Lite Invitational  119, 124–125, 128
Litsky, Frank  13, 17, 24, 26, 36, 42–45, 47, 52–53, 66, 132, 137
Little Zion Baptist Church  159
Lockett, Raymond Dr.  147
Long Branch High School  12
Los Angeles Rams  87–88, 94–95, 97
*Los Angeles Times*  158
Louis, Joe  62
Louisiana Sports Hall of Fame  151
Louisiana State University (LSU)  37, 87, 91, 93–94, 98, 145–146, 151

Madison Square Garden  117
Martin Luther King Games (Philadelphia)  33, 36, 38
Matson, Randy  86
Matthews, Vincent  31–32, 59–61, 78–81, 83, 87, 145
Mayor's Council for Youth Opportunity (Baton Rouge)  31
McCullough, Earl  28, 67, 84
McRae, Donald  63
Meet of Champions (Houston)  23, 34, 37

Meuillion, Harry  8
Michigan State University  17
Milan Invitational  140
Milburn, Alice  3, 26, 149, 154, 161
Milburn, Betty  113, 130–131, 141–144, 150–151, 154–156, 161
Milburn, Carolyn  44, 66
Milburn, Clary  3, 104
Milburn, Felicia  156
Milburn, Janice  110, 141, 157
Milburn, Jimmy  1, 3–11, 13, 15–16, 18, 20, 24–25, 52, 56–57, 66, 68, 80, 82, 87–88, 105, 111–112, 131, 149, 151, 153–155, 157–158
Milburn, Jonia  156–157, 159
Milburn, Lillie  3–4, 26, 46, 161
Milburn, Mary  3, 7–9, 26, 66, 82, 161
Milburn, Mary Ann  3, 8, 26, 66, 82 157, 159, 161
Milburn, Rodney  1–27, 29–30, 32–61, 65–78, 80–85, 87–100, 103–105, 107–162
Milburn, Rodney, Sr.  3–5, 8, 66
Milburn, Rodney, III  141, 152
Milburn, Russell  156, 161
Milburn, Stanislars Joseph  22, 159, 162
Milburn, Wilfred  3
Millrose Games  117
Minden High School  21
Modesto Relays  38, 48, 134
Moore, Kenny  68
Morehouse College  145
Morrison, Robert  12, 14–15, 17, 19–22, 25
Moses, Edwin  145
Munkelt, Thomas  105, 128
Murray, Godfrey  87

National Association of Intercollegiate Athletics (NAIA) Championships  33, 38, 41, 47, 49–50, 84, 91
National Basketball Association (NBA)  86
National Collegiate Athletic Association (NCAA) Championships  41, 84, 88, 91–94, 118–119, 126, 133
National Football League (NFL)  90, 109, 139
Nehemiah, Renaldo  1, 69, 91, 111, 113, 115–121, 125–129, 131–143, 145–146
Nelson, Bert  35–36, 109
*New Orleans Times-Picayune*  11, 81, 152

# Index

New York Athletic Club (NYAC) 63
*New York Times* 113, 132, 137
Newland, Bob 124
NORD (New Orleans Recreational Department) Meet of Champions 17–18
Norman, Peter 64
North Carolina Central University 38, 48, 145
Northwestern University 41

O'Hara, Mike 86, 102
Oklahoma University 146
Oldfield, Brian 31, 103, 108–109, 111, 115, 123, 125
Olympic Boycott Games 128
Olympic Games, 1912 (Stockholm) 62
Olympic Games, 1936 (Berlin) 62, 65
Olympic Games, 1968 (Mexico City) 29–31, 60, 63–64, 79–80, 89, 100
Olympic Games, 1972 (Munich) 1, 58–59, 61, 65–67, 69–85, 104, 111, 121, 129
Olympic Games, 1976 (Montreal) 99, 102, 105, 107–108
Olympic Games, 1980 (Moscow) 99, 110, 122–124
Olympic Games, 1984 (Los Angeles) 138
Olympic Games, 1996 (Atlanta) 155–156
Olympic Project for Human Rights (OPHR) 30, 63
Olympic Trials, 1968 (USA) 29
Olympic Trials, 1972 (USA) 52–59, 67, 74, 79, 133
Olympic Trials, 1976 (USA) 105–107
Olympic Trials, 1980 (USA) 113, 121–126
Opelousas, LA 2–7, 20–23, 25, 34, 44–45, 53, 66, 77–78, 85, 130, 144, 146–147, 151, 153–155, 159
Opelousas Cultural and Interpretive Museum 1, 151
*Opelousas Daily World* (newspaper) 19, 42, 154
Opelousas High School 25
Oregon Track Club 124
Ottoz, Eddy 29
Owens, James 106–107
Owens, Jesse 62–63, 65, 116

Pacific Coast Club 114
Pan-American Games 45, 142

Parks, Rosa 147
Pastorini, Dan 88
Paxton, Claude 10–15, 19–20, 23–24, 26, 30, 33–34, 36, 77, 83, 92, 98, 154–155
Pelican Relays 21, 24, 28, 33, 140
Penn Relays 93
Pepsi Invitational 120, 134–135
Pierson, Don 111, 117, 119
Poquette, Jean 130
*Pre: The Story of America's Greatest Running Legend* 101
Prefontaine, Steve 42, 68, 101–102, 124, 134
Preptacular track meet 17

Rhodesia (Zimbabwe) 61, 65, 73, 80
Rice University 112
Rice University Meet of Champions 134, 142
Rich, Charles 53, 55–56, 94
Robinson, Rey 70, 75
Rodney Milburn Boulevard 154
Roesler, Bob 81
Rogers, Bill 122
Romano, Yossef 71
Rosen, Byron 111
Rosenthal, Bert 125
Ross, Wilbur 92
Rudolph, Wilma 89
Ryun, Jim 37–38, 68, 86, 134

San Francisco 49ers 127, 139
San Jose City College 30
San Jose State University 114
Sang, Julius 78
Savoie, Kevin 147, 150
Scotch Plains Fanwood High School 129
Scott, Steve 129
Seagren, Bob 71, 86–87
Shipp, Larry 37, 45, 87, 91–94, 97–99, 106, 117, 145
Shorter, Frank 42, 68, 101–102, 134
Shreveport Steamer (football team) 104
Siebeck, Frank 69–70, 74–75, 105
Simpson, O.J. 84
Smith, John 79, 114–115, 123–125, 145
Smith, Tommie 23, 30–31, 64–65, 80, 89
South Eastern Conference (SEC) 91
Southern California Striders 99
Southern University 2, 21, 26–29, 31,

192

*Index*

33, 35, 39, 44, 48, 53, 60, 66, 83–86, 89, 91, 93, 98, 116, 130, 142, 144–151, 154, 156, 159, 162
South Western Athletic Conference (SWAC)  60, 91, 148
Southwest Louisiana Relays  48
Soviet Union  121–123
Spitz, Mark  90–91
*Sport* Magazine  101
Sports Festival  135, 141
*Sports Illustrated*  30
Stewart, Milan  141
Stones, Dwight  67–69, 84, 108–109, 114–115, 124, 139
Stubbs, Ricky  93–94
Sudan  128
Superstars Competition  114–115, 139

TAC (The Athletics Congress)  115, 123–125, 131, 139
TAC Championships  121, 123, 134, 141–142, 144
Tatum, Isaac  12
Taylor, Dick  41
Taylor, Robert  70
Texas Relays  60, 93, 147–148
Texas Southern University  26, 60, 140, 145
Thomas, Spencer  15, 17–18, 20–22, 33
Thompson, Aaron  24
Thompson, Woodrow  9
Thorpe, Jim  62–63
*Track & Field News* (*T&FN*)  35–37, 44–45, 52–53, 79, 86, 96, 103–104, 109–110, 130, 133
Turner, Sam  134–136, 138, 141–142
Turrini, Joseph  101, 115
Tyus, Wyomia  102

United States Olympic Committee (USOC)  31, 60, 64–65, 80, 110, 122, 124–125, 160
United States Track and Field Federation Championships (Wichita)  33, 93
University of Alabama  146
University of California at Los Angeles (UCLA)  100, 106, 114, 118–119, 134, 145

University of Florida  17
University of Houston  119
University of Maryland  118, 145
University of Oregon  106–107
University of Pennsylvania  128
University of Pittsburgh  142, 145
University of Southern California (USC)  17, 28, 36, 41, 53, 100, 114, 119, 145
University of Tennessee  17, 138, 145–146
University of Texas at El Paso (UTEP)  17, 34, 43, 48
Upton, Jimmy  21

Villanova University  37
VONS Invitational (Los Angeles)  50

Walker, Dr. Leroy  48, 60, 107
Walker, Marcus  32, 34–35, 38, 41, 60
Walter Cohen High School  32
Washington, Fran  92
Washington High School (Kansas City)  113
*Washington Post*  89, 110
Weinberg, Moshe  71
Weltklasse Meet  135–136, 138, 142
West Germany  128
Wheeler Avenue Baptist Church  113
White, Tommy  36, 38, 41–42, 47–49, 51, 53–56, 94
Whitfield, George, Dr.  29–30, 146–147
Wiley, Cliff  113, 116
Williams, Steve  129
Wilson, Jerry  41, 53, 56, 105
Winston Salem Teachers College (Winston Salem State University)  92, 145
World Football League  95, 97, 104
Wottle, Dave  103
Wright, Stan  59–60, 70

Xavier University  12

Zone 1 AAA Track & Field Championships  15
Zurich, Switzerland  135–136

www.ingramcontent.com/pod-product-compliance
Ingram Content Group UK Ltd.
Pitfield, Milton Keynes, MK11 3LW, UK
UKHW042009140426
5217IPUK00015B/1075